Afterlives of Indigenous Archives

D1605572

Edited by Ivy Schweitzer and Gordon Henry

AFTERLIVES

OF INDIGENOUS ARCHIVES

Essays in honor of *The Occom Circle*

Dartmouth College Press   Hanover, New Hampshire

Dartmouth College Press
© 2019 Trustees of Dartmouth College
All rights reserved
Manufactured in the United States of America
Designed by Mindy Basinger Hill
Typeset in Minion Pro by Westchester Publishing Services

For permission to reproduce any of the material in this book, contact
Permissions, Dartmouth College Press, 6025 Baker-Berry Library, Hanover,
NH 03755; or email university.press.new.england-author@dartmouth.edu

Library of Congress Cataloging-in-Publication Data available upon request

Hardcover ISBN: 978-1-5126-0364-4
Paperback ISBN: 978-1-5126-0365-1
Ebook ISBN: 978-1-5126-0366-8

5   4   3   2   1

FOR THE WATER PROTECTORS AT STANDING ROCK AND FOR ALL OF THOSE WHO PROTECT THE EARTH

WE ALSO DEDICATE THIS VOLUME TO OUR COLLEAGUE TIMOTHY POWELL, WHO DIED IN FALL 2018 AS THIS COLLECTION WAS IN PREPARATION. THE COLLABORATIVE AND INCLUSIVE APPROACH TO AMERICAN STUDIES YOU PIONEERED WAS A LIGHT AND A MODEL TO MANY OF US. MAY IT SHINE FOR A LONG TIME.

CONTENTS

The Afterlives of the Archive

Melanie Benson Taylor

What does a scholar of modern and contemporary literature have to say about the archive? This is not a rhetorical question; rhetorical questions don't demand answers quite so insistently, don't keep us up at night, haunted by the proverbial blinking cursor of a blank Word document.

When asked to participate in this project, I worried earnestly that I would have little to say and much to expose. I have always felt a little inferior to — and envious of — my brilliant colleagues in Native American Studies who take regular research trips to comb through dusty archives at far flung institutions, both settler and tribal, returning bleary-eyed but triumphant with sheaves of freshly drafted manuscript pages. Against mine, the work of my colleagues seems commendably grounded, rooted tangibly in the densities of history and the material conditions of community, altogether more constructive, purposeful, and noble. Wistfully, I wonder less about what they have found in their archival junkets than what they went searching for in the first place: what gaps in the record insisted on being filled? Where did they know to look for clues? How does one judge whether the discoveries are true? And — perhaps most bewildering of all — where does the quest begin and end?

There are obvious answers to these questions, supplied by intellectual logic and disciplinary methodologies; and while they are seductive, truthfully, none of them are fully convincing to me. If knowledge were a puzzle, I imagine the archive as a dazzling treasure chest filled with final missing pieces; yet, as a literary scholar admittedly ruined by poststructural theory, and an American Indian

Studies scholar inured to postmodern appropriations of the "real," I have long since jettisoned the very notion of final pieces, missing links, or the elusive clue that would solve the mystery.

The truth is that I don't trust the archives. Setting foot in any Special Collections storehouse, you can veritably smell the musty air of reverence, the profound care with which its precious contents are guarded from ink pens and coffee cups. I feel nervous there, and a little recalcitrant. My preferred texts are housed in the wide-open, defenseless field of the now, with all its awful silences and nagging mysteries, and my work is tuned to exposing rather than falsely patching the dark, permanent vacancies of the human condition.

So that haunting, blinking cursor plagued me. What could *I* say about this thing, this quest, this space that had never spoken to *me*?

I began by doing what all good literary scholars do and scurried to my own preferred archives: the vast alphabetic repositories of the *Oxford English Dictionary*. Archive — the entry was surprisingly, uncharacteristically, indeed distressingly spare. Two entries alone stared back at me: "1. A place in which public records or other important historic documents are kept"; and "2. A historical record or document so preserved."[1] (Imagined footnote: "It really is that simple, you idiot.") Yes, in some ways, it is exceedingly simple: the *archives* (rendered almost exclusively in the plural form) are both text and container: the records themselves, and the spaces where they are held. Voices and places — what could be a more simple synergy, a more appealingly Indigenous pairing, a more multi-throated expression of lively communities and textured pluralities?

Things got even better for me when I contemplated the verb form of "archive": "To place or store in an archive; in *Computing*, to transfer to a store containing infrequently used files, or to a lower level in the hierarchy of memories, esp. from disc to tape."[2] Here, *place* is elevated from static to dynamic, from the concrete to the abstract, and from the library basement to the (virtual but somehow literal) cloud of the internet — a shuttling energy to which the final two essays in this book attest with stunning symmetry. Indeed, the archive lives in the ancient coils of a birch tree, as Alan Corbiere beautifully documents in his essay, as well as the ever-growing stack of the World Wide Web that Jason Edward Lewis unravels in his. Both archives are rich, enduring, mutating things; both invite readers to engage with and translate them in order that they may go on living; and both are vulnerable to the sinking forces of hierarchy exerting downward pressure on the fragile roots and traces preserved therein.

Indeed, what all of the essays in this volume demonstrate, over and over again, is the ponderous weight of history and hierarchy threatening to eclipse forms of Indigenous knowledge forever and, thus, the urgency of archival methods to excavate, transliterate, and reboot them. In environments both digital and ecological, we battle the kind of opacity and "dangerous . . . blindnesses" that Lewis describes, the murky consequences of our post-settler condition. But traveling backward through the striations of history, no matter how energetic the archive, doesn't guarantee either clarity or survival. Nor does importing and updating the found nuggets of Indigenous wisdom. It is not simply that the orthographies are "obsolete," as Corbiere admits, but rather, as Lewis notes, that, "tinkering at the edges will not fix a system that is so deeply compromised." That is, surrendering to the inevitability of corrupted data, of the bungled translation, is perhaps the only way to ensure that communities, languages, and identities persist into the twenty-first century.

Tethered irremediably to a broken system, Lewis thus wonders, "how do we breathe humanity back into our computational creations?" Rather than answer this question with the genuine fervor that most Indigenous scholars do, I think we might do better to scramble the terms — to ask instead whether we might confront the vast computational and colonial creations themselves *as* the expression of humanity in this new millennium. Full stop. Such a revision would shift our focus from projects of reclamation or reversal, or even of decolonization, to a more sober but potentially nutritive emphasis on the heteroglot certainties of our present moment. There is no room in such a pursuit for the facile vocabularies of victimhood, nor for concepts of sovereignty illegible under advanced capitalism.

Perversely, then, the elusive trip to the archives becomes less a deep dive into the occlusions of history and instead an expedition into as yet unimagined futures. Elsewhere in this collection, Gordon Henry poses the arresting idea of the archive itself as agon: a perpetual site of struggle, a fragile tether between past and future, between the dust of irrelevance and the sign of regeneration. From that skirmish is born Gerald Vizenor's idea of the afterlife, an Indigenous eruption from the Derridean promise of what the archive represents — not history, but harbinger. For all of their revisionary spirit, what every one of these essays is concerned about, finally and vitally, is how the archives can serve living Indigenous communities today — how texts and languages and stacks might continuously populate their own fertile afterlives, in archives both physical and ethereal.

Indeed, the authors in this volume suggest collectively, sometimes profoundly, that our bodies themselves are the richest of archives. Even mine, I realized. Suddenly, a melancholy fact of my own history took on new relevance; growing up on Cape Cod in Massachusetts, my mother worked cleaning the homes of families we called "summer people," many of whom were absent three-quarters of the year and, thus, invisible to us, but we blotted and absorbed their traces. While my mother dusted and mopped, my sister and I would greedily devour the treasures of the fully stocked bookshelves in those vast houses. One particular spring in one particular house, I worked my way through *Gone with the Wind* (and thus was born my romance with US Southern literature, now my primary field of study); an entire set of mystery stories, whose author or whodunits I can no longer recall; and perhaps most influentially, a set of diaries written by one of the house's early occupants in the late nineteenth century. These journals were the quintessence of the mundane: recordings of weather patterns, inconsequential household purchases, registers of illnesses and deaths in the community. Occasionally, there was a glimmer of high drama — a romance, a marriage, the arrival or loss of a child — and these moments especially stayed with me, fixed in my head a vision of places and people I never knew in a world apparently right beneath my feet, and yet accessible only by imaginative projection and fancy. I was desperately hungry for the small details of luxury, leisure, and adventure that the entire library both contained and embodied. All of it, jumbled and stored together, has remained locked in my personal archives, has fed me in ways intimate, academic, ironic, and permanent.

Some years later, when I was a young teenager, we got a call telling us that that grand house was on fire. We rushed out and, from our side of the bay, watched the enormous structure go up in flames, faster than you could imagine. All of us wept — my mother for the house she had lovingly tended for years, and I for the books and letters I had claimed as my own. But although I would never read or touch them again, I wouldn't need to;[3] they were, and still are, indelibly recorded in my very being, have helped to give form and words to my life as a writer and scholar of economics and race in American literature. Perhaps the best way to conceive of the archives, in fact, are as ashes and dust — with our bodies themselves the recipients of their knowledge, the sometimes reluctant palimpsests.

Indeed, it is not the repossession but the abdication of spaces, texts, and even land itself that can prove paradoxically liberating. Accordingly, fresh new pathways in Indigenous criticism and theory seek to go beyond the settler studies paradigm of landed sovereignty: as Jared Sexton puts it, "the indigenous relation to land precedes and exceeds any regime of property — landlessness. And selfless-ness is the correlate. No ground for identity, no ground to stand (on) . . . This is not a politics of despair brought about by a failure to lament a loss, because it is not rooted in hope of winning. The flesh of the earth demands it: the landless inhabitation of selfless existence."[4] Landless, selfless existence — a history before history, a place without place to return to. Encumbered by history but not its terms, what ground do we stand on (both literally and figuratively)? Without the archive, how do we reconstitute ourselves? Can we both claim land and text, and expunge it all at once?

In *Designs of the Night Sky* (2002), Cherokee author Diane Glancy situates her protagonist, Ada, in an agonized position as librarian — as ambivalent keeper of the archives. She muses: "Are the books content in their encampment in the library? They are cataloged and in their place, yet they circulate. I like to think of them as camps lined up on the hills. One camp can hear others on the shelves. But why are they murmuring, more now than before?"[5]

Indeed, why are these texts so animated and restless "*now* more than before," and what sort of battle are they mobilizing for? And where, she wonders, would they go? Haunted, "I hear the books," Ada says, "Not with my ears, but in my imagination." She channels the voices most vividly in, of all places, a local roller-skating rink: "When I skate . . . I am the written word let loose in spoken story."[6] Pointedly named the Dust Bowl, the rink is uniquely American, evocative of its redundant trails of removal, evacuation, migration, deprivation; it is also decid-edly literary, conjuring the worlds of John Steinbeck and Frederick Manfred struggling westward alongside the so-called Five Civilized Tribes staggering out of the Southeast. At once figurative and literal, emancipated and corralled, desic-cated and fruitful, all of these voices together bear witness. Settler space unsettled.

These, then, are the afterlives of the archive: in texts and bodies that function broadly and encyclopedically as storehouses of knowledge and culture, who register the inevitable infections of being in the lived world, and who translate that experience in difficult, impacted, sometimes grotesque ways. As the Black-feet writer Stephen Graham Jones imagines it in a self-fashioned epigraph to his collection of short stories *Bleed into Me* (2005), "Columbus landed in the second grade for me, and my teacher made me swallow the names of the boats one by one until in the bathtub of my summer vacation I opened my mouth and they came back out — Niña, Pinta, Santa Maria — and bobbed on the surface of the water like toys. I clapped my hand over my mouth once, Indian style, then looked up, for my mother, so she could pull the plug, stop all this, but when I opened my mouth again it was just blood and blood and blood."[7] Jones's speaker vividly embodies the internalization of the American archives of knowledge and discovery, but also their eviction — from the Indigenous body that absorbed them, whose writings are both an exorcism and a prayer. From the ashes and dust of the history and the archives, our bodies explode with the "blood" both of loss and new life — the teeming new archives of the twenty-first century.

Notes

1. "archive, n." *OED Online*. March 2018. Oxford University Press. http://www.oed .com (accessed April 15, 2018).

2. "archive, v." *OED Online*. March 2018. Oxford University Press. http://www.oed.com (accessed April 15, 2018).

3. I am knowingly paraphrasing William Faulkner's protagonist Isaac McCaslin, who in *Go Down Moses* (1942; New York: Vintage, 1990) reads in a set of plantation ledgers about his own family's tortured history of slave owning and miscegenation. Faulkner tells us that Ike "would never need to look at the ledgers again nor did he; the yellowed pages in their fading implacable succession were as much a part of his consciousness and would remain so forever, as the fact of his own nativity" (259).

4. Jared Sexton, "The *Vel* of Slavery: Tracking the Figure of the Unsovereign," *Critical Sociology* (2014), 1–15.

5. Diane Glancy, from *Designs of the Night Sky*, in Gerald Vizenor, *Native Storiers: Five Selections* (Lincoln: University of Nebraska Press, 2009), 167.

6. Glancy, 169.

7. Stephen Graham Jones, *Bleed into Me: A Book of Stories* (Lincoln: University of Nebraska Press, 2005), front matter.

ACKNOWLEDGMENTS

We would like to thank Elizabeth Dillon, professor and Chair of English, Codirector of NULab for Texts, Maps, and Networks at Northeastern University, and Ellen Cushman, Cherokee, Associate Dean of Academic Affairs, Diversity and Inclusion at Northeastern University, for help in organizing the conference and inviting so many wonderful participants. Also many thanks to Kelly Palmer, the conference administrator, and Brooke Hadley, a student in Native American Studies at Dartmouth College, who was our capable assistant.

We are also grateful to the Society of Early Americanists for its sponsorship and guidance, the Dartmouth College Conference Fund for its generosity, the Native American Studies Program at Dartmouth, the Leslie Center for the Humanities at Dartmouth, and the Friends of the Dartmouth College Library.

A special thank you to members of *The Occom Circle* project team, who formed a community of diverse skills necessary to produce even this modest digital project: Peter Carini, College Archivist, Rauner Special Collections; Christina Dulude, Web Architect/Engineer; Hazel-Dawn Dumpert, Project Manager and Editor; William Ghezzi, Digital Production & Metadata Librarian; Deborah Howe, Conservationist; Paul Merchant, Senior Programmer. Mark Mounts, Business & Engineering Librarian; Maninder Rakhra, Cataloging and Metadata Services Librarian; David Seaman, former Associate Librarian for Information Management. And very special thanks to Laura Braunstein, our English and Digital Humanities Librarian, and Scott Millspaugh, Instructional Designer par excellence, whose knowledge, help, and friendship have been invaluable. Barbara de Felice gave important advice about publishing at a crucial moment.

We would also like to thank Richard Pult for his guidance and the folks at UPNE.

INTRODUCTION

"The Afterlives of Indigenous Archives"

Ivy Schweitzer

> We're not looking at an issue of paper by paper or record group
> by record group. It's a whole system of a way of life. Our knowledge
> systems don't make sense without spirituality. We are asking for
> respect for a system of knowledge.
>
> *Kim Lawson (Heiltsuk Nation), "Protocols for Native American Archival Materials"*[1]

As we enter the third decade of the twenty-first century, we can acknowledge a good deal of important work on decolonizing the archive of Western knowledge so that it is no longer singular, static, or monolithic. When Michel Foucault reconceived the archive as a "discursive formation" establishing an order of truth that societies accept as reality, he inextricably linked the archive to politics and power.[2] Jacques Derrida saw archives as riven by warring forces but he also confirmed that "there is no political power without control of the archive, or without memory."[3] In the wake of these interventions, scholars, digital humanists, librarians, and activists are rescuing the theory and practice of archives from the Western-dominated archive, born from the rampant nationalisms of Europe with its pretensions to neutrality, objectivity, and comprehension.[4]

Members of identity groups who do not find themselves accurately represented in the archive of the West subject it to a radical critical analysis. Not only have they confronted their own absence or distortion, they have traced the dominant regime's use of its archives to justify exclusionary policies. In 2012, Dana A. Williams and Marissa K. López celebrated the blossoming of ethnic archives as an opportunity to recast an entrenched paradigm: "If the archive has historically provided an opportunity to establish tradition, then the ethnic archive affords an opportunity to do the opposite: to challenge assumptions cultivated as truths; to contest the hegemony of the nation-state's imagined pasts and futures; and to invoke a multiethnic cacophony of voices that require reconsideration of established knowledge and knowledge production alike" (358). Rather than a harmony, ethnic archives produce a sometimes harsh and destabilizing clash of voices and truths. They require us to rethink the archive, not just in terms of who and what we include, but *how* we produce knowledge. That is, ethnic archives "must learn the lesson of transnational and diaspora studies" and develop archival methodologies "capable of meaningfully engaging distinctions of nonimperial cultures and traditions."[5] Emerging from these radical critiques is the understanding that archives are always acts of interpretation giving "rise to particular practices of reading."[6] Thus, we must always subject archives, even or especially those we create, to a critical interrogation of the politics of archiving.[7]

These developments have been particularly challenging for those of us working with Indigenous materials. Since the Enlightenment, archives assembled in the West included extensive records of colonialism and imperialism, in which Indigenous peoples around the world appeared as objects of study, collection, curation, and display — rarely as subjects. In the nineteenth century, as Siobhan Senier notes, major collections of Native American, First Nations, Aboriginal, and other Indigenous materials "are the products of a global, imperial enterprise to steal cultural materials wholesale from Indigenous communities, in service to the myth that those cultures were dying. Colonial theft and vanishing race stories may not have been invented during the nineteenth century, but this was the period of unprecedented and coordinated archive building in the service of settler colonial supremacy."[8]

Working in the earlier period of first contact, Drew Lopenzina argues that the archival written record left by Europeans is a form of "unwitnessing," in which settler-colonialists recognized Native existence and then denigrated or erased it. This unwitnessing is part of the hegemonic architecture Derrida calls "the house of the archive," and very often occurs through the writing, transmission, and domination of written texts over other forms of cultural meaning-making. As historian Michel de Certeau notes, writing allowed imperial powers to control Native peoples, even from great distances: "The power that writing's expansionism leaves intact is colonial in principle. It is extended without being changed. It is tautological, immunized against both any alterity that might transform it and whatever dares to resist it."[9] By unacknowledging Indigenous forms of writing, by destroying or collecting as objects (and thus redefining them as exotic and ahistorical) those they did find, and by imposing Western forms of literacy on Indigenous populations, settler colonists elevated writing, and the archives that preserved it, into the pre-eminent tool of conquest.

Scholars theorize different ways of countering this history. Lopenzina suggests we adopt an interpretive framework he calls "a *longhouse* of the archive, with roots in Native epistemologies." Alluding to the big house of Algonquian culture, Lopenzina explains that the longhouse "is the central location of ceremony and spirituality . . . a space of vision and memory, narrative and tradition" that can elude Western structures of knowledge and also augment them.[10] Another way of restoring what eludes the Western archive is through the distinction Diana Taylor makes between the archive and the repertoire, which is similar, but not quite equivalent, to the written/oral divide. In her terms, the archive encompasses "supposedly enduring materials (i.e. texts, documents, buildings, bones) and the so-called ephemeral *repertoire* [consists] of embodied practice/knowledges (i.e., spoken language, dance, sports, ritual)." The major issue for Taylor is "that archival memory succeeds in separating the source of 'knowledge' from the knower — in time and space. . . . Embodied memory, because it is live, exceeds the archive's ability to capture it."[11]

To return knowers to their knowledge in past, present, and future archives requires decolonizing our methodologies. This requires understanding Western archives not as neutral repositories, but as means of producing knowledge that is partial, distorting, and often erased the very existence, if not the richness, variety, and vitality of Native cultures. It requires seeing how Western archives and the whole range of their operations — their physical holdings, selective procedures of categorization and classification, interpretive practices and one-sided cultural representations — circumscribe, trivialize, and sometimes completely ignore Indigenous space, cultural practices, and knowledge systems that operate under different understandings of history, progress, time and space, notions of gender, and difference.

In her ground-breaking work *Decolonizing Methodologies* (1999), Maori scholar Linda Tuhiwai Smith draws on the work of British cultural studies theorist Stuart Hall to suggest that archives can be transformed by, and be transformative for, Indigenous people if they are created and utilized with the knowledge, concerns, and perspectives of Indigenous peoples and communities foremost in mind. Kim Lawson, a librarian active in a communal effort to produce protocols for Indigenous Archives, insists that the key to this transformation is recognizing and respecting that Indigenous archives embody many types of Indigenous ways of knowing, as well as embracing patience and collaboration. Given this as a foundation, Native scholars, writers, archivists, and community-based proponents of Indigenous thought and research are working to re-curate existing archives and create new ones to reinforce tribal and community interests and — in the process — redefine American history, literature, and culture.

Calls for decolonizing the archive have also extended to the most recent developments in archival work, the production of digital archives. Although supporters tout cyberspace and digital technology as the new democratic frontier, many scholars and activists argue that tech companies and holding institutions like universities, museums, and libraries develop and use digital technologies in ways that reproduce the colonialist paradigm of Western, white, male, and individualist dominance. A cultural turn that supports innovative archives focused on tribal needs, not the general pursuit of profit or knowledge according to Western academic standards, becomes even harder to sustain as universities become corporatized in times of economic downturn and cultural conservatism. In such a climate, Timothy Powell argues, it will require "a new kind of creativity, an expansion of the digital imaginary, to implement archives based on cultures that do not descend from the Euro-American tradition of print culture."[12] Over the past few decades, digital archivists and humanists have stepped up to this challenge, adapting existing digital tools and creating new ones as part of what Kim Christen identifies as "the emergence of a global politics of indigeneity, a boom in cultural tourism, and the increased debates over what constitutes — and who owns — intellectual property and cultural knowledge."[13]

Working with insights garnered from her extensive collaboration with the Warumunga people of northern Australia, Christen headed a group that created the *Mukurtu* content management system, which is based on and can be adapted to the different cultures and needs of Native communities.[14] Not only do Native communities co-curate their materials, because collaboration is structured into this system of archiving, but they can control different levels of access, depending on the ritual sensitivity of documents and communities' understanding of the public/private opposition not as a binary, but as a spectrum.

Digital projects can preserve and disseminate Indigenous languages, literatures, and cultures in ways that are not based on the Euro-American tradition of print culture. A model of this is *Gibagadinamaagoom*, a partnership among

"Medicine Men, Sacred Pipe Carriers, language-keepers, deans and faculty at four tribal and community colleges, filmmakers, and hundreds of Ojibwe students across northern Minnesota" as well as the University of Pennsylvania's Museum of Archaeology and Anthropology, the Minnesota Historical Society, and the American Philosophical Society.[15] Created to address the survivance and pedagogical needs articulated by the Ojibwe community, its design incorporates Ojibwe codes of conduct and belief: users navigate the site according to the seven sacred directions of the Ojibwe cosmos and can access unscripted videos of Ojibwe elders speaking about their culture. Considering "how the Ojibwe wisdom-keepers recontextualize digital technology — utilizing it as part of a cultural continuum that can be traced back hundreds, if not thousands, of years," Timothy Powell concludes, from "their perspective, digital videos record the oral tradition much more accurately than print media ever did."[16]

Another notable example is the *Yale Indian Papers Project (YIPP)*.[17] Curated and annotated by Native and non-Native archivists and scholars working collaboratively, this large database of primary source material from several New England collections and the National Archives of the United Kingdom aspires to be what the editors call "a communal dish or 'common pot,'" a term based on an ancient northeastern Native notion of space that encompasses relations across different communities and their needs within that space.[18] YIPP describes its contemporary version of the common pot as "a shared history, a kind of communal liminal space, neither solely Euro-American nor completely Native."[19] Projects such as these give wider audiences unprecedented access to Indigenous archival materials and knowledge about Indigenous lives, past, present, and future.

Still, as Christen notes, not all digital projects involving Indigenous archives recognize the importance of reflecting Indigenous values or succeed in collaboration or agree to re-curation of Indigenous culture. Rather, "They also provoke paralysis and end negotiation when their trajectories seem only future-oriented and fast-paced, when they are seen as a cultural threat, invasion, or the inevitable catalyst for the erasure of tradition." Many Indigenous cultural artifacts held in universities and other large collections are subject to conventional Western archival protocols. What happens to sensitive materials that, for reasons of tribal history and religion, should not be made public? Archivists do not routinely consult Indigenous communities about the handling of artifacts, though there are movements afoot to encourage Native people to become archivists, to train archivists in cultural awareness, and to support Native communities in creating and maintaining their own archives.[20]

In a 2014 survey of the field titled "Digitizing Indigenous History: Trends and Challenges," Senier traces some of these movements but sees a worrisome trend: that the large state-sponsored granting institutions are funding digital projects mostly for "*non*-Native institutions: museums, universities and antiquarian societies, which hold collections from donors who may have come by their Native materials unethically, or fabricated them in the first place." Such institutions do not as a rule critique their process of knowledge production; the archives they produce, though important in preserving Native cultures, reinforce the status quo and, more dangerously, occlude the existence and importance of homegrown "insurgent" archives. Senier is concerned that, despite some interventions such as those described above, current trends do not look hopeful: "'Indigenous digital archives,' as they are broadly understood at the moment, thus continue to marginalize non-colonial collections and non-colonial practices — newsletters saved in tribal offices, photographs cherished in family collections, artworks still in current use, and living oral traditions. These tell a very different story."[21]

Elucidating the different dimensions of that story is one of the purposes of this collection of essays, which draws on papers delivered at the conference, "Indigenous Archives in the Digital Age," held at Dartmouth College, Hanover, New Hampshire, in September 2016. The occasion of the conference was to celebrate the launch of *The Occom Circle*, a scholarly digital edition of handwritten documents held in Dartmouth's libraries by and about Samson Occom (1723–1792), which I edited with a large team of more than forty scholars, editors, archivists, librarians, IT specialists, and student and graduate student assistants, with input from members of the Mohegan and Brothertown Tribes.[22]

Occom was a Mohegan Indian, Presbyterian minister, political activist, and one of the foremost Native writers in eighteenth-century North America. He studied for four years with Eleazar Wheelock, who was a New Lights Congregational minister in Connecticut before becoming a missionary to several New England tribes. Occom's academic and ministerial success gave Wheelock the idea to start an Indian "charity" school to educate and acculturate other Native boys from the northeast as missionaries and schoolmasters, and Native girls as their wives. This school operated from 1754 to 1769, when Wheelock became disillusioned with his "great design" and moved his base of operations to Hanover, New Hampshire, where he merged the school with Dartmouth College, which he founded to educate Anglo-American men as missionaries. Scholars now agree that despite Wheelock's racist intentions to assimilate his Native students to Anglo-American culture, his school produced a large cohort of educated Christian Indians who were instrumental in creating a Native form of Christianity and a Native English that adapted imperial literacy technologies — reading, writing and the use of Latin and Greek — to their own purposes of communal resistance, response, and survival.[23]

This aspect of Dartmouth's history echoes the histories of our earliest and most prestigious academic institutions — Harvard, Brown, Columbia, and William and Mary — which reflect Eurocentric settler colonial values. One has only to visit Brown's extensive website "Slavery and Justice" to realize the extent of its founders' involvement — not just as slave owners but as slave traders.[24] At Dartmouth, the College lionizes as its founder Wheelock, who, in fact, owned slaves and brought them up to the New Hampshire wilderness to build the College. In fact, Occom never set foot on Dartmouth campus and finally broke with Wheelock over his decision to abandon his original purpose of educating Native children, though Wheelock still used over £12,000 of funds he sent Occom to solicit for the Indian school in England and Scotland between 1765 and 1768.[25] In Dartmouth College's charter, Wheelock cannily presented its mission first and foremost as "the education and instruction of youth of the Indian tribes in this land in reading, writing, and all parts of learning," though this did not become a reality until the establishment of the Native American Studies Program in 1972.[26]

When this project began in 2006, I originally wanted easier access to the Occom papers in Dartmouth's Special Collections Library to use in my courses in Early American literatures, but the project quickly took on a larger scope. I originally planned to digitize all the writings by Occom held in Dartmouth libraries. The publication in 2007 of Joanna Brooks's canonical edition, *The Collected Writings of Samson Occom*, forced me to rethink the purpose of a *digital* edition. Instead of reproducing Brooks's edition in digital form, I decided to change the original scope of the project to include documents from the voluminous materials in *The Wheelock Papers* held at Dartmouth and related to Occom and his circle. That is, I decided to create an archive with a Native figure at the center of a large network of associations, correspondences, and activities. Because digital platforms allow users several options of display, organization, and retrieval, a digital archive would approximate the multiple transatlantic and transcultural *networks* of association that constituted Occom's world. It would illustrate just how wide and varied Occom's "Native space" had become.

When Wheelock occupies the center of this story, Occom's career appears to end with the dissolution of his relationship with Wheelock in the early 1770s over the founding and financing of Dartmouth College. But that is when Occom's celebrity and noteworthy activism and leadership begin, working with other graduates of Wheelock's school to establish the Brothertown settlement of Christian Indians on Oneida lands in upstate New York. Occom's collaborative work and his sense of himself as part of larger collective are crucial to his world. By contrast, the means by which we canonize authors in the west, through edited collections of their works, evolved from a romantic belief in individual genius and writers striving in isolation. In the case of Native writers, such canonization may be politically strategic. Brooks's *Collected Writings* validates Occom and gives him the visibility of other eighteenth century Anglo-American writers, but it wrenches him out of the "common pot" and community identity he deliberately embraced as an activist and leader. A digital edition like *The Occom Circle* allows users to access networks of correspondence, thus amplifying the limited linear and sequential presentation of print technologies.

Yet, for all its attempts to be post-Eurocentric, *The Occom Circle* is still an act of interpretation, using documents whose collection may not have been authorized, housed in an institution with a largely unacknowledged colonialist-settler past, using digital technologies that have a strong potential to re-inscribe a Western paradigm of dominance.[27] This brings me to the conference in September 2016.

The two-day gathering, which was organized with the help of Ellen Cushman and Elizabeth Maddock Dillon, under the auspices of the Society of Early Americanists, brought together an international and interdisciplinary group of scholars of Native American and early American literature and culture, librarians, curators, archivists, digital humanists, poets, and storytellers. We wanted to offer multiple technical, critical, community, and institutional perspectives on Indigenous archives, from leading scholars and practitioners, Native and non-Native alike. It is important to work across disciplines and fields, but it is also demanding: we do not necessarily share the same terms, perspectives, or values. Alongside academic papers, we scheduled a roundtable and a digital projects session. Participants also got a taste of Dartmouth's extensive and contentious Indian history with an exhibit of Occom materials from our archives entitled "'Power, Honor, and Authority,' Samson Occom and the Founding of Dartmouth College," a walk to and reception at Occom Pond, and tours of the Orozco Murals and their institutionally sanctioned response, the infamous Hovey Murals, which can only be visited with a Hood Museum curator.[28]

It was also a week of momentous events at Standing Rock, North Dakota, where hundreds of activists, Native and non-Native, had gathered to protest the building of the Dakota Access pipeline near the Sioux Tribe's reservation, threatening water sources and their way of life. On September 9, the first day our meetings, three Federal Agencies responded to a US District Court Judge's ruling to allow construction to continue by publishing a joint statement calling for a halt in the construction.[29] We began in a mood of hopefulness, buoyed by the courageous efforts of the water protectors and the possibility that their hard work might prove successful in stopping the construction.

Our proceedings opened with remarks by Donna Moody, a tribal elder of the Abenaki Nation, and John Moody, who are joint directors of the *Winter Center for Indigenous Traditions*, located in the Upper Valley, a place that fits Senier's definition of a non-colonial site for the collection and preservation of local culture. The Moodys set the tone for a deeply engaged discussion that urged us to think critically about the politics of archives and digitality. Donna Moody began by observing that Indigenous people have long resisted the archiving of Native materials: they consider archives "evil" — sites of concentrated knowledge, not communal ownership. Some archives contain privileged knowledge. Who controls the dissemination? she asked. Some Native Nations want their materials returned, as cultural patrimony. The solution, she said, is to put Native communities in control of their own histories: create archives compatible with Indigenous values. John Moody brought us into the Native space of the Abenakis by observing that Mink Brook in Hanover, New Hampshire, where Dartmouth College is located, is the dead center of Abenaki lands. To make this concrete, he passed around a box of local blueberries and asked everyone to partake — a manifestation of Native traditions connecting us to the place, its history of sustenance, and to each other. He observed that across the Connecticut River, the Norwich (Vermont) firefighters are Abenaki, with long tradition of fire keeping. This knowledge resides in families, not in archives, he said.

Reinforcing this point, Stephanie Fitzgerald, who gave the first paper on the first panel, reminded us that when the First Archivist Circle proposed protocols for Native American materials, from which the epigraph to this Introduction comes, they were not warmly received. Libraries feared they would lose control of the documents they held. But, Fitzgerald asked, "whose documents are they?" She went on to make the crucial distinction: "The archive (small a) is colonial paper knowledge, inanimate. It is wielded to control those people it presents. Archive (capital A) is animate; it can only be captured through memory and doing: it is an embodied Archive." She gave the example of her grandfather, who was a singer and would warm up by "digging deep into his Archive" — that is, his memory of songs. She asked us to think about how the North Dakota encampment will be documented; will we record how many diverse groups came together, and how do we digitize all that social media?

Patricia Norby, who is a curator at the Newberry Library in Chicago, illustrated a quite different embodied response *to* the archives in her presentation. She argued that archives *come* alive when Indigenous peoples work with archives and talk about them in their own languages. Then, she said, emotions run high and force archivists to think outside the box. She told how, for example, K'iche' people annually visit the Library's copy of the *Popul Vuh,* a narrative of creation written before the Spanish conquest of what is now Guatemala, and bless the librarians as archive keepers, because otherwise this ancient text would have perished.

Not all the presentations given at the conference were transformed into essays. The essays collected here represent a serendipitous gathering of humanistic approaches to decolonizing and historically resituating past, present, and future Indigenous archives. They do not constitute a unified or comprehensive, or even technical view of Indigenous archives and archiving. But they all share deep commitments to the salience of decolonizing critiques and putting Indigenous knowledge and ethics at the center of archival activities. Although librarians, curators, and archivists contributed to the conference, only two papers by librarians and archivists made it into the collection. The majority of essays are written by literary scholars, scholars of Native American studies, and historians who use archives to further their research into specific figures or texts, and their activism in areas like language preservation, the creation of community-centered pedagogical materials, and the connection of ancient stories to current experiences. Similarly, although we strove for a broad geographical representation in the conference, the collected essays cluster around the Northeast, with a few essays focusing on the First Nation peoples in Canada and the Cherokees in the Southeast. Still, the essays reflect a broad range of interests in Indigenous history and culture, and while not always specifically driven by questions about archival practices, explore the broader implications of Natives' engagement with archival materials and subjects, and Natives researching and writing as archival subjects from within and without archival holdings and from inside and outside tribal communities.

Because the occasion of the conference was to celebrate the launch of *The Occom Circle,* a publicly accessible digital humanities project, we asked participants to think not only about Indigenous archives, but also about the benefits and drawbacks of digital tools, digital literacy, and digital access in relation to archival materials and practices. Each essay touches on digital possibilities with regard to Indigenous archives, while several projects in the final part make extensive use of digital tools and the landscape of cyberspace to re-center Native knowledge and agency.

The essays are organized into three parts: Critiques; Methods; and Interventions. Although, in reality, all the essays mount critiques of the Western archive, describe new or revalued methodologies, and offer recommendations for decolonizing and re-centering Native knowledge and agency. We grouped the essays in terms of their overriding concerns, hoping to produce overlapping conversations from several different perspectives. Framing the collection is a short reflection by Melanie Benson that grounds the collection in an interrogation of the Western archive and what she calls, after Gerald Vizenor, "its afterlives." The title of our collection is a play on Benson's central idea: exploring the conditions necessary to produce the afterlives, often digital, of Indigenous archives.

Part 1 begins with an essay by Timothy Powell, an academic and digital humanist active in a process he calls "culturally diversifying both the humanities and Western archives with significant Indigenous holdings." In his stint as director of the Center for Native American Indigenous Research at the American Philosophical Society and as the founder of EPIC (Educational Partnerships with Indigenous Communities) at the Penn Language Center in the School of Arts and Sciences at the University of Pennsylvania, Powell brought many stakeholders, including Native communities, into the shaping of digital projects, such as *Gibagadinamaagoom* discussed above. But he was also well aware of the pitfalls and precarity of the process. His essay is a good introduction to the current state of the field of digital Indigenous archives, where he surveys the two primary forms they are taking at the moment: the more advanced and robustly funded institution- and university-based partnerships and the more precarious, poorly funded Native community-based digital archives managed by tribes. Through a series of anecdotes about his experiences in brokering these partnerships, Powell illustrates the absolute necessity for Western archives to recognize tribal protocols as having standing equal to their own, and for striving to integrate them — while also keeping them separate by acknowledging Native ritual practice: that is the tricky part. More realistic than optimistic, but a strong supporter of the value of digital tools, Powell concludes with a call for granting institutions to recognize and support the decolonizing self-archiving work of tribes and nations.

The next essay, titled "Making Native Ethics the Norm: Critique and Decolonization," delves more particularly into critiques and attempts to decolonize archives. Jennifer O'Neal has been working for years on the front lines as a historian, archivist, and member of the Confederated Tribes of Grand Ronde in Oregon to decolonize specific archives. She works collectively with other archivists on best practices for the respectful treatment of Native American materials. Her essay analyzes the politics of knowledge production that governs Western archives and foregrounds aspects of traditional Indigenous knowledge systems that constitute a foundation for redressing archival practices in non-tribal repositories. She argues that destructive practices stem from a lack not only of a working knowledge of Native history, which our educational systems fail to integrate into their curricula, but of a visceral appreciation of the effects of long-term discrimination and erasure. Archivists need to be educated in this history and its effects and trained to apply a decolonizing Indigenous research methodology to their archival practices. O'Neal champions the foundational work of Linda Tuhiwai Smith and also recommends frameworks developed by the aboriginal educator Margaret Kovach, who rejects the descriptor of Native culture as post-colonial and, thus, not requiring historical analysis or contexts. Drawing on a wealth of scenarios she has experienced with curators and archivists, O'Neal ends with a call to action and provides practical steps.

Citing the work of Powell, O'Neal, and others, Ellen Cushman applies a decolonizing approach to Indigenous archives with a digital platform. For years, she has been doing ethnohistorical research with her tribe, the Cherokee Nation, in support of their attempts at language preservation and the historical importance of the Cherokee writing system. Her essay describes her current project, the development of a Digital Archive for Ojibwe and Cherokee manuscript translation, which she hopes will aid the translation and respectful preservation of Indian manuscripts held in museums and libraries around the country. The team she works with designed the specific features of their digital interface to create an online space that allows for "collaborative translations" of Native materials; not just viewing documents but being able "to interact with them at a linguistic level." Cushman is optimistic about this technological development: "Digital archiving technologies represent a crucial strategic step for libraries and an integral new set of technical opportunities that will expand research, education, and communication within Indigenous communities." With these opportunities, she concludes, "we see the beginning of the creation of Indigenous archives."

Christine DeLucia explores the digital turn in Indigenous archives not through interfaces, but through the materiality of what she calls "memory houses," which tell us much more about settler-colonialist attitudes and misconstructions than the words of documents ever do. Her goal is to illuminate early Native-colonial relations in the Northeast by ferreting out "more Indigenous-centered understandings of multi-tribal resistances of the late seventeenth century." To do so, she visits a large number of "minor" archives, small repositories in tiny town historical societies, cultural heritage centers run by sovereign tribal nations, and anthropological museums held at colleges and universities, whose collections may have been obtained unethically. What she finds is profoundly disturbing: libraries built on Native burial grounds, rumors about historical documents ending up in dumpsters during a contentious legal battle over land and sovereignty, restricting access to documents based on their fragility, or the opposite — unfettered access to sensitive documents by unauthorized researchers. She asks searching questions about how we factor these material traces of dispossession and trauma into the digitization process and offers some possibilities "for leveraging digital tools to enable more holistic, even restorative, approaches to history and memory."

The second part, "Methods," thinks about recovering lost or occluded archives and uncovering both resistance to and adaption of the Western archival paradigm and its digital incarnation. We begin this part with Thomas Peace's essay, which introduces many of the arguments presented in later essays in the group and offers a compelling historical critique of Dartmouth's archive. He brings into conversation scholars of the colonial past, such as Drew Lopenzina, who uncover the "false histories" of the Western archive, and Native American studies scholars, who acknowledge the necessity of a nuts-and-bolts approach to reclaiming Indigenous archives. He does so through his account of his own historiographical practices and interventions researching the biography of one of Dartmouth's earliest Indian students, Louis Vincent Sawatanen. What he finds, through careful comparison with biographies of other Native writers like Occom, is that archives produce their own distorted versions of reality and ignore important contexts. Addressing this means acknowledging networks of northeastern Indigenous intellectual influence, like that of attendees or graduates of Wheelock's Indian Charity School and Dartmouth College, that cross borders and nations, and also decenter the focus away from the schools themselves. The strategy of a "non-narrative alternative to historiography" appears in Peace's vision of the promise of digital archives, which, he concludes, "lies in the creation of new archival relationships in order to recover historical interconnections by bringing together material related to people, places, communities, or cultures not envisioned by any single archive's organizational structure."

Next, Kelly Wisecup unearths the existence of a collection of materials, including word lists for five southeastern Indigenous languages, created by Cherokee spokesman John Ridge in 1825, within the larger collection of linguistic materials gathered by Albert Gallatin, a statesman interested in Native linguistics who thought to expand on Thomas Jefferson's call in *Notes on the State of Virginia* to collect and study Native languages. Wisecup finds that, far from the scholarly goal Jefferson evinced of discovering the origins of Native people, Gallatin's lists would be put to the service of developing theories to support efforts to remove Native nations like the Cherokees from their ancestral lands. Furthermore, she argues that Ridge worked out of a different set of "memory practices" that did not "fix Indigenous tribes in archival or geographic place." How do we treat Indigenous materials that are encompassed within larger archives created by Euro-Americans, but that differ markedly in their assumptions, goals, and methods? One solution is to recontextualize collected materials in their original, communal circumstances. Wisecup concludes by asking how digital archives can reflect such restorative embeddedness.

Marie Taylor attempts to clear a "Native space" within Western methodologies by using kinship as a means of excavating Native relations often obscured in settler-colonial accounts and archives. First, she argues, we need to understand what kinship meant in Native communities and how it was often erased in the accounts of early American missionaries, who wanted to trace a very different set of relations for Native converts. Using Wequash, a Pequot and the Massachusetts Bay colony's first convert, as an example, Taylor works through the Puritan archive in which Wequash appears to have voluntarily given up his Native connections. But using digital tools, she manages to uncover what historian Jean O'Brien calls "unexpected archives" that, when read from Indigenous perspectives, reveal the difference between genealogies, recorded by settlers and thus limited, and kinship ties which expand beyond genealogical affiliations. By reading the digital archive differently, Taylor performs a "de-familiarization of familiar archives" and produces an enriched understanding of Wequash's relations and the methodological possibilities of kinship for illuminating Native networks.

Susan Glover raises another troubling question about the digitization of archives, which she calls the "receding archive." What happens when a particular archive loses its embodiment? In nineteenth-century northern Canada, a missionary named James Evans developed a written syllabary for the Cree language so his converts could read scripture and prayers. As a result, literacy flourished in these communities. Churches in this region have preserved these materials, but Glover encounters problems of access, ownership, and translation discussed by O'Neal, Cushman, and DeLucia. Digitization of these materials addresses some of these issues but, as Glover says, it "brings its own challenges of deracination, loss of control of access and textual integrity, and a further remove from any land-text nexus that might locate meaning." More pressing and less tangible is: "how might we recover that reciprocal exchange of the spiritual imaginary" as Indigenous teachers and clergy carried the texts of the English churches into other languages and cultures? Finally, Glover reports that the younger generations of Cree are increasingly not able to read the Cree syllabics. With modernity, they have adopted French and English and schools are not currently teaching the Cree language. What can digitalization do in the face of a receding archive?

As both an academic and storyteller, Gordon Henry is acutely sensitive to the origins, status, and mobility of texts. In his essay, he turns that sensitivity to teasing out the tangled history of Gerald Vizenor's *Summer in Spring*, which he treats as a palimpsest, a series of re-curations of Anishinaabe dream songs collected by ethnographer Frances Densmore, reused by Vizenor himself in various ways, then recorded and uploaded to the website of Drumhop Music, where they are disseminated digitally. Through language that reflects the dizzying spirals of recursivness, Henry shows the archive as agonistic, a site of connection and struggle. In this newly evolving digital world, he argues, we can glimpse what he identifies as a "Native curatorial subjectivity," exploring the effects of transvaluation, overwriting, and Native hermeneutics, a tribal imaginary without jurisdiction.

The third part, "Interventions," offers essays that outline four very different digital projects focused on bringing the past or present into the future by using non-Eurocentric, decolonial modes of knowledge production. The first is an account of making an archive by Laura R. Braunstein, Dartmouth's digital humanities librarian, Peter Carini, Dartmouth's archivist, and Hazel-Dawn Dumpert, a freelance editor and writer, who were part of the management team of *The Occom Circle* project, charged with bringing the vision of that project into reality. Their essay gives more background on Occom and the genesis of the project and serves as a case study in how specialists from inside and outside an institution can learn new skills and bring their expertise to the common pot of digital projects that require many minds and hands working across our disciplines and specialties to reach fruition.

Alan Corbiere explains that his digital archive came about unintentionally, driven by his pedagogical needs, but is an "embodied archive" in ways that echo Powell's collaboration with Ojibwe elders. Working at an elementary school at the M'Chigeeng First Nation on Manitoulin Island, Ontario, Corbiere was charged with devising "culturally enhanced curriculum through the medium of language instruction," which involved translating documents, creating lessons, and recording the speech of the elders who are fluent, so that the younger generation will learn their dialect and Anishinaabe language, and also have the benefit of their *aansookaan* (sacred stories) and traditional knowledge and skills. In the course of constructing this serendipitous archive, he realizes that these stories are not just the standard "morality" or "creation/origin" tales. At the end of his essay, Corbiere tells how he tagged along with a native speaker to record him speaking in Anishinaabemowin while collecting birchbark for his wife, who is a renowned quillbox crafter. From this man's experience and knowledge of harvesting practices, Corbiere realizes that the stories *he* has harvested contain what people call "traditional ecological knowledge," which he is in a unique position to preserve.

Next, Damián Baca outlines an inventive digital project based on his scholarly research into ancient nonalphabetic story systems known as codices, or *amoxtli*, of Mesoamerica, which rely completely on pictures, figures, and symbols. In order to offer students a deeper engagement with these ancient writing systems and a different way to think about their own lives and contemporary moment, Baca has devised a graphical user interface (GUI) that allows users to write stories with pictures — that is, to create their own codex. He offers the model of *Codex Delilah: Journey from Mexicatl to Chicana* by Mexican American and Chicana feminist artist Delilah Montoya, who created it in 1992 for the quincentenary of the European invasion of the Americas. Although still in prototype, Baca's Codex project not only makes accessible a forgotten and vibrant history of literacy not based on European textuality, but also asks users to employ elements of that literacy to "affirm the importance of both historical and contemporary intermixing for Mexican and Chicana cultural survival."

Finally, Jason Lewis takes us into the very "stack" of modern computing systems to think about the "unwitnessing" and cultural erasures of Indigenous peoples and others that take place there and how we can replenish this "digital earth" so that Indigenous peoples can flourish here. In effect, he takes us beyond the longhouses of the digital archive, and beyond archives, into analyses about algorithmic bias and encoded bias and whether and how we can reconfigure these processes to include the Indigenous imaginary. This means the very terrain of political action has changed. Because computational philosophers contend we now think through "the thoughts of systems," Lewis argues that, "defining protocols that guide those thoughts is a political act." That is, Lewis proposes that we apply decolonial critiques of the archive to "human-computer interaction." To do so, in 2006 he founded the Aboriginal Territories in Cyberspace (ABTEC) research network, which works to "consciously shape cyberspace to serve Indigenous ends" — that is, to "tell their stories their way." In 2014, ABTEC founded the Initiative for Indigenous Futures (IIF) to explore ways of reclaiming virtual territory, not just being "Indians *in* cyberspace" but becoming "Indians who *make* cyberspace." You will have to read Lewis's essay to see just how he envisions this and puts it into practice.

The conference and the essays in this collection leave us with several questions going forward. Colonial archives exist and require re-curation and, in some cases, repatriation, while digitization is happening apace. How can we intervene to turn these juggernauts to the benefit of Native communities, which in the end benefits us all as a nation based in justice for all? We can work through our scholarship and teaching, through our curation and archival practices, through our storytelling and activism, to recognize and bring attention to the importance of embodied archives, which means honoring the wisdom of elders and those fluent in Native languages threatened with disappearance. It also means exploring and experimenting with different methodologies, casting off the familiar in some cases, and inviting in the new and unfamiliar. In our various modes of work, we can demand the acknowledgement of contexts — of power relations, history, space, and place — in our treatment of Indigenous materials. We can demand from colleagues an acknowledgement that Native protocols for archiving are equally as important as the conventional protocols of Western archives — that is, we can recognize our differences and the different assumptions under which we operate and collaborate around them; recognizing that it is not a zero-sum game in which one way of doing things is the right and only way. To do this, we have to learn to live with discomfort and unfamiliarity, with improvisation and humility. These are not the usual conditions promoted by the academy, or by large and entrenched institutions, or by funding organizations, or by the prevailing digital community. Still, we can nurture these attributes and sharpen our critiques.

We can also nurture the expansion of a post-Eurocentric digital imaginary. We can share or encourage shifting resources from large, institutional holdings to the small, local collections that are overseen by sovereign tribes or communities. For example, in recent discussions about a second phase of *The Occom*

Circle as part of the upcoming 250th anniversary of the founding of Dartmouth College, the planning committee will reach out to smaller libraries and historical societies that hold documents by and about Occom, as well as small regional museums like Mashantucket Pequot Museum and Research Center and the Tantaquidgeon Museum run by the Mohegan Tribe. We can encourage and promote in our courses and institutions community-based learning projects in which our students with digital skills reach out to Native communities to see what their needs are and how we might support and advance the long-term work of cataloguing and digital preservation. The conference papers, and now this collection of essays, provide blueprints for decolonial critique, models for informed archival work, cautions, aspirations, and questions, always questions.

Notes

1. http://www.firstarchivistscircle.org/files/index.html accessed March 31, 2018.

2. Michel Foucault, *The Archeology of Knowledge*. Trans. A. M. Sheridan Smith (London: Tavistock, 1972), 129, 191–92.

3. Jacques Derrida, *Archive Fever: A Freudian Impression*. Trans. Eric Prenowitz (Chicago: University of Chicago Press, 1998), 4.

4. Linda Ferreira-Buckley, "Archivists with an Attitude: Rescuing the Archives from Foucault," *College English* 61:5 (1999): 577–85. I draw here on arguments I develop further in "Native Sovereignty and the Archive: Samson Occom and Digital Humanities," *Resources in American Literary Studies* 38 (2015): 21–52.

5. Dana A. Williams and Marissa K. López, "More Than a Fever: Toward a Theory of the Ethnic Archive," *PMLA* 127:2 (2012): 357–59, 358.

6. Carolyn Steedman, *Dust: The Archive and Cultural History* (New Brunswick, NJ: Rutgers University Press, 2002), 150.

7. For an exemplary illustration of such self-scrutiny, see David J. Kim and Jacqueline Wernimont, "'Performing Archive': Identity, Participation, and Responsibility in the Ethnic Archive," *Archive Journal* (April 2014), http://www.archivejournal.net/essays/performing-archive-identity-participation-and-responsibility-in-the-ethnic-archive/ accessed May 1, 2018.

8. Siobhan Senier, "Digitizing Indigenous History: Trends and Challenges," *Journal of Victorian Culture* 19:3 (2014): 396–402, 396. DOI: 10.1080/13555502.2014.947188 accessed March 19, 2018.

9. Michel de Certeau, *Heterologies: Discourse on the Other*, Trans. Brian Massumi (Minneapolis: University of Minnesota Press, 1995), 216.

10. Drew Lopenzina, *Red Ink: Native Americans Picking Up the Pen in the Colonial Period* (Albany: State University of New York Press, 2012), 18. See "Introduction, Survival Writing: Contesting the 'Pen and Ink Work' of Colonialism," 1–29, for an excellent analysis of the colonial archive and Native responses to it.

11. Diana Taylor, *The Archive and the Repertoire: Performing Cultural Memory in the Americas* (Durham, NC: Duke University Press, 2003), 19–20.

12. Timothy Powell, "Negotiating the Cultural Turn as Universities Adopt a Corporate Model in an Economic Downturn." OpenStax CNX. May 14, 2010 http://cnx.org/contents /e63d4643-0975-4d1b-b5b2-770511886438@2 accessed March 19, 2018.

13. Kimberly Christen, "Gone Digital: Aboriginal Remix and the Cultural Commons," *International Journal of Cultural Property* 12:3 (2005), 315–345, 317.

14. See http://www.mukurtu.org accessed March 19, 2018.

15. *Gibagadinamaagoom* (2012), http://ojibwearchive.sas.upenn.edu/ accessed March 19, 2018. Powell, "Negotiating."

16. Powell, "Negotiating."

17. *Yale Indian Papers Project*. https://yipp.yale.edu accessed March 19, 2018.

18. Grant-Costa, Paul, Tobias Glaza, and Michael Sletcher, "The Common Pot: Editing Native American Materials," *Scholarly Editing: The Annual of the Association for Documentary Editing* 33 (2012): 1–18. http://www.scholarlyediting.org/2012/essays/essay .commonpot.html accessed March 19, 2018 For a larger discussion of "the common pot," see, Lisa Brooks, *The Common Pot: The Recovery of Native Space in the Northeast* (Minneapolis: University of Minnesota Press, 2008), esp. 3–8.

19. Grant-Costa, et al., "The Common Pot," 2.

20. See, for example, https://news.dartmouth.edu/news/2017/11/hood-receives-grant -diversify-art-museum-leadership accessed March 24, 2018. Dartmouth's Hood Museum of Art will use a recently announced Diversifying Art Museum Leadership Initiative grants from the Walton Family Foundation and the Ford Foundation to hire an associate curator of Native American art, a Native American art graduate fellow, and a Native American art undergraduate intern to work with their collections and train the next generation.

21. Senier, "Digitizing Indigenous History," 397.

22. *The Occom Circle*, https://www.dartmouth.edu/~occom. For more on the history of the project and make-up of the various teams, go to the website under "Project" and "Staff."

23. On Native uses of literacy, see Hilary Wyss, *English Letters and Indian Literacies: Reading, Writing, and New England Missionary Schools, 1750–1830* (Philadelphia: University of Pennsylvania Press, 2012). See also E. J. Vance, "Latin Education and the Brothertown Nation of Indians," *American Indian Quarterly* 40:2 (2016): 138–174. Vance was a student research assistant on *The Occom Circle*; this essay derived from the award-winning Honors Thesis in Classics they wrote, using the Occom and Wheelock materials at Dartmouth.

24. Brown University, "Steering Committee on Slavery and Justice," http://www.brown.edu/Research/Slavery_Justice accessed March 31, 2018. For more on this history, see Craig Wilder, *Ebony and Ivy: Race, Slavery, and the Troubled History of America's Universities* (New York: Bloomsbury Press, 2013).

25. See, for example, Occom's letter of July 24, 1771, to Wheelock, where he angrily castigates Wheelock for abandoning his original design and for impugning his reputation among their European supporters: https://collections.dartmouth.edu/occom/html/diplomatic/771424-diplomatic.html accessed May 1, 2018.

26. "Dartmouth College Charter," https://www.dartmouth.edu/~library/rauner/dartmouth/dc-charter.html accessed March 20, 2018. For an account Native American attendance at and graduation from Dartmouth, see Colin Calloway, *Indian History of an American Institution: Native Americans and Dartmouth* (Hanover, NH: University Press of New England, 2010).

27. For an exploration of a post-Eurocentric approach to American Studies, see Timothy Powell, ed. *Beyond the Binary: Reconstructing Cultural Identity in a Multicultural Context* (New Brunswick, NJ: Rutgers University Press, 1999), 2. In order to decenter the dominant national and European perspectives, Powell recommends that scholars work to "reconfigure American Studies not as a series of distinct and disparate identities that are categorically separate but as a critical site that will allow for the theorization of difference and conflict as well as commonality and community."

28. For the Orozo murals, see http://hoodmuseum.dartmouth.edu/explore/news/jose-clemente-orozco-epic-american-civilization and scroll down to the inaugural lecture by Professor Mary Coffey, who gave the conference participants our tour. To read about the Hovey Murals, see https://www.dartmouth.edu/~library/digital/publishing/books/kennedy2011, a free epub book, accessed May 1, 2018

29. Carla Javier, "A Timeline of the Year of Resistance at Standing Rock," *Splinter*, https://splinternews.com/a-timeline-of-the-year-of-resistance-at-standing-rock-1794269727 accessed March 20, 2018

PART I *Critiques*

ONE

The Role of Indigenous Communities in Building Digital Archives

Timothy B. Powell

The first generation of large-scale digital archives focused primarily on canonical American literary figures and historical events such as Walt Whitman, Emily Dickinson, and the Civil War.[1] With the publication of *Digital Debates in the Humanities* (2012), scholars led by Alan Liu, Amy E. Earhart, and Tara McPherson launched an important critique, pointedly captured by the title of McPherson's essay: "Why are the Digital Humanities So White?"[2] Indigenous cultures, in particular, seemed once again to be left out of the digital reconstruction of American history and literature. Happily, this has begun to change. As Jennifer O'Neal notes in "'The Right to Know': Decolonizing Native American Archives" (2015), "Over the past decade Native American archives have witnessed a significant transformation across the United States. . . . [N]umerous non-tribal repositories are collaborating with and developing shared stewardship protocols with tribal communities regarding Native American collections." O'Neal goes on to observe an even more recent trend: "More than any time before tribal communities are establishing strong, growing archival collections documenting their histories."[3] This essay will provide an overview of both these phenomena — digital repositories created by archives and/or universities in partnership with Indigenous communities and community-based digital archives managed and maintained by tribal entities. Because the first movement is further along, an overview of some of the more successful archives will demonstrate their importance to culturally diversifying both the humanities and Western archives with significant Indigenous holdings. Community-based digital archives, however, have not been as fully developed and so the emphasis here will be placed on how scholars, archivists, and community members can work together to strengthen this nascent movement. In both cases, Indigenous communities play a fundamentally important, albeit sometimes precarious, role. By way of addressing how such partnerships can be put into place and the problems that can occur along the way, the intent of this essay is to share stories meant to further both these movements.

A Brief Overview of Indigenous Archives

Digital technology has revolutionized the stewardship of Indigenous materials at Western archives. Funded by forward-looking grant institutions, archives with some of the largest Native American collections in the country are in the midst of digitizing massive quantities of Indigenous materials. The American Philosophical Society, for example, recently digitized more than 3,000 hours of its Native American audio collection. The Archive of Traditional Music at Indiana University is in the process of digitizing its entire audio collection, which includes one of the largest collections of wax cylinder recordings of Indigenous languages.[4] The National Anthropological Archive at the Smithsonian is in the midst of a long-term project to digitize "endangered cultures and languages, indigenous environmental knowledge, and the connections between these subjects."[5] Simultaneously, the California Language Archive is digitizing its valuable collection of recordings of Indigenous languages.[6] Long inaccessible to Native communities, the availability of these manuscripts, photographs, and audio recordings has produced unprecedented partnerships between scholars, archivists, and community members that have, in just a short time, already resulted in remarkable outcomes.[7]

At the same time, Indigenous communities across the continent are in the midst of a wave of cultural revitalization. Although reasons vary from one community to the next, this historical phenomenon has undoubtedly been strengthened by the fact that the first generations in living memory are being raised free from the forced assimilation and cultural genocide inflicted by the boarding school system in the United States and the residential schools in Canada. Truly extraordinary developments in cultural revitalization are unfolding, as in the case of Jessie Little Doe's work to bring back the Wampanoag language, considered extinct for more than 200 years, for which she received a MacArthur genius grant.[8] In the Tuscarora Nation on the Niagara River, the community has broken ground on the first Longhouse to be built in the community in more than 150 years, providing a place for the stories to be kept and passed on according to well established and highly sophisticated Haudenosaunee protocols. Projects like these, large and small, are being undertaken by hundreds of Indigenous communities ranging from the Kwakwaka'wakw on Vancouver Island to the Penobscot on the northeast coast, from Inuit communities within the Arctic Circle to the Tunica in the southern Mississippi valley.

This confluence of digitization and revitalization has led to the creation of a number of large-scale projects that demonstrate the promise of this unique historical moment. The *Plateau Peoples' Web Portal*, for example, is one of the oldest and most successful examples of collaborations between archives, scholars, and Indigenous communities. Tribal partners include the Spokane Tribe of Indians, the Confederated Tribes of the Colville Reservation, the Confederated Tribes of the Umatilla Indian Reservation, the Coeur d'Alene Tribe of Indians, the Confederated Tribes of Warm Springs, and the Confederated Tribes and Bands of the Yakama Nation. Scholarly collaboration is directed by the Center for Digital Scholarship and Curation and Native American Programs at Washington State University (WSU). And the participating archives are WSU's Manuscripts, Archives, and Special Collections; the Northwest Museum of Art and Culture; the National Anthropological Archives; and the National Museum of the American Indian at the Smithsonian Institution.[9] The archive uses the *Mukurtu* content management system designed by Kimberly Christen and her team. The viewer gains access to the archive through "tribal paths" that foreground the cultures rather than the names of the predominantly non-Native people who collected the archival materials.[10] Baskets are juxtaposed with videos of community members entitled "What does Sovereignty Mean to You?" to provide a rich cultural context that effectively reminds the viewer that Native people are not trapped within the borders of black and white photographs, but are vital partners in the process of retelling the history of Indigenous peoples in the digital age.

On the east coast, the *Yale Indian Papers Project* (YIPP) is a similarly vast collaborative endeavor focused on the New England region that includes seven institutional partners, nine contributing partners, and five tribal/First Nation partners.[11] More focused on primary archival materials, the YIPP's stated goal is:

To provide greater access to primary source materials by, on, or about New England Native Americans by editing a foundational set of documents that explores various aspects of Native history and culture, including sovereignty, land, gender, race, identity, religion, migration, law, and politics, and publishing them in an open-access virtual repository . . . to facilitate greater intellectual access to the documents . . . [and] to re-inscribe indigeneity into a collection of documents that represents a shared history between Americans, Native Americans, Britons, and the Atlantic World by fostering participation of Indian scholars and tribal members . . . [and] by acknowledging them as colleagues, scholars, intellectuals, and representatives of the Native voice.[12]

This recognition of "Indian scholars and tribal members" as equals to academic scholars is a monumentally important step forward. The oft-cited goal of "decolonizing the archive" is not, however, easily achieved.[13] As is so often the case, the researcher trying to locate materials through archival websites is initially confronted by an empty box, which requires a good deal of knowledge about how Western archival systems work in order to find the name of, say, an ancestor who is not recognized as an "author" in the system. Even the search for prominent figures like King Philip produces the answer: "No entries found." If one knows to type in his Indian name, Metacom, this produces two hits: "Letter from Wait Winthrop to John Winthrop, Jr." and "Letter from Roger Williams to Robert Car." Clicking on either entry leads to a long string of Library of Congress subject headings, with a note, "Metacom [Mentioned within document]."[14] The problem, simply stated, is that the knowledge system underlying archival search engines (e.g., Library of Congress headings, Encoded Archival Description [EAD] Finding Aids, or Dublin Core metadata schema) differs sharply from the way that communities remember their own history based on a very different knowledge system (e.g., clan affiliation, genealogy, or stories and songs associated with certain ceremonies).[15] I will come back, in the third section of this chapter, to strategies for reconciling the Western archival and Indigenous knowledge systems.

Another approach to making large-scale digital repositories of Indigenous holdings accessible to Indigenous audiences is the California Language Archive's (CLA's) map-based interface. Like the *Plateau Peoples' Web Portal* and YIPP, CLA is made up of large and prestigious contributing repositories including the Bancroft Library, the Berkeley Language Center, Phoebe A. Hearst Museum of Anthropology, and Survey of California and Other Languages. Regionally focused like the two repositories described above, CLA, as the name would suggest, concentrates more narrowly on Indigenous languages from the western coast. The map, in contrast to the blank box that serves as a point of entry for so many other archives, hews much more closely to an Indigenous way of understanding culture in relation to the land. As one zooms in on the map, more and more geographical features and points of identification become recognizable, each designated by tribe/language, thus making the Indigenous communities more immediately present rather than a subfield to the non-Native author or contributor. Clicking on any given point reveals all the material available for that particular language with a metadata scheme that features "contributors," noted parenthetically as (donor), (consultant), and (researcher), such that the collaborative nature of the work between scholars and fluent speakers is more effectively highlighted.[16] This, in turn, allows a member of the tribe to search through a single page for the name of family members or neighbors and, thus, works much more effectively for a community-based audience.

A fourth example of a highly successful digital archive of Indigenous materials is *The Occom Circle*, which digitizes and annotates archival documents by Mohegan author Samson Occom (1723–1794) located in Dartmouth College's collections. Like the Walt Whitman or Emily Dickinson archives, it is tightly focused on one distinguished character in the broader framework of American literary history, though in this case, the author is Native American. Samson Occom is one of the most important early figures in Native American literature written in English, and his work has not received the attention it deserves in part because of its eighteenth-century prose and regionally specific subject matter. *The Occom Circle*'s curated annotations thus make the work much more accessible by transcribing the handwritten documents and utilizing hypertext to identify people, places, organizations, and events related to Occom's life. The project also exemplifies how to train undergraduates to utilize primary research and the digital humanities to more successfully integrate Native American writers into early American literary history. Especially welcome is the way the archive helps American literature students and scholars to appreciate connections to the contemporary Mohegan Nation by linking tribal projects such as "Restoring our Language," "Connecting to our Culture," and "Preserving our Culture," which highlight the wave of cultural revitalization taking place in the community.[17]

Finally, one of the most important and inspiring digital archives to date is Darryl Baldwin's exemplary work at the Myaamia Center at Miami University on behalf of the Miami Tribe of Oklahoma. This digital archive includes an online dictionary, "Telling Our Story: A Living History of the Myaamia," which contributed to bringing the Myaamia language back from extinction and teaching scholars that Native languages, though moribund, can be revitalized through carefully thought-out collaborations between academic, community-based, and digital humanities scholars. The Myaamia Center has also successfully developed an app called niiki ("My Home") that has helped bring the Myaamia language into classrooms and homes outside the academy's walls.[18] Darryl Baldwin has also been instrumental, through his work with the Smithsonian's Recovering Voices and Breath of Life programs, in getting other communities involved with archives and linguists to create partnerships to strengthen language revitalization programs.[19]

I have been fortunate to have worked at a Western archive that possessed state-of-the-art digital infrastructure, a deep-seated commitment to digitally repatriating its holdings to the communities of origin, and a grant officer who raised more than three million dollars to support this work in partnership with distinguished scholars and highly innovative tribal partners. The grants produced a digital archive at the American Philosophical Society that includes more than 3,000 hours of Indigenous audio recordings and hundreds of photographs with information provided by Indigenous communities. The new finding aid for the Native American collection includes a map interface and the names of more than 100 Indigenous contributors, not previously recognized by the older cataloguing system.[20] Having described the results of those projects elsewhere, I want to concentrate on telling some of the stories that did not find their way into the final grant reports or the PR announcements.[21] Moments when the whole enterprise teetered on the brink of collapse until Indigenous elders, teachers, and young people stepped in to help us focus on what mattered most — realizing the extraordinary opportunity created by the simultaneous rise of digital technology and community-based revitalization movements. I do so not to criticize the American Philosophical Society, but rather in the hope that by being honest, these stories may help other institutions and Indigenous communities work together more effectively.

The Role of Elders and Storytelling in Building Digital Archives

The American Philosophical Society (APS) represents the epitome of an august archive, deeply rooted in the colonial tradition. Founded by Benjamin Franklin in 1743, the Native American collection began when Thomas Jefferson, who served concurrently as the president of the APS and president of the country, sent Lewis and Clark off across the continent to collect Indigenous languages.[22]

During the eight years I worked at the APS (2008–2016), projects related to the Native American collections resulted in two Mellon grants to digitize the library's entire Indigenous audio collection of more than 3,000 hours, a Getty grant to gain intellectual control over more than 200,000 images of Native Americans in the collections, and a National Endowment for the Humanities (NEH) grant to endow a Center for Native American and Indigenous Research (CNAIR). APS librarian, Martin Levitt, deserves a great deal of credit for overseeing all these projects and building partnerships with Indigenous communities into an enduring part of the institution, as do archivist extraordinaire Brian Carpenter and the development officer, Nanette Holben. None of this would have been possible, however, without the invaluable assistance of elders and community members. These partnerships did not come easily, and so I want to begin by recounting a culturally insensitive but nonetheless revealing moment, which occurred the very first time the APS administration and staff sat down with representatives from the Indigenous Nations whose traditional knowledge was housed in the library.

In 2010, the APS hosted a conference entitled "Building Bridges between Archives and Indigenous Communities," which came at the end of a Mellon grant that digitized the first half, roughly 1,500 hours, of the Native American audio collection.[23] Invited guests included representatives from twelve Indigenous communities, leading scholars in the field such as Kimberly Christen and Jennifer O'Neal, and archivists from peer institutions including the National Anthropological Archives at the Smithsonian Institution, the Folklife Center at the Library of Congress, and Scott Stevens, who was at the time the director of the McNickle Center for American Indian and Indigenous Studies at the Newberry Library. But despite the fact that all the right people were assembled, things went wrong almost immediately.

To demonstrate their commitment to the project, the APS asked that one of its senior library staff speak first. The staff member, who had worked at the APS for many years and delivered dozens of similar presentations to non-Native audiences, began by asking an Indigenous guest to read from one of the books in Franklin's personal library, which impressively lined the walls of the room where we were sitting. Unfortunately, the staff member selected a text that included numerous usages of the word "squaw," which many Indigenous people believe translates into a vulgar term for vagina, or at the very least, a demeaning term for Indian women.[24] It was clear that the Native people in the room were deeply offended, though they remained politely silent, waiting until we were alone to express their dismay. In sharp contrast, the staff member remained utterly oblivious, having naively assumed that Indigenous people, like other guests, would be impressed by the APS's colonial origins. I honestly do not think any of the APS administrators were aware of the gaff, which would have horrified them as a gross violation of the Society's protocols for treating distinguished guests. And yet, unintended cultural misunderstandings like this one are precisely what make it so challenging to bring together archives and Indigenous communities that can clash without making a sound.

Knowing that the whole endeavor could have imploded almost literally before it began, I quickly jumped to my feet and apologized (fortunately, the staff member had departed the room). I then asked Larry Aitken, an Ojibwe elder from Cass Lake who has been my mentor for many years, to speak. In preparation for this moment, I had invited Aitken to come to the APS a year earlier to see the collections and to seek his advice about forming partnerships between Western archives and Indigenous communities. Based on this earlier visit, Aitken had requested, in advance of the conference's introductory meeting, that a large pictographic map of the Ojibwe migration story from the A. Irving Hallowell collection be spread out across the table.[25] Speaking in the cadences of traditional oratory, Aitken explained to the APS administration: "this story does not belong to the APS. We still possess the birchbark scrolls in our *Midewiwin* (Grand Medicine Society) lodges from which this map was copied." Because the *Midewiwin* teachings are culturally sensitive, Aitken did not discuss the meanings of the story, nor will I, in keeping with his community's protocols. Aitken's point, rather, was that this pictographic map, recounting a story that had occurred more than 500 years ago, clearly demonstrated that "the Ojibwe are the archivists of our people, the keepers of the sacred scrolls. There is nothing that is not archived about our people. It's just an archive with a different symbol, with a different way. And if Western society knew that, they would stop saying that Native people do not keep track of their own history, that we need Western archives to do that for us."[26] He then pointed to the place where the migration ends, Otter Tail Point on Leech Lake (Hallowell annotated the map with the expert assistance of elders) and said: "This is where I'm from, Leech Lake. We remember well that an important *Midewiwin* Lodge stood on this site and we continue to honor and protect Otter Tail Point to this day."[27]

Watie Akins, a Penobscot elder who had never met Aitken before this moment, then rose to speak. Akins pointed to the pictograph where the migration began. "I am from this place, on the east coast. The Penobscot too are Anishinaabeg and we remember well when the Ojibwe were our neighbors" (the Anishinaabeg are a larger cultural group that include both the Ojibwe and Penobscot).[28] Then, in an immensely touching moment, Aitken apologized to Akins for leaving his people behind, more than 500 years ago, when the time came for the Ojibwe to move west on the migration. The gesture invoked an even older story of the Seven Fires Prophecy, which instructed the Ojibwe, before Europeans arrived, to take the Sacred Scrolls to safety by migrating west until they arrived at a place where food grew in the water (*manonmin*, or wild rice, that, in this scroll's version of the migration, led them to Leech Lake). The prophet of the First Fire foretold that a light-skinned race would come during the period of the Fourth Fire when the Anishinaabeg, who remained on the coast, would nearly be destroyed.[29] For this reason, the Ojibwe were instructed to take the sacred scrolls away to protect them from the foretold European encroachment. Akins nodded in affirmation, since he knew the Seven Fires Prophecy as well.

Watie Akins and Larry Aitken's stories demonstrated very powerfully to the APS administration and staff how traditional knowledge, in the hands of elders, could span the thousand miles that separates Leech Lake in Minnesota from the Penobscot reservation in Maine and, even more impressively, collapse the thousand years between the present moment and the last time the Ojibwe and Penobscot were neighbors. With artful subtlety, Aitken revealed how the traditional knowledge kept in the library (e.g., the pictographic map in the Hallowell collection) and the traditional knowledge kept by the communities (e.g., the stories and scrolls passed down for countless generations) can come to life when reconnected. Even though the APS administration was almost certainly unaware of the intricacies of the Anishinaabe traditional knowledge system, the stories nevertheless worked in the sense that they reassured the Native guests in the aftermath of the staff member's mistake and convinced the APS to apply for a second Mellon grant to complete the digitization of the APS audio recordings and to build digital archives in four partnering communities.

Significantly, the APS also benefitted from these partnerships. The second Mellon grant funded fellowships that allowed representatives from the partnering tribes to come to the APS to select materials for their own digital archives and to share their knowledge of the APS collections. I think it is safe to say that no one at the APS anticipated how mutually beneficial these collaborations would turn out to be. Communities provided the names of relatives in dozens of old photographs, significantly enhancing the metadata and thus making the APS holdings more valuable to researchers. In some cases, elders graciously agreed to make new recordings telling stories about the people in the photographs or explaining how they felt about listening to recordings of ancestors whose voices they had never heard before the wax cylinders were digitized.[30] Many of the elders who attended the "Building Bridges" conference went on to serve on the APS's Native American advisory board, which established protocols to protect culturally sensitive materials in the Indigenous collections for the first time in the Society's more than 270-year history. In return, the APS allowed their tribal partners to digitize tens of thousands of manuscript pages, audio recordings, and old photographs to begin the process of building their own digital archives.

Reviewing these outcomes, however, it is easy to forget how close all this came to not happening. Digitization of archival materials alone will not suffice. Elders and community members played a vital role in the success of the grant and in convincing the APS to share its resources. Before continuing in the next section to a more detailed discussion of how the communities set up their digital archives, it is important to go deeper into the question of how the stories *worked* to convince the APS to form these partnerships.

About a year after the "Building Bridges between Archives and Indigenous Communities," I went to see Aitken at Leech Lake to ask for his help in understanding how the stories healed the wound inflicted by the staff member's cultural insensitivity and, in turn, helped to create the partnerships that led to the second Mellon grant. Aitken laughed and teased me about being an "academaniac" who studied stories but did not understand how they worked. He then explained, "the preservation of our language, our culture, our history, our people, and our ways to acquire knowledge all ought to be retained, not only for the good of our people . . . but so they can be shared, so you will no longer be a foreigner, a stranger, but you'll be a neighbor." He pointedly reminded me that "we've been neighbors for 500 years and [we have patiently endured this] stifling encroachment on our people . . . our language . . . our epistemology . . . our medicine." Aitken explained that we are now living in the time of the Seventh Fire when, it was prophesized, the dominant whites would either choose the "right road," which leads to a new era of respectful cohabitation with Indigenous peoples, or the "wrong road," which leads to the destruction of the environment and ultimately the human race.[31] "Don't kill our culture," he implored, "embrace it and understand it."[32]

With all due humility, I want to try to address this challenge of finding a way for Western archives and Indigenous communities to work together to return the cultural heritage that has been withheld for so long.[33] I speak here not on Aitken's behalf, but only for myself. Based on my research and what Aitken has taught me about Ojibwe cosmology and epistemology, I know that the pictographic migration story at the APS, which begins in primordial times and recounts the actions of *manidoog* (spirits), is a form of *aadizookaanag*, which translates roughly to empowered stories about legendary ancestors or dream spirits.[34] Such stories have their own system of protocols. They should, for example, only be told in winter when the thunderbirds migrate south and the bear are sleeping, to minimize the risk the *manidoog* will overhear these stories and be offended.

Another quality *aadizookaanag* possess is animacy. As the anthropologist Tim Ingold explains, myths "tell the lives of non-human persons [e.g., spirits or thunderbirds] — or, to be more precise, the myths *are* those persons, who, in the telling, are not merely commemorated but actually made present for the assembled audience, as though they had been brought to life and invited in." Discussing the animacy of stones in the context of Ojibwe ceremonies, Ingold writes, "animacy . . . is a property not of stones *as such*, but of their positioning within a relational field which includes persons as foci of power."[35] This is why the stories only work their magic in the presence of elders like Aitken, who was formally trained by the Medicine Man Jim Jackson to act as an *oshkabewis*, or someone authorized to translate from one world to another; in this case, to speak on behalf of the ancestral spirits embodied by the pictographic narrative to the APS administrators, who watched with rapt attention.

Having situated the stories within the context of the Ojibwe traditional knowledge system, my hope is that we can now better understand how and why the ancient stories performed so effectively in a contemporary, non-Native environment like the "Building Bridges" conference. Note that Aitken begins by boldly declaring of the migration narrative, "This story does not belong to the APS." I do not believe Aitken intended to challenge US copyright law's definition of ownership, since this would have immediately caused the APS to pull back and, thus, negate the possibility of the traditional knowledge being returned to the communities of origin in digital form. Rather, my impression is that Aitken thoughtfully initiates a process to establish Ojibwe protocols as having equal standing with those of the APS. "We still possess the birchbark scrolls," Aitken continues, "the Ojibwe are the archivists of our people." Here he begins the process of creating a common vocabulary so that the APS and Ojibwe could speak to one another as fellow archivists. The fact that the Ojibwe possessed the sacred scrolls hundreds of years before Ben Franklin founded the APS and continue to care for them to the present day subtly elevates the Anishinaabe system of *aadizookaanag* and, in doing so, silently subverts the hierarchy of ownership enshrined in US copyright law.[36] That is to say, Aitken shifts the frame of reference so that what the APS metadata refers to as an "oversized map" in the "A. Irving Hallowell Papers" now becomes situated in relation to the much longer continuum of Ojibwe archival history.

Aitken accomplishes this, I believe, by using the word "story" in a highly strategic manner. For once you begin to think about the archival object as a story, it quickly becomes evident that it had a long life prior to coming to the APS as one of the most powerful stories in Ojibwe culture and, moreover, that it is still alive according to the logic of *aadizookaanag*. Or, as Aitken puts it, "whenever we are telling a story, the story itself comes to life." I firmly believe, having witnessed this phenomenon many times, that the stories do come back to life when they are returned to the community of origin and that we need to take this dynamic quality into consideration when building community-based archives. Another quality of *aadizookaanag* that deserves attention is the power of these animate stories to shape-shift. As Ingold observes in "A Circumpolar Night's Dream," the spirits that inhabit these empowered stories also possess the ability to transform in the hands of an elder trained to do this highly specialized work: "this capacity for metamorphosis is . . . a critical index of power: the more powerful the person, the more readily a change of form may be effected."[37] These qualities of metamorphosis and animacy, as we will see in the next section, share a surprising affinity with digital technology that is important to understand as we turn to the question of how digital technology can be most effectively utilized in Indigenous communities.

I do not, however, want to conclude this section by making it seem like digital technology or contributions by elders and community members can rid Western archives of colonization's problematic legacy. Yes, the collaboration had some positive outcomes. The pictographic map, along with more than 300 photographs from the A. Irving Hallowell collection, would become part of a United Nations Educational, Scientific, and Cultural Organization (UNESCO) World Heritage Site nomination submitted by the Pimachiowin Aki Corporation—made up of four Anishinaabe communities, the provincial governments of Ontario and Manitoba, and the Canadian government—to protect almost 24,000 square kilometers of boreal forest and the cultural landscape of the Anishinaabeg ancestral homeland.[38] The Penobscot would use a digitized version of a previously unpublished Penobscot-English dictionary written by Frank Siebert to win two grants totaling $800,000 that would enable them to revitalize their language after the last fluent speaker died in 2006.[39] Despite these accomplishments, the end of the grant cycle (2011–2014), as is often the case, led to a sharp drop off in the Digital Knowledge Sharing initiative. When the Mellon Foundation approached the APS in 2016 about writing a third grant focused on Native American research, the previous administration had retired and the new administration insisted on returning to a system where only scholars in a PhD track or beyond are eligible for the Native American fellowships. As a result, elders like Larry Aitken and Watie Akins, who played such a crucial role in forming the partnerships and were skilled archival researchers in their own right, have been excluded, as were members of the upcoming generation who chose to work on revitalization efforts in their communities rather than leaving the reservation for a multi-year commitment to graduate studies.

Rather than abandoning the partnerships with Indigenous communities, I retired from the APS to start Educational Partnerships with Indigenous Communities (EPIC) at the Penn Language Center in the School of Arts and Sciences at the University of Pennsylvania.[40] EPIC is dedicated to writing grants through tribal institutions (e.g., museums or tribal colleges) that support community-based scholars. EPIC has also expanded the archival consortium to include the APS, Archive of Traditional Music at Indiana University, Bloomington, the Folklife Center at the Library of Congress, and the National Anthropological Archives and Recovering Voices Program at the Smithsonian Institution. A new NEH grant from the Office of Digital Humanities is funding community-based scholars doing innovative work with digital technology to travel to the participating archives and work together to build digital archives in Indian Country. In the next section, I will review some ongoing projects that, taken together, provide a sketch of the complex and diverse ways communities are using digital technology and hopefully inspire other communities to work with archives to take advantage of this unprecedented historical opportunity.

Following the Stories Back Home

By way of conclusion, I want to shift the focus from decolonizing Western archives to building digital archives in Indigenous communities. Rather than seeing it as something inherently Western and new, it may prove more productive to situate digital technology as an extension of the historical continuum of Nations managing their own unique systems of collective memory. Surprisingly, for example, digital technology is able to represent Indigenous instances of the oral tradition much more effectively than print culture, which is unable to record the cadences of traditional oratory or the movement of the dance. Digital recordings and video, on the other hand, reflect more accurately the animate qualities of traditional knowledge. As the Cherokee elder Tom Belt said, after listening to a newly digitized recording of an ancestor who had died more than 60 years earlier: "The manner in which he spoke was an older form of addressing people. . . . It is a very melodic way of speaking. . . . We learned or know in the Cherokee language how that kind of information is best received. . . . After all, we practiced this for millennia upon millennia." In this sense, Tom Belt concluded, digital technology is able to connect the speaker and the listener across "time and . . . death itself."[41] It is this ability of digital technology to become part of the historical continuum of Cherokee elders passing down animate stories from one generation to the next for "millennia upon millennia" that is so intriguing and suggestive of the exciting possibilities that lie ahead.

STORY #1: WHAT DOES AN ANIMATED, FOUR-THOUSAND-YEAR-OLD ARCHIVE LOOK LIKE?

The Franz Boas Professional Papers at the APS contain more than 10,000 pages of ethnographic notes collected by George Hunt, a Tlingit ethnographer who married into two prominent Kwakwaka'wakw families, with the guidance of Boas, the founding father of American anthropology. Much of the Hunt-Boas collection was never published and therefore has remained unavailable to the communities for a century or more. Kwakwaka'wakw community leaders worked closely with my colleague Brian Carpenter to select hundreds of pages to be digitized with the goal of supporting cultural revitalization in four Kwakwaka'wakw bands. Interestingly, the community did not want the materials in digital form. So we printed out the digital files into two books and made 200 copies of each book to present to the elders and hereditary chiefs at a potlatch ceremony. It was a remarkable opportunity to witness the moment when papers preserved by a Western archive transform to become part of the living archive maintained by the Kwakwaka'wakw for *four millennia*.[42] Within the Big House, where the potlatch ceremony took place, the stories came to life as elaborate dances performed with elegantly carved masks, accompanied by songs sung to the pulsating rhythm of ten men drumming on a hollowed-out cedar log. At either end of the lodge, Sis-kiutl, the two-headed serpent, watched over the feast in the form of a beautifully carved cedar trunk painted in the palette of the Northwest coast. The dancers wore hats with eagle down sprinkled onto the crown so that with each step, the downy white feathers would fly into the air, become caught in the hot air rising from the fire and then, as they reached the roof of cedar beams, float down and gently touch each person in the Big House.

What this story tells us is that, once returned, the Western archival materials shapeshift almost immediately into the forms preserved by traditional Kwakwaka'wakw archives — dances, regalia, carvings, songs, oral tradition, and so on.[43] Boas's importance is eclipsed by George Hunt, whose family remains prominent within the community. This shift can be read as metaphor for how the ownership of the materials is transformed as it leaves the "Franz Boas Professional Papers" collection at the APS and becomes part of the Kwakwaka'wakw archives being performed to affirm the Kwakwaka'wakw relation to the land. Given that the potlatch ceremony was banned by the Canadian government from 1885 to 1951, when thousands of masks and carvings were stolen from communities and placed in museum collections throughout the Western world, the return of stories constitutes an important affirmation of Kwakwaka'wakw sovereignty.[44] The restoration of the potlatch system as a traditional form of governance is an extraordinary accomplishment. And even though digital technology plays a very small role in the process, the outcomes of returning the stories back to the community are extraordinary.

There is an important lesson here for the digital humanities, which can sometimes become infatuated with big data projects and the capabilities of supercomputers.[45] What we need, I would argue, is to understand how digital technology can best serve the community. This varies greatly from one community to the next, even within the Kwakwaka'wakw. The community-based U'mista Cultural Centre in Alert Bay, British Columbia, for example, is working with the Archive of Traditional Music (ATM) at Indiana University to oversee the return of digital copies of wax cylinder recordings of Kwakwaka'wakw songs made by Hunt and Boas.[46] Here, then, a very different set of challenges arises, raising important questions about how best to make digital archives accessible to the community. Should the ATM's catalogue descriptions simply be imported, even though this system would be completely foreign to how the Kwakwaka'wakw understand their own traditional archive? Or should a new kind of digital archive be devised that would allow Kwakwaka'wakw people to search the collection based on the genealogies of the families or communities who own the traditional rights to the materials? Or would the community be better served by a relational database that would connect descriptions of masks, regalia, and songs associated with specific ceremonies? All this remains to be pondered. What is important here is to begin the discussion about how to find ways for the archives or institutions of higher education to train community members to build their own digital archives, based on their own traditional archival systems, so that the knowledge can be passed on to the coming generations who will almost undoubtedly possess much more vivid digital imaginations.

The Frances Densmore collection of wax cylinder recordings of Chippewa (Ojibwe) music in the Folklife Center at the Library of Congress (LOC) was originally recorded in the first decade of the twentieth century and was digitally repatriated to Fond du Lac Tribal and Community College (FDLTCC) 106 years later, in 2014.[47] Lyz Jaakola, the director of the Ojibwemowining Resource Center ("Ojibwe is Spoken Here") at FDLTCC, exemplifies the new generation of community-based, tech-savvy Indigenous scholars who are able to imagine digital possibilities that stretch well beyond the limits of Western archives.[48] Jaakola and I co-wrote an NEH Humanities Initiatives with Tribal Colleges and Universities grant, through FDLTCC, to digitize the Densmore recordings and bring them back to the communities where the recordings had originally been made. When FDLTCC received the digital recordings from the LoC, they were in massive files that made it difficult to correlate each song with Densmore's exquisite ethnographic descriptions. Two graduate students at Vanderbilt and Princeton (Juliet Larkin Gilmore and Joshua Garrett-Davis, respectively) worked for two years to build a digital database that embedded each individual recording with Densmore's notes so that the information would be searchable and, thus, of much greater use to the community. This, however, was just the beginning of songs' journey.

Because many of the songs are associated with the *Midewiwin* (Grand Medicine Society), Jaakola has taken them to a number of lodges to identify which ones should be restricted as culturally sensitive and see whether they could be of use to contemporary *Midewiwin* practices. Jaakola then began working with those songs designated as not culturally sensitive, transforming them from barely audible, scratchy recordings back into living entities that then circulate through the community in fascinating patterns. Jaakola accomplished this by enlisting elders and students at the college to help re-record the songs. These new digital files are being incorporated into curriculum for use by Native and non-Native students throughout northern Minnesota. Jaakola and FDLTCC are currently working with the World Indigenous Nations Higher Education Consortium

(WINHEC) to create new curricula for elementary education, an Environmental Institute, and the American Indian Studies program at FDLTCC, all developed in consultation with Ojibwe elders. Jaakola is also incorporating some of the Densmore recordings and re-recordings into "An Ojibwe-Anishinaabe Music Curriculum" in accordance with grade-level state standards to be used by music educators in the Minnesota public school system. As Jaakola wrote in an article we copublished in the *Oxford Handbook of Musical Repatriation* (2017): "Music in Ojibwe-Anishinaabe culture is more than just a form of entertainment. Music is a living spiritual being."[49]

This story illustrates the complex interplay of digital and traditional archives and the need to coordinate the two carefully in close consultation with the community. The Densmore collection is unique in that it includes descriptions of how both a Western-trained ethnomusicologist documented the songs and the Ojibwe themselves archived the songs. Densmore's meticulous ethnography thus includes musical scores and an analysis of "varied measure lengths and rapid metric unit[s]."[50] In addition, her notes include the name of the singer, the lyrics written in the Ojibwe language, the Ojibwe elder's description of the song's meaning, and even pictographs for each song that would have been etched in birchbark scrolls that Aitken identifies as the original "Ojibwe archive." Beneath each pictograph is a quotation from an elder explaining the symbols. This pictographic system has not been "lost" or "forgotten," as the myth of the Vanishing Indian would have us believe. When I showed Densmore's book, *Chippewa Music*, to an Ojibwe Medicine Man who had been raised in a remote region of Canada and who could not read English, he took one look at the pictographs and immediately began singing the song. Thus, because FDLTCC maintains a robust digital infrastructure, it becomes possible to integrate Western and Indigenous archives and, just as importantly, to keep them separate in accordance with *Midewiwin* protocols.

We stand on the edge of an unprecedented historical moment when it has become possible to return thousands of archival recordings, photographs, and manuscripts to the communities just as a wave of cultural revitalization is sweeping across the continent. We are seeing archival recordings used in the Tuscarora Toddlers program and digital copies of old photographs used by their communities to preserve their ancestral homelands through UNESCO World Heritage nominations. It is the proverbial win-win-win situation for scholars, archives, and communities.

But we still need some help. In closing, I would ask the granting agencies, archives, colleges, and universities to recognize the important work being done by elders, dancers, drummers, and K–12 teachers. Archival and university fellowships need to be rethought so they do not require a PhD, nor do they require community-based scholars to leave the reservation so they can be in residence somewhere far away. As Richard Hill, the director of the Deyohahá:ge Indigenous Knowledge Centre at Six Nations Polytechnic, told me when we were discussing a new grant application, we need to be concentrating on developing community-based digital humanities scholars who will be able to imagine new ways for Western archival materials to take on new life to benefit those, as the Haudenosaunee say, seven generations in the future.[51]

Notes

1. See, for example, Walt Whitman Archive, http://whitmanarchive.org; Emily Dickinson Archive, http://www.edickinson.org; Valley of the Shadow: Two Communities in the American Civil War, http://valley.lib.virginia.edu.

2. See Alan Liu, "Where Is Cultural Criticism in the Digital Humanities?" *Debates in the Digital Humanities*, ed. Matthew K. Gold (Minneapolis: University of Minnesota Press, 2012), 490–507. Amy E. Earhart, "Can Information Be Unfettered? Race and the New Digital Humanities Canon," *Debates in DH*: 309–318. Tara McPherson, "Why Are the Digital Humanities So White? Or Thinking the Histories of Race and Computation," *Debates in DH*: 139–160.

3. Jennifer R. O'Neal, "'The Right to Know': Decolonizing Native American Archives," *Journal of Western Archives* 5:1 (2015): 1.

4. "ATM and MDPI to Preserve Wax Cylinder Collections," *IU Newsroom* (April 20, 2015), https://repository.upenn.edu/cgi/viewcontent.cgi?referer=https://www.google.com/&httpsredir=1&article=1013&context=rs_papers.

5. "National Anthropological Archives, in Partnership with the Recovering Voices Initiative, Awarded $1 Million Grant to Digitize Materials," Smithsonian National Museum of Natural History, https://newsdesk.si.edu/releases/national-museum-natural-history-receives-1-million-increase-global-access-endangered-langua.

6. California Language Archive, http://cla.berkeley.edu/about-us.

7. Siobhan Senier, "Digitizing Indigenous History: Trends and Challenges," *Journal of Victorian Culture* 19:3 (2014): 396–402; Joshua A. Bell, Kimberley Christen, Mark Turin, "Introduction: After the Return," *Museum Anthropology Review* 7:1–2 (2013): 1–21; Guha Shankar and Corelia Hooee, "Zuni Cultural Heritage Materials in the American Folklife Center: The Potential of Return," *Museum Anthropology Review* 7:1–2 (2013): 74–84;

Timothy B. Powell, "Digital Knowledge Sharing," *Museum Anthropology Review* 10:2 (2016): 66–90.

8. "Jessie Little Doe Baird," *MacArthur Foundation*, https://www.macfound.org/fellows/24/.

9. *Plateau Peoples' Web Portal*, https://plateauportal.libraries.wsu.edu.

10. Kimberly Christen, "Opening Archives: Respectful Repatriation," *The American Archivist* 74 (Spring/Summer 2011): 185–210.

11. Paul Grant-Costa, Tobias Glaza, and Michael Sletcher, "The Common Pot: Editing Native American Materials," *The Annual of the Association for Documentary Editing* 33 (2012): 1–18.

12. "Mission Statement," *Yale Indian Papers Project*, https://yipp.yale.edu/mission-statement accessed January 3, 2018.

13. See Linda Tuhiwai Smith, *Decolonizing Methodologies: Research and Indigenous Peoples* (London: Zed Books Ltd, 2008); Ellen Cushman, "Wampum, Sequoyan, and Story: Decolonizing the Digital Archive," *College English* 76:2: 115–135; Elizabeth A. Povinelli, "The Woman on the Other Side of the Wall: Archiving the Otherwise in Postcolonial Digital Archives, *A Journal of Feminist Cultural Studies* 11:1 (2011): 146–171.

14. http://findit.library.yale.edu/yipp/?utf8=%E2%9C%93&search_field=all_fields&q=metacom.

15. For a fuller discussion of this problem see O'Neal, "'The Right to Know'", 2–10; Gywneira Isaac, "Perclusive Alliances: Digital 3-D, Museums, and the Reconciling of Culturally Diverse Knowledges," *Current Anthropology* 56, supplement 12 (December 2015): S286-S296; Kimberly Christen, "Opening Archives: Respectful Repatriation," *The American Archivist* 74:1 (2011): 185–210.

16. http://cla.berkeley.edu/explorer.

17. "The Occom Circle," Dartmouth College, http://www.dartmouth.edu/~occom/; Mohegan Nation website, https://www.mohegan.nsn.us/

18. "Mission & Statement of Purpose," *Myaamia Center: Researching Myaamia Language, Culture and History*, http://myaamiacenter.org/statement-of-purpose/.

19. *Recovering Voices*, http://recoveringvoices.si.edu; *National Breath of Life Archival Institute for Indigenous Languages*, http://nationalbreathoflife.org. See also Darryl Baldwin, David J. Costa, Douglas Troy, "Myaamiaataweenki eekincikoonihkiinki eeyoonk aapisaataweeki: A Miami Language Digital Tool for Language Reclamation," *Language Documentation & Conservation* 10 (2016): 394–410.

20. "Guide to the Indigenous Materials at the American Philosophical Society," https://search.amphilsoc.org//natam/search.

21. Powell, "Digital Knowledge Sharing," 72–78.

22. Timothy B. Powell, "Steering a Course Set by Thomas Jefferson: New Developments in the Native American Collections at the American Philosophical Society," *Proceedings of the American Philosophical Society* 159 (Spring 2015): 282–295.

23. Timothy B. Powell, "Building Bridges between Archives and Indian Communities," *News from the American Philosophical Society* 12:1 (2010): 2–3.

24. "Squaw," *Wikipedia*, accessed December 19, 2017, https://en.wikipedia.org/wiki /Squaw.

25. Map can be found in the A. Irving Hallowell collection at the American Philosophical Society library, Mss.ms.Coll.26. It has been deemed culturally sensitive and reproduction is prohibited.

26. The quotations from Larry Aitken come from two sources, personal memory of the event and an interview I did with Larry in 2009, in which we discuss many of the same issues that Larry discussed at the APS in 2010. Those videos have been donated to the American Philosophical Society. Other videos of Larry Aitken are available on the "Ojibwe Digital Archive" YouTube channel, including excerpts of the 2009 interview. See for example, https://youtu.be/mHdQNPiBzhs. Hereafter cited as Larry Aitken, pers. comm., May, 2010.

27. Larry Aitken, pers. comm., May 2010.

28. Watie Akins, personal correspondence, May 2010.

29. Eddie Benton-Banai, *The Mishomis Book: The Voice of the Ojibway* (Minneapolis: University of Minnesota Press, 2010), 89–93.

30. For more on the value of such collaborations see: Diana E. Marsh, Ricardo L. Punzalan, Robert Leopold, Brian Butler, and Masssimo Petrozzie, "Stories of Impact: The Role of Narrative in Understanding the Value and Impact of Digital Collections," *Archival Science* 16:4 (2016): 327–372.

31. Benton-Banai, *Mishomis*, 93.

32. Aitken, personal correspondence November 2011.

33. For more on this subject see Kate Hennessy, "Virtual Repatriation and Digital Cultural Heritage," *Anthropology News* (April 2009): 5–6; Siobhan Senier, "Decolonizing the Archive: Digitizing Native Literature with Students and Tribal Communities," *Resilience: A Journal of the Environmental Humanities* 1:3 (Fall 2014), http://www.jstor.org /stable/10.5250/resilience.1.3.006?seq=1&cid=pdf- reference#references_tab_contents; for an alternative view see Robin Boast and Jim Enote, " 'Virtual Repatriation: It is Neither Virtual nor Repatriation,' Heritage in the Context of Globalization," *SpringerBriefs in Archaeology* 8 (2013): 103–113

34. Maureen Matthews, *Naamiwan's Drum: The Story of a Contested Repatriation of Anishinaabe Artefacts* (Toronto, ON: University of Toronto Press, 2016), 112.

35. Tim Ingold, "A Circumpolar Night's Dream," *The Perception of the Environment: Essays on Livelihood, Dwelling and Skill* (New York: Routledge, 2000), 92, 95.

36. See Peter B. Hirtle, Emily Hudson, and Andrew T. Kenyon, "Case Study 1: Interview and Oral Histories," *Copyright and Cultural Institutions: Guidelines for Digitization for*

U.S. Libraries, Archives, and Museums (Ithaca, NY: Cornell University Library, 2009); Jane Anderson, "Intellectual Property and the Safeguarding of Traditional Cultures," *Heritage & Society* 4:2 (2012): 253–260; Jane Anderson and Kimberly Christen, "'Chuck a Copyright on It': Dilemmas of Digital Return and the Possibilities for Traditional Knowledge Licenses and Labels," *Museum Anthropology Review* 7:1–2 (2013):105–126.

37. Ingold, "Circumpolar's Night Dream," 91.

38. *Pimachiowin Aki*, http://pimachiowinaki.org.

39. Powell, "Digital Knowledge Sharing," 75–76.

40. Jacquie Posey, "Penn's Timothy Powell: Forging Partnerships to Promote Native Languages, Culture," (February 8, 2017), https://news.upenn.edu/news/penns-timothy -powell-forging-partnerships-promote-native-languages-culture; The EPIC website (http://pennds.org/epic) is still in the early stages of development. When complete it will bring together several pre-existing archives, curated by Powell including the Gibagadinaamaagoom site with a digital archive prototype based on the seven directions of the Ojibwe cosmology. The new site will feature Scalar-based digital exhibits created in partnerships with tribal partners.

41. Tom Belt, "Commentary on Will West Long's 'Long Life and Going to Heaven,'" recording, American Philosophical Society digital library.

42. Four thousand years was the age of Kwakwaka'wakw culture given at the potlatch ceremonies. Estimates vary widely. The *Canadian Encyclopedia* states: "Archaeological evidence shows habitation in the Kwak'wala-speaking area for at least 8,000 years," http:// www.thecanadianencyclopedia.ca/en/article/kwakiutl.

43. Diana Taylor makes an interesting distinction between "archive" and "repertoire." She associates the latter with "embodied memory, because it is live, [and] exceeds the archive's ability to capture it," *The Archive and the Repertoire: Performing Cultural Memory in the Americas* (Durham, NC: Duke University Press), 20.

44. "Our Masks Come Home," *Living Tradition: the Kwakwaka'wakw Potlatch on the Northwest Coast*, https://umistapotlatch.ca/nos_masques_come_home-our_masks_come _home-eng.php.

45. See Frédéric Kaplan, "A Map for Big Data Research in Digital Humanities," *Frontiers in the Digital Humanities*, May 6, 2015, https://www.frontiersin.org/articles/10.3389/fdigh .2015.00001/full; Tim Hitchcock, "Big Data, Small Data and Meaning," *Histoyonics*, http:// historyonics.blogspot.com/2014/11/big-data-small-data-and-meaning_9.html.

46. Personal Correspondence with Alan Burdette, director of Archive of Traditional Music, June 2014.

47. Lyz Jaakola and Timothy B. Powell, "'The Songs Are Alive': Bringing Frances Densmore's Recordings Back Home," *The Oxford Handbook of Musical Repatriation* (New York: Oxford University Press, June 2018).

48. Ojibwemowining Resource Center, http://fdltcc.edu/ojibwemowiningresource center.

49. Jaakola, "'The Songs Are Alive.'"

50. Frances Densmore, *Chippewa Music* (Washington, D.C.: Bureau of American Ethnology, 1910), 83.

51. "Chiefs," *Onondaga Nation: People of the Hills*, http://www.onondaganation.org /government/chiefs.

TWO

From Time Immemorial: Centering Indigenous Traditional Knowledge and Ways of Knowing in the Archival Paradigm

Jennifer R. O'Neal

"We wish our ethics were the norm and not the exception."[1]

First Nation, Inuit, and Metis peoples reiterated this maxim at the "Working Better Together Conference on Indigenous Research Ethics" hosted by Simon Fraser University in Vancouver, BC, in February 2015.[2] Making this statement a reality and reconciling hundreds of years of colonization of Native American and Indigenous people is not easy, especially in countries that have tried systemically to eradicate our culture, lifeways, and traditions. Yet our communities are rising stronger than ever, fighting for our inherent sovereignty and traditional ways after years of oppression, genocide, assimilation, and termination. Now there is a distinct urgency to make right the atrocities and injustices against so many for far too long. This call to action appears across North America, both formally as part of official federal truth and reconciliation processes, and also as more focused calls for immediate changes in the way academics, researchers, and curators engage with, approach, and collaborate with Indigenous communities. This is part of a larger movement to educate the academy about approaching research and the management of collections with openness and empathy by ethically and respectfully centering Indigenous knowledge and traditional ways of knowing.

I have dedicated my career to bringing awareness about the historical legacy of displaced Native American archives and the reconciliation work that has emerged within the context of Indigenous activism. Throughout my teaching, research, and publications, I have argued for the respectful care of Indigenous archives held at non-tribal repositories and called for decolonizing Native American archives as a form of respect, reciprocity, and reconciliation.[3] In this chapter, I seek to build upon this work by examining one specific aspect of my decolonizing effort, the centering of Indigenous traditional knowledge systems, which, I argue, is the foundation and key to embodying these changes in the archival paradigm and beyond. I will highlight recent developments in Indigenous activism surrounding policies regarding Indigenous archives, research ethics, and collaborative stewardship. I examine the thinking of various Indigenous scholars, elders, and policy makers to argue that we must apply the same methodologies, policies, and recommendations utilized for Indigenous research ethics to the management and stewardship of Indigenous archives.

"The Protocols for Native American Archival Materials:" Then and Now

The publication of "The Protocols for Native American Archival Materials" (PNAAM) in 2006 generated important discussions and debate both nationally and internationally about the proper care of Native American cultural heritage archives housed at non-Tribal repositories. PNAAM served as a catalyst for a larger paradigm shift, generally within the archival profession, that called for new non-Western perspectives and methodologies, including, but not limited to, participatory and community archiving in archival education and practices for managing archival collections.[4] Although some organizations and repositories endorsed and successfully implemented PNAAM, not all archive professional groups agreed with the document, specifically with guidelines concerning access, use, and repatriation.[5] Still, the document highlighted issues surrounding Native American archives and began much needed conversations about their care and preservation. More importantly, it broadened discussions and viewpoints about ways of managing these archival collections from a Native perspective.

Significant activist work has continued since that time, and in the summer of 2015, a small group gathered at the yearly conference for the Association of Tribal Archives, Libraries, and Museums (ATALM) for an "Archives Summit" to review and assess PNAAM after ten years, discussing successes, challenges, and possible next steps for further implementation across the United States. Based on the original intent of PNAAM as a living document, this pre-conference summit brought together some of the original drafters of PNAAM, as well as key archivist allies in the United States and Canada, to review and reflect on lessons learned from PNAAM and other key international documents, for general overall discussions of specific sections, and to determine possible next steps and updates to the document based on recent case studies, conversations, and research. A larger overall goal of the gathering was to utilize this momentum as a call to action about human rights through the framework of the United Nations Declaration on the Rights of Indigenous Peoples, with the objective of contributing to the efforts of decolonizing Indigenous archives. Both United States and Canadian Indigenous archivists gave presentations that highlighted major accomplishments in each country to date, including the development and implementation of various guidelines, such as PNAAM in the United States and the Canadian Aboriginal Archives Guide, as well as major groundbreaking initiatives such as the Canadian Truth and Reconciliation Commission. Presenters also made clear the inherent need to enhance and expand these resources even further to ensure the implementation of the guidelines across various repositories, the creation of practical tools for managing Indigenous archives, and the inclusion of these guidelines in various educational programs.

The group collectively determined that the following next steps should be taken regarding PNAAM: include specific case studies into each section, develop a practical implementation guide, continue dialogue through presentations at conferences, and collaborate with other groups working on similar initiatives, including, among others, the ATALM Museum Summit. The group has now undertaken these goals within the auspices of ATALM and the Society of American Archivists Native American Archives Section.

Recontextulizing Archives through Centering Indigenous Knowledge

As a participant in the original drafting of PNAAM and then organizer of the Archives Summit, I have a unique perspective on the development, implementation, evolution, and varied perspectives of the guidelines over the past ten years. PNAAM has led to an increased awareness of the importance of incorporating notions of stewardship, rather than just custodianship, into the traditional procedures and roles of an archivist and curator. Since PNAAM launched in 2006, it has become evident that the guidelines contradict various aspects of conventional archival practice, namely issues of open access and ownership. Over the years, as a part of various conference presentations on PNAAM urging for its implementation, I witnessed non-Indigenous archivists express their strong opinions and concerns about these issues, especially regarding the specific guidelines calling for limiting access to Indigenous collections, the possible return of materials, and the development of stewardship and consultation policies.[6] These concerns speak to the core of the inherent historic problem within archival repositories that have served as sites of power over Indigenous history, culture, and lifeways, by controlling and disseminating our history according to the repositories' interpretation, often based upon the individuals (i.e., anthropologists, ethnographers, historians, etc.) who appropriated the materials, rather than by and with Indigenous communities. Archives have not been historically neutral entities for these collections, and the power dynamics within the management of these collections needs to shift to ensure the implementation of PNAAM. These important changes are not just about restricting access or returning collections, but finally giving Indigenous communities control over their histories, centering their traditional knowledge, and undoing historic trauma.

Despite initial reactionary responses, numerous non-Tribal repositories have successfully implemented or are seeking to implement PNAAM.[7] This indicates that the archival profession continues to evolve and expand theoretical and practical frameworks to include approaches that are outside the conventional Western ways of knowing and operating. The information profession is finally embracing alternative ways of knowing and managing collections, which gives power back to source communities to provide some form of social justice through reconciliation. This is also evident in the larger conversations about and implementation of the post-modern, post-custodial, and participatory archiving methodology for various ethnic and community archives, not just Indigenous archives.[8]

While some have adopted and implemented PNAAM, many non-Indigenous archives and archivists have yet failed to do so or are still wrestling with some of the core recommendations outlined in PNAAM. Despite these concerns, it is time archival repositories and archivists stop wondering about how to address the recommendations of PNAAM and simply begin doing the work. Information professionals must now listen to repeated requests from those in the Indigenous communities who are pleading for proper care of these collections and for implementation of stewardship changes in repositories containing Indigenous materials. These recommendations must be implemented, not in the future, but *now*. After years of colonization, assimilation, termination, and restoration, Indigenous communities have waited far too long to reconnect with these collections and to provide the missing Indigenous context and traditional knowledge required to treat those collections respectfully and in accord with the cultural, spiritual, and epistemological needs and concerns of Indigenous people. Addressing this need will ensure a beginning to social justice and reconciliation for this historic trauma.

Throughout the nearly ten years between the drafting of PNAAM and the summit gathering, the drafters and supporters have always emphasized that the foundation of the guidelines is collaboration, relationship building, and shared stewardship. However, while archivists and library professionals may be more open to general ideas of collaboration and relationship building, I have often found that a deterrent or uncertainty regarding Indigenous collections stems from a lack of knowledge or understanding of Native American history and the importance of centering Indigenous sovereignty and traditional knowledge within the archival paradigm to show why these collections need to be approached differently. Furthermore, most archivists do not know exactly how to begin this work. I have experienced this frequently when speaking with library information professionals about Indigenous collections, especially with non-Indigenous archivists who are often hesitant to implement PNAAM, or who may not know where to start.

While some archivists have a general understanding of Native American history, education at the secondary level often lacks and overlooks knowledge of key elements of Indigenous history and existence, including community specific historical trauma and pain; hundreds of years of destruction and genocide faced by our communities; why our sovereign status sets us apart; the uniqueness of our tribally specific histories; and the importance of traditional knowledge specific to each Tribal community. Some states have finally passed laws to ensure that secondary schools appropriately teach basic location-based Native American history, but we should require this knowledge and training at the undergraduate and graduate levels as well.[9] Various graduate schools have implemented significant changes, incorporating different approaches to the stewardship of collections, including post-custodial frameworks and PNAAM. In order to ensure that these changes persist, we must infuse the basics of Indigenous history, traditional ways of knowing, and research methodologies into the larger Library and Information Science (LIS) curriculum. And for those that are already practicing in the profession, repositories and organizations should require workshops or cultural competency trainings to train staff in these issues as well.

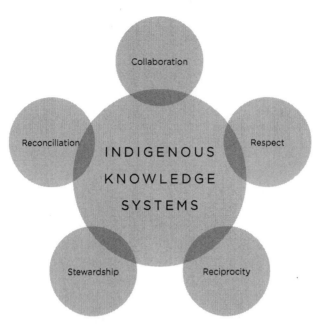

FIGURE 2.1. Centering Indigenous Knowledge Systems: The Five Pillars

Over the past fifteen years, through my work and activism as a Native American historian and archivist, I have traveled to various Indigenous and Aboriginal locations for conferences, discussions, and consultations. Through these unique interactions, I have determined that the one unifying factor in ensuring a successful collaboration for both Tribal and non-Tribal participants is making collaboration, stewardship, respect, reciprocity and reconciliation the key anchors of Indigenous knowledge systems and relationship building that honors sovereignty (see Figure 2.1). This means entering into these relationships with purpose, intent, and with the goal of making a significant social change and, most importantly, putting Indigenous communities and traditional knowledge at the center of the work, driving the project.

In addition to this core foundation, I have also determined that in order for information professionals to implement new non-Western ways of managing Indigenous archives, they must first learn and respect our unique Indigenous histories and our traditional practices in order to center them within archival collections. We can define Indigenous systems of knowledge as "the philosophies and community practices of Indigenous peoples as they maintain connections to place, language, history, and ceremony. These are the systems of knowledge — the philosophies and practices — that have formed the foundation for Indian survivance for generations."[10] These traditional ways of knowing include storytelling, dreaming/visualization, oral history, observations, listening, lived inter-generational experiences, and various other methods for orally passing down our histories and cultural practices. All of these approaches are tied to our sacred history, land, language, and ceremony.

Making these changes in the profession means recognizing the historical Indigenous-settler relationship that often governs these collections and revealing the relational power dynamics between Indigenous and Western science that permeates archival repositories today. Thus, we must *recontextualize* the historical narrative by placing Indigenous history and knowledge at the center of the archival paradigm. To do this, the profession must stop privileging the Western, non-Indigenous narrative and perspective in information education, repositories, and among granting agencies. Indigenous researchers, academics, informational professionals, and professors are calling on professional archivists and librarians to be leaders in this effort to undo hundreds of years of colonization and oppression and to finally center traditional Indigenous knowledge in collections and the curriculum through collaboration, stewardship, respectful relationships, reciprocity, and finally reconciliation.

Implementing a Decolonizing Indigenous Research Model into the Archival Paradigm

> The purpose of decolonization is to create space in everyday life, research, academia, and society for an Indigenous perspective without it being neglected, shunted aside, mocked, or dismissed.[11]
>
> *Margaret Kovach*

Building on the decolonizing research methodologies of renowned Indigenous scholar Linda Tuhiwai Smith,[12] I argue that we must also apply the Indigenous knowledge research methodologies and frameworks espoused by Aboriginal educator, researcher, and professor Margaret Kovach, to the archival paradigm. We should apply the same recommendations she provides for conducting Indigenous research to archivists stewarding Indigenous collections in non-Tribal repositories. While archivists may find these research methodologies challenging, they have proved successful and ensure that Tribal knowledge and epistemologies are respected and remain at the center of the research. I examine Kovach's methodology for centering traditional cultural knowledge in Indigenous archives, and provide some practical frameworks for its implementation.

As Kovach argues, those studying or working with Indigenous communities encounter inherent politics of knowledge (i.e. what knowledge gets privileged?), as Western research processes often already define these communities as marginalized. To counteract this, Kovach notes the groundbreaking work of Smith, which "applies a decolonizing analysis to reveal the degree to which Indigenous knowledges have been marginalized within Western research processes." She concludes that "while few non-Indigenous scholars would contest marginalization and colonization, much has been written about this concept yet action has been minimal by a smaller community of allies, but it seems to be growing." This provides hope to Indigenous researchers, academics, and curators who have been calling for this type of work for numerous years. However, it also provides a lens through which to measure major challenges and how much work still remains to be done, especially in relation to how we foundationally approach curation when stewarding Indigenous collections.[13]

Kovach further contends that part of the challenge of applying decolonizing approaches within an academic environment stems from the theoretical positioning of Indigenous studies, which obscures the necessity of historical analysis. As she correctly concludes, some critical theorists have applied "post-colonial" to some Indigenous studies and stop there. But from an Indigenous perspective, applying the prefix "post" does not mean that it is finished business or no longer requires historical analysis. She argues that "in actuality this causes numerous challenges within a United States context, where non-Indigenous scholars are adept at ignoring, forgetting, and often reproducing the colonial past, when in fact that very complex colonial past influences daily Indigenous life."[14] This point supports my argument noted above, that it is critical to learn unique Indigenous histories and knowledge systems. These histories provide key and sometimes missing contexts for understanding Indigenous archival collections. We need context to determine how the collection was gathered, by whom, and why, since outsiders gathered many of the items in archives, sometimes as a manifestation of colonization, to define Indigenous communities as vanishing. The context matters because only Tribal members may know the importance of the history and knowledge the collection contains. It is imperative that we preserve this context and present it in conjunction with Tribal community partners.

Acknowledging context matters not only in remembering the historical colonial past, but also acknowledging the present and future, since, as Kovach

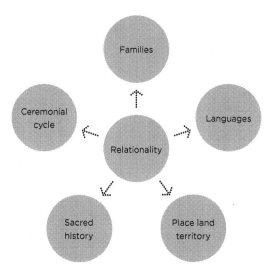

FIGURE 2.2. The Core Components of Indigenous Relationality

argues, there is "no way to address tribal knowledge and epistemologies without considering continued colonial interruptions, including but not limited to globalization and consumerism, and the continued effects of historic and current settler colonialism on Indigenous communities." Learning and providing historical context, then, ensures that we also acknowledge the continued effects of colonization still pervading Indigenous communities today.[15]

In addition to centering Indigenous historical context, we need to recognize another key concept in centering Indigenous knowledge systems into the archival paradigm — the concept of relationality. Indigenous researcher Shawn Wilson states that building relationships and relationality is what it means to be Indigenous. This refers to our various relationships with our families, importance of sacred histories, ceremonies, and languages, as well as the ties we have to place and land. It is all interconnected and related to who we are (see Figure 2.2). Wilson reflects on the importance of land and space to Indigenous peoples rather than just our history: "Identity for Indigenous peoples is grounded in their relationships with the land, with their ancestors who have returned to the land, with future generations who will come into being on the land. Rather than viewing ourselves as being *in* relationship with other people or things, we *are* the relationships that we hold and are part of."[16] Thus, the concept of relationality should be applied to how archival repositories approach, manage, curate, and disseminate archival holdings. Relationality is at the core of centering Indigenous knowledge systems into archival collections.

An Indigenous Archives "Call To Action"

After spending numerous years working in the archives and history field, as well as dedicating my career to advocating for the respectful and proper care of Indigenous collections, I share here what I have learned during my career, what I have learned from important Indigenous thinkers, and what, thus, fuels my call to action for curators, collections managers, archivists, etc. working with Indigenous archives. This builds on my previous arguments about context and Indigenous ways of knowing that must be at the center of this work. Before I detail some specific suggestions for ways forward, I want first to present a few scenarios that I often encounter in the field as some examples, again to provide context.

Curators, especially those who are non-Indigenous or who have been in the profession for a long time, are often fearful of how to properly care for these collections. They may be under the assumption that their efforts in collaborative stewardship are going to be too difficult and, thus, often fail to act and continue operating under conventional Western ways of managing collections. Then, another staff member, Indigenous curator, or a Tribal researcher creates the impetus for change. This situation covers a small percentage of curators or collection managers, and is increasingly rare, with a newer, younger, more diversely educated generation coming into the profession.

Another scenario I see frequently is that curators, especially Indigenous curators, have to strike a challenging ethical balance between our own inherent societal and financial needs (i.e. having a job to earn money to care for ourselves, our families, our future, etc.), yet find ourselves working for organizations that house Indigenous collections at non-Tribal repositories such as historical societies, local archives, universities, colleges, federal repositories, and various others. Thus, many Indigenous curators find themselves torn between their inherent need and desire to engage in proper, respectful, and ethical work and the historic colonial bureaucratic infrastructure created in the organizations we work for. Although we personally have the ethics and dedication to implement changes in the stewardship of these collections, we are faced with navigating the bureaucracy of colonial institutions that lack the malleability to support these changes.

Although each of the above scenarios presents unique challenges, there are some basic foundational steps and concepts that we can follow as we move forward to implement important changes in our repositories. The key is to do *something*. Do not wait for someone else to implement changes or wait for someone who fills your positions after you to do this work. If you see something wrong with how collections are being cared for or if you see something wrong in how collections display, interpret, or contextualize Indigenous materials, say and do something about it.

There are many archivists, both Indigenous and non-Indigenous, who have devoted their careers to doing this work and have shared guidance, lessons learned, and ways to move forward. It is important to become familiar with this work and a variety of related topics. PNAAM serves as one of the key foundations to learning about the beauty and complexities of Indigenous archives, and offers guidelines for how to care for Indigenous holdings in non-Tribal repositories. However, since the first publication of PNAAM in 2006, numerous other resources and publications have advanced examples of successful projects and guidance.[17] In addition, there are a growing number of Indigenous information professionals and professors who are producing very important research on the topic of imagining and centering Indigenous ways of knowing in the profession. This includes, but is not limited to, Cheryl Metoyer, Loriene Roy, Miranda Belarde-Lewis, Marisa Elena Durante, Sandy Littletree, Camille Callison, and Kim Lawson, as well as those that have already walked on, including Ally Krebs and Ann Massmann.[18]

If this is the first time you are beginning this type of work or project, it can often feel overwhelming. Therefore, I have highlighted some basic key steps to guide you. I have found these to be the foundation to successful stewardship of Indigenous collections. These stem both from key concepts and issues addressed in PNAAM, as well as lessons I learned in my own work and research and, most importantly, lessons I learned from other Indigenous scholars, curators, educators, and spiritual leaders.

First, **the foundation is Indigenous context and history**. You must learn and understand why Indigenous communities are unique, how these collections were often illegally acquired or displaced from their original source community, and the legacy of colonization for our communities. Colonization is real and our people and collections are affected by it to this day. This is why these collections are different, and why you must do something to address the effects of hundreds of years of colonization on our history, heritage, and lifeways.

Our sovereignty must be respected. Tribes have had their own traditional governments since time immemorial and prior to colonization. These governments determine their own laws and legal restrictions surrounding cultural issues. While some tribes have federal recognition, others hold state recognition. Information professionals should understand and respect Native American rights and laws, as recognized in the United States constitution and treaties.

Each Indigenous community is different and unique. It is critically important to remember that as a researcher, instructor, curator, or practitioner, you must always take into account the unique nature of each Indigenous community's histories, laws, practices, and culture. Thus, figure out, learn, and respect the community's specific histories and needs as you embark on working with a community, whether in terms of a collection, item, interview, etc. What works for one community may not work for another because each has different histories, cultures, traditions, and stories that constitute the uniqueness of their communities.

Respect and implement our traditional knowledge systems. One of the most important actions in this process is to learn as much as possible about that community, their history, lifeways, traditions, and beliefs. This should always serve as your foundation as each community is different and each one requires different ways of approaching the stewardship of its archive. This knowledge and understanding will in turn guide how you enter and build trust in the relationship. Begin implementing our knowledge-keeping systems into our collections housed at your repositories. For example, if you house documents or recordings that include stories that should only be told certain times of the year or only told by a certain gender, begin assigning certain cultural access protocols to these items to ensure adherence to the needs of the community and to their unique knowledge-keeping systems.

Indigenous people should determine next steps. As you enter these relationships and collaborations, the Indigenous community should always provide the central perspective and drive the project. This also means determining and accepting what your role is or may not be in the process. Perhaps you take on the role of facilitator, rather than project manager. Listen and understand what your role is and how you can coordinate with the community. The Tribal community members must always be the ones shaping the research and project.

If you are feeling overwhelmed and not sure where to start, simply **select one Indigenous collection as a pilot project** to test how your repository can begin working collaboratively with Indigenous communities to steward the collection.

Although this work is very challenging, it will always be rewarding and important to Indigenous communities. It pushes archivists and researchers to make themselves vulnerable, to step out of their comfort zones, to understand hidden histories and different ways of knowing. It opens their eyes to different ways of seeing themselves and the Indigenous peoples who have been here since time immemorial. At the center of this work must be Indigenous traditional knowledge. This knowledge is medicine and will help to bring a form of reconciliation to our people.

Notes

1. "Working Better Together Conference on Indigenous Research." Simon Fraser University, February 18–20, 2015, Vancouver, BC. https://www.sfu.ca/ipinch/events/ipinch -events/working-better-together-conference-indigenous-research-ethics/ accessed February 1, 2018.

2. Throughout this paper I use the term "Indigenous" to refer to the original inhabitants of North America. More specifically, I use "First Nation," "Inuit" and "Metis" to refer to the Aboriginal people of Canada, and "Native American," "American Indian," "Indian," and "Tribal" to refer to the Indigenous peoples of the United States. And more importantly, when known, I identify specific Tribal or Aboriginal community names or names they prefer.

3. Jennifer R. O'Neal, "The Right to Know: Decolonizing Native American Archives," *Journal of Western Archives* 6:1 (2015); "Respect, Recognition, and Reciprocity: The Protocols for Native American Archival Materials," in *Identity Palimpsests: Archiving Ethnicity in the US and Canada*, eds. Dominique Daniel and Amalia Levi (Sacramento: Litwin Press, 2014), 125–142.

4. First Archivists Circle, "The Protocols for Native American Archival Materials," 2006. http://www2.nau.edu/libnap-p/ accessed February 1, 2018. For a full overview of PNAAM see, Karen J. Underhill, "Protocols for Native American Archival Materials," *RBM: A Journal of Rare Books, Manuscripts, and Cultural Heritage* 7:2 (2006): 134–145.

5. The following organizations, institutions, and Native American communities endorsed the principles expressed in PNAAM: American Association for State and Local History, First Archivists Circle, Union of British Columbia Indian Chiefs, Union of British Indian Chiefs Resource Centre, Native American Archives Roundtable (Society of American Archivists), and Cline Library, Northern Arizona University. Later on, others followed their lead, but these were some of the first to endorse the document.

6. See the Native American Protocols Forum Working Group held at the Society of American Archivists Annual Meetings, 2008–2012. The first forum was held August 27,

2008, "Forum on 'Protocols for Native American Archival Materials.'" For a full summary of the three forums, see the groups' final report, http://www2.archivists.org/sites/all/files/0112-V-I-NativeAmProtocolsForum.pdf accessed February 1, 2018. See also, John Bolcer, "*The Protocols for Native American Archival Materials*: Considerations and Concerns from the Perspective of a Non-Tribal Archivist," *Easy Access: Newsletter of the Northwest Archivists, Inc.* 34 (2009): 3–6. "During the drafting of this article, the Society of American Archivists finally officially endorsed PNAAM on August 13, 2018, see statement, https://www2.archivists.org/statements/saa-council-endorsement-of-protocols-for-native-american-archival-materials, accessed January 26, 2019.

7. Elizabeth Joffrion and Natalia Fernandez, "Collaborations between Tribal and Non-Tribal Organizations: Suggested Best Practices for Sharing Expertise, Cultural Resources, and Knowledge." *The American Archivist* 78:1 (Spring/Summer 2015): 192–237.

8. Katie Shilton and Ramesh Srinivasan, "Participatory Appraisal and Arrangement for Multicultural Archival Collections," *Archivaria* 63 (Spring 2007): 87–101.

9. Washington, Montana, and Oregon now require that place-based Native American history be taught at the K–12 level.

10. G. R. Vizenor, *Fugitive Poses: Native American Indian Scenes of Absence and Presence* (Lincoln: University of Nebraska Press, 1998); Sandy Littletree, Society of American Archivists Annual Conference Presentation, July, 2018.

11. Margaret Kovach, *Indigenous Methodologies: Characteristics, Conversations, and Contexts* (Toronto: University of Toronto Press, 2009), 85.

12. Linda Tuhiwai Smith, *Decolonizing Research Methodologies: Research and Indigenous Peoples* (London: Zed Books, 1999).

13. Kovach, *Indigenous Methodologies*, 75.

14. Kovach, *Indigenous Methodologies*, 75–76.

15. Kovach, *Indigenous Methodologies*, 76. See also, Kimberly Christen. "Tribal Archives, Traditional Knowledge, and Local Contexts: Why the 's' Matters," *Journal of Western Archives* 6:1 (2015).

16. Shawn Wilson, *Research is Ceremony: Indigenous Research Methods* (Halifax: Fenwood Publishing, 2008), 80.

17. See examples in Elizabeth Joffrion and Natalia Fernandez, "Collaborations between Tribal and Non-Tribal Organizations: Suggested Best Practices for Sharing Expertise, Cultural Resources, and Knowledge." *The American Archivist* 78:1 Spring/Summer (2015) and in Kimberly Christen, "Tribal Archives, Traditional Knowledge, and Local Contexts: Why the 's' Matters."

18. Cheryl A. Metoyer and Ann M. Doyle, "Introduction to Special Issues: Cataloging & Classification Quarterly Special Issue — Indigenous Knowledge Organization," *Cataloging & Classification Quarterly* 53, no. 5–6 (2015): 475–478; Cheryl Metoyer and Sandy Littletree, "Knowledge Organization from an Indigenous Perspective: The Mashantucket

Pequot Thesaurus of American Indian Terminology Project." *Cataloging & Classification Quarterly* 53, no. 5–6 (2015): 640–657; Marisa Elena Duarte and Miranda Belarde-Lewis. "Imagining: Creating Spaces for Indigenous Ontologies." *Cataloging & Classification Quarterly* 53, no. 5–6 (2015): 677–702; Brett Lougheed, Ry Moran, and Camille Callison, "Reconciliation through Description: Using Metadata to Realize the Vision of the National Research Centre for Truth and Reconciliation," *Cataloging & Classification Quarterly* 53, no. 5–6 (2015): 596–614; Camille Callison, Loriene Roy, and Gretchen Alice LeCheminant, eds., *Indigenous Notions of Ownership and Libraries, Archives, and Museums* (Berlin: De Gruyter, 2016); Allison Boucher Krebs, "Native America's twenty-first-century right to know" *Archival Science* 12, no. 2 (2012): 173–190; Ann Massmann, "Center for Southwest Research, university libraries, University of New Mexico: An interdisciplinary archive" *Journal of the West* 47, no. 1 (2008): 43; Ann M. Doyle, Kimberly Lawson, and Sarah Dupont, "Indigenization of Knowledge Organization at the Xwi7xwa Library," *Journal of Library and Information Studies* 13, no. 2 (December 2015): 107–134.

THREE

Decolonizing the Imperialist Archive: Translating Cherokee Manuscripts

Ellen Cushman

In ongoing efforts to decolonize the archive, the goal has been to build alliances between scholars, archivists, and the peoples represented in archives. This work has led to important advances in the creation of protocols for working with Native communities to identify culturally sensitive materials and to select metadata categories for those materials.[1] An important next step in decolonizing the archive is to design user interfaces for the translation of Indigenous language manuscripts. This chapter offers an initial realization of the decolonial potentials in digital archives and considers the potential for creating spaces to facilitate translation as a practice in language perseverance work undertaken with collaborators from Indigenous communities, universities, museums, and libraries. Language perseverance focuses on the everyday Indigenous language practices of speakers, learners, readers, and writers necessary to ensure the continuing vitality of the language, while language preservation is aimed primarily at documentation and formal analysis of linguistic features of Indigenous languages.

The essay opens with a brief consideration of the imperial legacy of archives before moving into a discussion of processes used to create a click-through mockup of a user interface. Features of the user interface were designed in light of the goals, audiences, purposes, and practices of Indigenous Nation translators and curators of Indigenous language manuscript archives. The essay ends with a consideration of the impact this user interface might have for the collaborative authoring of translations of Indigenous language manuscripts. When peoples, languages, and knowledges come to be appreciated in and on their own terms, and when archival materials can be meaningfully integrated into ongoing practices, then, I argue, archives, museums, and libraries move ever closer to the creation of Indigenous archives. Decolonial digital archive designs and translation methodologies help to ensure the ongoing creation of native knowledges, interpretations, and representations of the past.

Decolonizing the Digital Archive User Interface

As part of my consulting work with the Cherokee Nation Johnson O'Malley Program in 2012, I was asked to lead a team of Cherokee scholars in building a comprehensive curriculum based on the teachings of a selection of the Cherokee wampum belts to be used in schools and communities of the Cherokee Nation's fourteen-county jurisdiction. The need for this curriculum developed after one of the wampum belts was unethically obtained by a national museum. Partially in protest to the unethical purchase of the belts and partially as a protective measure, our elders decided to stop reading the belts at stomp grounds. Since these belts are traditionally read aloud in a formal register of Cherokee — a register that museum curators would not likely be able to speak or understand — my team needed to open each one of the sections of the curriculum with stories written in Cherokee with appropriate English translations provided by the language translators on the team. Regardless of the material artifacts that prompt stories, be they wampum belts, manuscripts in digital archives, or social networking sites, decolonizing the archive demands that we pay attention to the way archives were imperialist creations from the beginning. As soon as the word "archive" is used, it evokes four imperialist tenets of thought: tradition; collection; artifacts; preservation. These tenets of imperialist thought structure archives whether in material or digital forms.[2]

The idea of tradition, in its singular form, evolved under the framing narrative of enunciating knowledge in, on, and through Western terms — particularly through the use of alphabetic scripts to codify Indigenous languages. The notion of a tradition, in the singular, "was invented in the process of building modernity" and "was used to disavow the legitimacy of the 'traditions,'" in the plural, of Indigenous peoples who were colonized.[3] Modernist thinking creates its own singular tradition of knowledge, by identifying necessarily othered traditions of Indigenous peoples, whose meaningful objects are then archived in and on alphabetic terms and categorized into systems and taxonomies more familiar to Western readers and writers.

If the first move in decolonizing the archive is to challenge Western understandings of time as a necessary underpinning for tradition, the second move takes up the problem of collecting artifacts. The actions involved in the collection of artifacts damage them in three ways: (1) the item is taken out of its context of use; (2) it is no longer understood in relation to the stories that place the item in its context and in relation to the people who use it; and (3) the people who would ostensibly have uses for the item are necessarily presumed to be no longer living. Whoever it was that sought to collect the Cherokee wampum belts in the first place worked from these assumptions. The second move to decolonize this tenet of the imperialist archive would be to replace the object within the context of its use. This means locating the object as much as possible within the day-to-day practices that give it meaning in people's lives.

The third move in decolonizing the archive emerges directly from the second when trying to understand how these "artifacts" work to mediate knowledge for the people who use them. What does this object mean to the people who use it? Even though a collector has succeeded in obtaining a Cherokee wampum belt, that person is not likely to know how to read it, how it works, or what it *means*. The Cherokee word for wampum belt, ᏕᎦᏅᎤ /dekanvnu/, means roughly to "look this way," or "a way to look toward." Because they are lived, spoken, read, enacted, and taught, and because they provide a history or way to look toward, the Cherokee wampum belts represent our continued survival as a tribe.

This brings me to a fourth move necessary to decolonize the digital archive: Indigenous languages. The language used to tell the stories in archives matters a great deal because English has been key to establishing Western thinking and histories. The Cherokee Nation creates and transmits its knowledge with and through these objects using Cherokee.

Recent work considers ways archives might be decolonized through respect, recognition, and reciprocity with American Indian nations[4] and through building collaboratives to guide the selection of culturally sensitive materials to be digitized.[5] These are positive steps in enacting decolonial methods for building partnerships and making available digital copies of holdings to American Indian Nations. In the next section, I advance these lines of work in anticipation of a necessary next step for redressing the imperialist legacy of archives: designing an interface for a digital archive that allows for the collaborative translation of Indigenous language manuscripts. What types of user interfaces will permit the collaborative translations of the digital copies of songs, stories, oral histories, and linguistic materials in archives and libraries? This question is particularly timely in light of the National Endowment for the Humanities Challenge Grant that the American Philosophical Society Center for Native American and Indigenous Research (CNAIR) recently received with the goal of helping to strengthen Indigenous Nations' language perseverance efforts using digital copies of holdings.[6] Future work will take up the question of what a decolonial translation methodology entails. Before such translation work might unfold, it is necessary to create the online space that permits the collaborative generation of translations according to the various needs of potential users.

Indigenous Language Translation in The Digital Archive

The Indigenous Language Manuscript Translation Project seeks to create a collective space for the translation of Indigenous language manuscripts within partnering libraries, museums, and archives. Working with a team of Indigenous nation-citizen scholars and representatives from the Cherokee Nation and White Earth Chippewa Tribe of Minnesota, our team developed a prototype of a graphical user interface for a digital archive in which tribally based translators and language learners can work together with librarians and scholars to develop, refine, and preserve translations of Cherokee and Anishinaabemowin language manuscripts from repositories around the country.

With funding from the Institute of Museum and Library Services (IMLS) Sparks Ignition Grant, our team explored methods of selecting and protocols for translating manuscripts that respond to the complex needs of these constituencies and has designed an interface responsive to translators' workflows, as well as needs ranging from technological to tribal. We collected representative samples of manuscripts already translated in the existing literature in both Anishinaabemowin and Cherokee, developed a prototype of an interface that will support translation of these documents and the needs of various stakeholders and users with whom we tested the interface prototype. We accomplished this in four phases of landscape analysis, stakeholder interviews, prototyping, and user testing.

LANDSCAPE ANALYSIS

Our team completed the task of selecting and analyzing ten documents in each language from museums and libraries. We analyzed a subset of two documents from each language using existing translations from both Anishinaabemowin and Cherokee. We selected documents on the basis of their historical import for the respective Nations and because they were pieces that had already been translated and incorporated into publications. At this point, we vetted documents with our respective Nations to better understand if concerns would arise from the selection of these already digitized Anishinaabemowin and Cherokee language manuscripts. We presumed that the relevant Indigenous Nation leaders appropriately vetted the manuscripts that were selected and included in the online database. As discussed later, we learned from citizens of the Eastern Band of the Cherokee Indians (EBCI) that our presumption was false. The National Anthropological Archive (NAA) had not spoken with any citizens of the EBCI before digitizing and uploading these manuscripts. As a result, they included culturally sensitive materials in the online catalog of the NAA, and the EBCI had requested an immediate take down of these digital images. To redress our mistake in using one of these documents as part of the mockup of the interface design, the team concluded we would change the mockup of the interface design to draw upon another document we were assured was vetted properly (this one from the Gilcrease Museum and vetted by the Cherokee Nation). Going forward, our collaborative will not include digital images of manuscripts from the NAA, nor seek partnership with them until an understanding is reached with the EBCI.

STAKEHOLDER INTERVIEWS

Using a series of informal interviews and site visits, our team gathered a better understanding of current translation processes employed by teams of language experts from our respective nations who routinely translate manuscripts or collaborate with archives. Our hope was to design a user interface that was well matched to the workflows already in place for these translation teams and individual translators. To accomplish this, we conducted informal individual stakeholder interviews with a select group of subject matter experts from the advisory board. We focused these discussions on creating a prototype that would aid in exploring and translating Anishinaabemowin and Cherokee manuscripts.

PROTOTYPING PHASE

With information from the first two phases in place, team members set about prototyping the interface. They designed an interface that allows users to translate and tag metadata for manuscripts in Anishinaabemowin and Cherokee. They provided interaction tips that allowed for this exploration and learning, including word analysis and visual connection between the language and the text. They then built a prototype that allowed us to see the interface design and features with our users and subject matter experts.

USER TESTING

We had originally proposed in this stage to bring the entire advisory board to campus to conduct a thorough and extensive user-testing session during a forum that would have been sponsored with funds provided through a sister IMLS planning grant. Instead, we conducted user testing of the prototype with a subset of board members who were translators, teachers, and subject matter experts. We showed advisory board members a PDF click-through of a mockup user interface and we asked them to note its more and less useful features. The red arrows suggested to them where they might click as a user. We updated the final screens to address any user issues as appropriate.

In addition to the user experience testing, I traveled to Oklahoma to discuss the interface with advisory board members Roy Boney and John Ross. In two one-hour meetings, we walked through the features of the interface, noting its strengths and areas for improvement. We confirmed and helped develop its usefulness given the workflow of translation practices happening in day-to-day activities within the Cherokee Nation. Advisory board members also recommended additional features they would appreciate adding to the interface as well as suggested that I speak with Dr. Duane King, then the Director of the Helmerich Center for American Indian Research at the Gilcrease Museum in Tulsa, Oklahoma,[7] with whom Ross and Boney worked to translate a recently acquired Cherokee manuscript. Dr. King was gracious with his time, reiterated and confirmed the usefulness of alternative conventions of translation, and agreed to join the advisory board for this project.

The process of developing this prototype yielded three major results we analyze in turn below: 1. A method for selecting culturally sensitive manuscripts to be translated that respected Nations' and archives' pre-existing agreements; 2. A method of translation consistent with present conventions that will be discussed elsewhere;[8] and 3. A prototype for an interface that will help address several needs in the ongoing efforts of nations, libraries, and museums to work together to make accessible, when appropriate, documents and manuscripts significant to the ongoing perseverance of Native peoples.

It was important to carefully consider the decisions related to the selection of documents to translate. We knew our respective Nations had encouraged limited access stewardship of several Cherokee and Anishinaabemowin manuscripts with several archives around the country. For instance, translation teams of the three federally recognized Cherokee Nations established a formal understanding with the American Philosophical Society (APS), among other archives. Teams of elders and language translators pre-selected documents from several collections that can be made available to readers.

These documents are housed in archives, such as at the National Archives; the Helmerich Center for American Research; The Newberry Library, housing the Bread manuscripts; the American Philosophical Society Center for Native American and Indigenous Research, housing manuscripts in the Frank Speck collection; and the Yale University Beinecke Rare Book and Manuscript Library. However, permission to translate these selected documents depends on the culturally sensitive nature of the content in the document and the authority of the translator as already defined by the Nations. To understand the nuances of the conventions governing the document selection, Gordon Henry and I created an initial decision tree to use in the design of this prototype and work with manuscripts in the future.

Using this decision tree, we chose to select documents that had already been translated, published, digitized, and widely disseminated. We selected one found in the papers of anthropologist James Mooney in the Belt manuscript housed in the Smithsonian's NAA. Its digital copy is available online through the Smithsonian Institute Research Information System (SIRIS).[9] For the purposes of illustrating an interface, we believed the selection of this manuscript posed limited risk of violating conventions for the selection of documents to translate set forth in agreements between team members' respective Nations and various archives. I initiated the selection of this document and translations of the first four lines with the Cherokee Nation translation team.

In October 2015, I delivered a talk at Wake Forest University where I presented initial findings from this research on a panel with Thomas Belt, elder from the Eastern Band of Cherokee Indians (EBCI) and Coordinator of the Western Carolina University Cherokee Language Program. Belt pointed out the APS and the EBCI had created a memorandum of understanding (MOU) that could provide a model for best practices for selecting culturally sensitive documents to import and translate for this interface. Subsequent contact with Dr. Timothy Powell, Director of Center for Native American and Indigenous Research (CNAIR) at the APS, and Brian Carpenter, Senior Archivist at the CNAIR at the APS, led to a clearer understanding of the concerns related to the potentially culturally sensitive nature of the document we had selected for use in this mockup. They shared with us the "APS Protocols for the Treatment of Indigenous Materials," which they had developed in collaboration with their Native American Advisory Board to outline best practices in stewarding culturally sensitive manuscripts in their collections with relevant Nations. They define culturally sensitive as:

> Any indigenous material that depicts a tribal spiritual or religious place (e.g., kiva or Midewiwin map), object (e.g., Iroquois masks), belief or activity (e.g., Cherokee sacred formulae). A spiritual or religious activity may include prayers, ceremonies, burials, songs, dancing, healings, and medicine rituals. The definition of "culturally sensitive" may include any other definition provided in writing by a specific tribe with respect to any indigenous materials held by APS depicting that tribe's culture or from which the materials originate. APS will then determine whether the tribe's definition falls within the spirit of the definition set forth herein.[10]

Finally, they also suggested I speak with T. J. Holland, the Cultural Resource Supervisor of the EBCI, who had helped develop a model MOU between the APS and EBCI, currently being finalized with EBCI's legal team. This MOU will provide a model of the type we might use as we begin coordinating efforts across Nations, translators, libraries and archives, and our respective universities.

In light of these subsequent conversations, we have revised the decision tree that our team will use in the future to select manuscripts for possible importation into this translation space. We will ask:

1. Do the legal restrictions of the document outlined by the archives permit viewing, reproduction or online publishing? If yes, proceed to 2. If no, stop.
2. Was the manuscript vetted by relevant Nations to determine its culturally sensitive nature? If yes, proceed to 3. If no, stop and secure one of three designations of the manuscript, in whole or part, in concert with archivists and librarians, if they have not already done so:
   a. not culturally sensitive. If yes, a) proceed to 3;

b. potentially culturally sensitive. If yes, secure permissions and next steps with relevant Nations' IRB and/or cultural supervisors as well as archives in shared MOU.

c. culturally sensitive. Stop.

3. Is there insufficient information to categorize materials as culturally sensitive? If yes, request information from nations. If no response from nations is received in sixty days, consult tribal contacts and representatives on advisory board.

4. Has an MOU or other written or verbal agreement governing the use of this manuscript been established with the relevant Nation and/or Nations? If yes, and permission is therein granted, the document can be used to populate the interface with appropriate permissions and attributions present on the site. If no, return to steps outlined in 2.

For the Anishinaabemowin sample of a user interface text (see Figure 3.2), we selected a copy of a handwritten letter from a member of the Odawa tribe who served in the American Civil War. We used this text as a sample text for the interface, since the text is historically and culturally important across cultures, and since it offers material relevant to the deeper translation and linguistic concerns of our project. Though it is an untranslated text, it is written in Anishinaabemowin and, thus, offers points of analysis for linguists and researchers as they consider how the text might be translated and reviewed decisions about how a nineteenth century Anishinaabemowin speaker chose to write the language, according to a particular view of how Anishinaabemowin words might be phonetically represented as text.

This method for determining best practices in selecting documents to potentially populate this translation will help to ensure that sacred knowledge and formula will remain practiced and understood by Nations, with respect and deference to the culturally sensitive nature of these documents. It will allow novices to train quickly in standard operating procedures for ethical selection of documents and manuscripts appropriate for translation. Perhaps most importantly, this decision tree will make it possible for those involved in translation to be assured that the digital copies of documents they are working with have been provided in line with the terms and conditions specified in MOUs with partnering archives, libraries, museums, and Nations. Along the way, the team will be able to ensure that they have followed protocols developed by libraries and museums governing the use, designation, and dissemination of culturally sensitive manuscripts in this interface.

During the initial prototype creation, we worked to develop an interface that would allow users to add, edit, modify, translate, curate, describe, and view documents. This interface would allow users to curate the Anishinaabemowin and Cherokee language manuscripts they were interested in translating. In creating these prototypes, we based our ideas on design patterns that already exist for online archives, while taking into consideration cultural differences and modifications for our specific communities. During the usability testing phase, we set out to create a test scenario that would represent a day in the life of an archivist. We asked participants to imagine that they were charged with viewing, updating, translating, tagging, and modifying a set of Cherokee or Anishinaabemowin language manuscripts within the system. The usability testing team then reported their findings to the designer so she could update and modify the screens based on our participant feedback.

Our first interface proved difficult for language translators to navigate. They didn't understand how a personal archive could become populated with manuscripts selected from partner libraries. They also didn't understand the workflow of the order of the pages and wanted it to match theirs. They asked that this translation highlight lines, word for word, and that it remove former translations. They also asked for a tab showing the history of translations made by each person. Finally, each page needed a save button at the top. Most importantly, they thought that trying to make this a pedagogical site for language learners proved too complex in the translation section. They suggested making this site for users that included scholars, librarians, and translators. Our Anishinaabemowin speakers wanted to see an Anishinaabemowin document in the mockup as well. As a result, we added, reordered, and rewrote four screens and made several in-line changes as well.

The outcomes from this process resulted in a click-through PDF of a user interface design. The interface design opens with a prompt for a user name and password and allows users to self-select their primary purposes for entering the archive as language learners and translators, researchers, and/or librarians.

The second page of the user interface design brings users to their dashboards and archives. Here users locate and select manuscripts in the particular Indigenous language of their choice from among those donated to this project by participating libraries, archives, and museums. The manuscripts selected and loaded into the user's dashboard are digital images of manuscripts housed at

FIGURE 3.1. Entry Portal to Indigenous Language Manuscript
Collaborative Translation Space

archives, museums, and libraries that have agreed to be collaborators in an MOU about selection and use of the digital images of these manuscripts. Only those manuscripts vetted by Indigenous Nations and approved as non-culturally sensitive will be available for and open to translation.

When users have selected particular manuscripts to import into their own dashboards, they begin to see their dashboards populate with these manuscripts, along with an indication of how much of the translation of these manuscripts they or other users have completed. When users select a manuscript within their dashboard, they are then taken to an edit document window that presents the image of the manuscript along with clickable fields in menu bars that read metadata, translation, history, and sources. When selected, each of these fields in the menu bar reveals a half-screen interface with fields waiting to be populated by the user. For example, the metadata subfield prompts the user for the title, description, library, authors, tribes, date, translators, editors, genres; any additional sources related to the manuscript are pictured to the left of these empty fields (see Figure 3.3).

This particular page proved important to several of our users. For Indigenous Nations' representatives, they hoped to begin to categorize knowledge in and

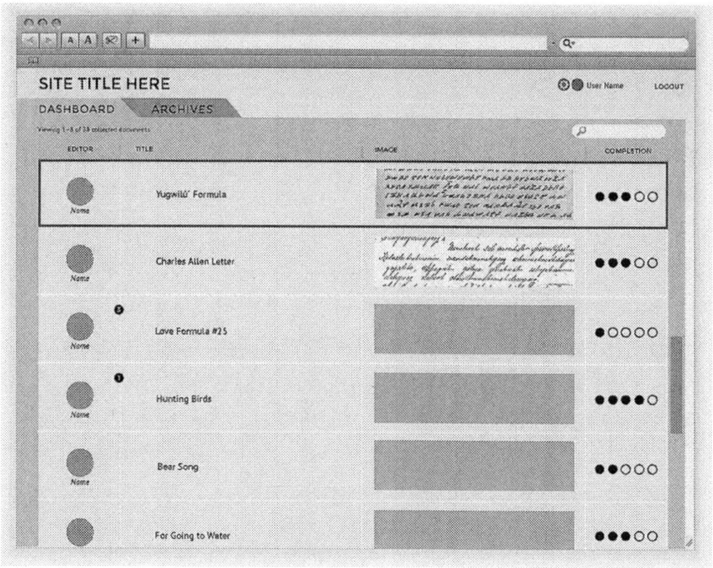

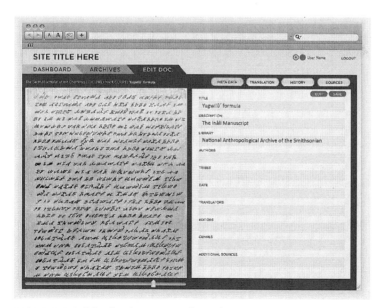

FIGURE 3.2. Dashboard and Task Interface Design

FIGURE 3.3. Metadata input page and sample manuscript

on their own terms. For the museum and archives curators on our team, they hoped to include more robust metadata information for each of their holdings and to correct faulty entries. For scholars, they hoped to create metadata tags that would facilitate their search of these Indigenous language manuscripts according to key terms within the content of these manuscripts.

The translation space allows users to create interlinear translations of words or phrases selected in the manuscript. Indigenous communities and scholars will set up transcription conventions. When compiled and exported, the translations can include transliterations of each character of the word into ISO 9660 recognized writing systems and fonts, literal translations of morphemes, glossed translations into English, and identification of linguistic units for verb forms. Translation conventions can be pre-established as part of the MOU between Nations and archives who donate digital representations of manuscripts for translation in this space. A separate tab will record the histories of who has contributed to each translation so that users can identify translators, sources for the manuscript, and last edit dates of the manuscript, as well as any notes or concerns that emerge as part of the ongoing collaborative translation process.

The development of this interface provides a space to facilitate the workflow and coordination of translation efforts of individuals and teams from Indigenous Nations, scholars, and librarians across archival holdings. It will provide scholars, translators, and interested users with access to reliable, co-created translations. It will allow translators to discuss their work, refine other translations, and offer alternative understandings. Further developments and additions to this interface may include audio files, as well as exporting of words and verb forms into online lexicons currently in use in Nations.

Museums and libraries with substantial holdings of Anishinaabemowin and Cherokee manuscripts have attempted to create accessible digital archives of these manuscripts. However, users may not have access to word-for-word translations of these documents. These digital holdings also tend to be images of documents with overall glosses of meaning. If a Cherokee speaker (e.g. Anna Gritts Kilpatrick) made a translation, those translations exist separately from the manuscripts and offer rough translations of overall content. In other words, these glosses are not directly linked to the words or phrases themselves; thus, they fail to incorporate the vast amount of linguistic information in these documents. Learners and users encounter access issues as well when they seek to pair the printed translations, published in an essay for the NAA, to the actual manuscript image. While libraries and museums may beautifully digitize and catalog images of Anishinaabemowin and Cherokee manuscripts, work remains to be done on deciding which of these may be culturally sensitive and making these useful across institutions to scholars and language translators alike. This interface will be populated with manuscripts using protocols that protect culturally sensitive documents and with permissions and collaborations with libraries and museums.

Next Steps in Decolonizing the Digital Archive: Toward an Indigenous Archive

We are now working with Northeastern University's Digital Scholarship Group (DSG) with four goals in mind:

1. Develop an **online environment for transcribing, translating, and contextualizing historical Cherokee language documents** written in the Cherokee syllabary, designed and developed in partnership with the Cherokee language learning community, and drawing from archival sources.
2. Support **sustainable programs of language learning**.
3. Over time, **build a large digital collection of Cherokee manuscript documents** with transcriptions and translations that serve as a resource for language learning and for linguistic and historical research.
4. Develop a **framework of linguistic and cultural tools and resources** that enable learners to find and compare word usages, learn about word formations, and read discussions of specific connotations and contextual meaning inflections as well as make it possible for scholars to make comparisons to other manuscripts and across languages.

Phase 1 of our project will lay the foundation necessary to document language resources found in Native language manuscripts by developing both a front-end interface and back-end framework capable of supporting collectively authored, word-by-word annotated translations and manuscript analysis to reveal and restore words and understandings lost to our peoples. For American Indian language learners, Phase 2 of this project promises to provide a wealth of opportunity to interact alongside language teachers and with manuscripts, offering a much-needed place to practice with these languages.

As the number of Indigenous community language speakers has decreased, the practice of digital archiving has increased, affording a uniquely modern opportunity: to strengthen the shared projects of Indigenous communities, museums, and libraries across digital repositories and to further develop lexicons, translations, and understandings of Cherokee and Anishinaabemowin peoples — providing an unprecedented avenue of access to primary sources of Indigenous communities' histories and cultures. Digital archiving technologies represent a crucial strategic step for libraries and an integral new set of technical opportunities that will expand research, education, and communication within Indigenous communities. We seek to prototype a sustainable, cumulative, and participatory home for the collective translation of Cherokee and Anishinaabemowin language manuscripts. Being able not only to view these documents, but to actually interact with them at a linguistic level would advance both cultural understandings and translation efforts.

This interface would also afford a shared pedagogical environment where language learners could hone their translation abilities in collaboration with fluent speakers and teachers, and where graduate students and scholars in the digital humanities could continue learning best curatorial practices by collaborating with Indigenous peoples. In addition to developing modern translation skills and facilitating cultural enrichment through the preservation of documents themselves, users in this space could enhance understanding of their histories and revitalize bonds in Indigenous communities by creating connections not just within certain borders but across the many miles and states that digital collaboration allows. Content that is so high stakes requires very careful handling at many levels.

Any platform for archiving, curating, and publishing tribal documents and cultural heritage materials must handle issues of access with great sensitivity both to the nature of the materials themselves and to the role and perspective of contributors, readers, and users. Additionally, because of the fragile and unique nature of these materials, such systems must avoid future obsolescence at all costs; we need to do deliberate advance planning and design to ensure that the data and tools are carefully curated and migrated forward into accessible and sustainable future formats. We also need to anticipate multiple-purpose usage, such as study and pedagogy by scholars and community members, potential reuse of selected data for larger-scale linguistic studies, and other linked open data applications. This platform will need to take into account the depositor roles, content creation roles, editor roles, and administrative/curatorial roles that users of this collaborative translation space may need to fill.

Finally, the computational framework must be hosted by an institutional partner that is ready to make a long-term commitment to the data and the infrastructure, and that has the requisite expertise to develop and support the technology and scholarship effectively. The organizational structure supporting this interface will have to allow for a range of workflows, tools, and associated interfaces that can guide the intake, transformation, encoding, indexing, and organization of these digital representations of Indigenous language manuscripts.

Doing so, this decolonized archive promises to help preserve and sustain native languages by creating a digital archive around the words and content in these manuscripts as they are understood today. Digital spaces like these might further the activist work of language perseverance in Indigenous communities and the ongoing efforts with colleagues in museums and libraries to decolonize imperialist legacies of archives.

Closing Thoughts

Insofar as this digital collaborative space for the translation of Indigenous language manuscripts affords users equal access to and opportunities for the engagement with Indigenous language manuscripts, we see the beginning of the creation of Indigenous archives. Importantly, this digital translation site will make possible the collaborative creation of knowledge in and on terms important to Indigenous communities, scholars, and curators. The extent to which collaborators share the language resources and cultural understandings in these manuscripts depends largely on the careful selection of manuscripts to ensure that culturally sensitive materials are available to the appropriate individuals. While this may run counter to the belief that all information on the Web should be made publicly available, it is crucial to recognize that Indigenous peoples are the keepers of their wisdom and maintain rhetorical sovereignty over this legacy. That being said, it is also crucial to recognize that the collaborators in this space are equal, though necessarily having different privileges based on the types and kinds of uses and practices relevant to the purposes they self-select. In other words, a language translator will have a different role and access within this site than a scholar or a librarian might. The differences in roles ensure consistent integration of the translation products across various user interactions and in relation to the computational infrastructure that supports the creation of content within the site.

While it is important to recognize that the practices of developing the site needed to be collaborative, the processes of translating manuscripts must also recognize the imperial legacy of translation. Translation has a long legacy of facilitating imperial and settler agendas throughout the world. As Tejaswini

Niranjana has argued: "Translation . . . produces strategies of containment. By employing certain modes of representing the other — which it thereby also brings into being — translation reinforces hegemonic versions of the colonized."[11] Representing the other is necessary to the work of controlling subjects, to containing them within whatever structuring mode of modernity one works from and from any direction one chooses. Translation by white outsiders to control Cherokees took place at several historical moments, however, I choose to overview only two for the sake of brevity and to serve as an illustration that the target direction the translation does not affect the instrumental value of translation as a key method in imperialist agendas. Employing certain modes of representing the other in Christianity and intellectual disciplines, missionaries and academics represent their civilizing missions and enunciations of superior knowledge through translation. Such was the goal of the translation of the bible into Cherokee. For example, John Pickering was the first translator, who created an orthography to represent all American Indian languages in order to translate the bible in them. The second was Samuel Worcester, who entered Indian Territory to learn Cherokee in order to preach in Cherokee. The American Board of Foreign Commissioners supported both efforts in the early and mid-1800s. Similarly, anthropologists undertook translation work to preserve the language, manuscripts, and artifacts of Indigenous others in order to create an imperial tradition from Othered traditions.

James Mooney's rationale for his anthropological study of the Cherokees also advanced imperial agendas. For him, the greater the difference from white men's ways, the greater the anthropological interest in translating primitive knowledges to white outsiders, to clearly distinguish Western traditions from Cherokee traditions. Mooney set his sights on the remote Carolina hills where "the ancient things have been preserved," rather than studying the Western Cherokees.[12] It would be easier to show the clearly visible differences of Cherokees in the Carolinas, through the considerable effort he undertook to translate their history, myths, and sacred formulas. In this way, by illustrating others as primitive and largely all the same — non-civilizing — Mooney totalizes the reality of Western culture. He gathered the complex world views and ways of non-white peoples, and then dismissed and erased them as primitive, with the stated goal of demonstrating the clear superiority of white men's ways.

I chose these instances to illustrate a subtle point about language itself as medium of translation. It matters little if the target language for translation was English or Cherokee. The target audience, purpose, and desired outcome are what matter most to the translation effort. In either direction the translation went (the Bible into Cherokee or Cherokee stories into disciplinary knowledge in English), translation served to contain Cherokee subjects. On the one hand, we see the containment of Cherokee ceremonial knowledge by Christian theology; on the other hand, we see the containment of Cherokee stories into myths and legends (not living knowledge, but quaint traditions and representations of the primitive oral culture). Regardless of the direction the translation goes, in other words, it serves to enunciate Western theologies and knowledge couched in narratives of conversion and representation of "primitive" people. Indigenous people cannot escape the imperial legacy of translation, even as the exigencies of creating collaborative translation spaces for Indigenous language manuscripts demands using translation. What is to be done?

Elsewhere, I develop a methodology for decolonial translation practices that necessarily involves members from the Cherokee nations. This method of translation will be important to the development of conventions for interlinear translation within this digital interface. Translation itself must necessarily be an inclusive practice that also recognizes the diversity in purpose, method, and knowledge base that users bring to this interface. It will also recognize the need for consistent and reliable translation practices and products that are internally validated within the site through collaborative dialogue. Finally, it will recognize the need for us to document translations and iterations of these translations for the sake of transparency and reliability, and to safeguard against the possibility of one person's translation becoming authorized to the detriment of understanding the potential variations of meaning found in these manuscripts. To be certain, the development of decolonial digital interfaces and Indigenous archives is but a first step in the process of creating shared collaborative spaces for the important work of responsibly translating these manuscripts.

Notes

1. See Timothy B. Powell, "Digital Knowledge Sharing: Forging Partnerships between Scholars, Archives, and Indigenous Communities," *Museum Anthropology Review* 10: 2 (2016): 66–99; Sonya Atalay, *Community-Based Archaeology: Research With, By, and for Indigenous and Local Communities* (Berkeley: University of California Press, 2012); Jennifer R. O'Neal, "Respect, Recognition, and Reciprocity: The Protocols for Native American Archival Materials," in *Identity Palimpsests: Archiving Ethnicity in the US and Canada*, ed. Dominique Daniel and Amalia Levi (Sacramento: Litwin Press, 2014), 125–142;

Jennifer R. O'Neal, "'The Right to Know': Decolonizing Native American Archives," *Journal of Western Archives* 6:1 (2015): 1–17.

2. See Ellen Cushman, "Wampum, Sequoyan, and Story: Decolonizing the Digital Archive," *College English* 76:2 (2013): 115–135; Amy Lonetree, *Decolonizing Museums: Representing Native America in National and Tribal Museums* (Raleigh: University of North Carolina Press, 2012).

3. Walter D. Mignolo, *The Darker Side of Western Modernity: Global Futures, Decolonial Options* (Durham, NC: Duke University Press, 2011), 160.

4. See O'Neal, "Respect, Recognition, and Reciprocity"; O'Neal, "'Right to Know'"; Timothy B. Powell, "The American Philosophical Society Protocols for the Treatment of Indigenous Materials," *Proceedings of the American Philosophical Society; Philadelphia* 158:4 (2014): 411–420; Powell, "Digital Knowledge Sharing"; Swan, Daniel C. and Michael Paul Jordan, "Contingent Collaborations: Patterns of Reciprocity in Museum-Community Partnerships." Journal of Folklore Research 52:1 (2015): 39-84.

5. See Robert Leopold, "Articulating Culturally Sensitive Knowledge Online: A Chero-kee Case Study," *Museum Anthropology Review* 7:1-2 (2013): 85-104.

6. Powell, "Digital Knowledge Sharing".

7. This chapter is dedicated to Dr. Duane King, who passed away on September 17, 2017, in honor of the legacy he left as a premiere scholar of Cherokee language and history, and curator of manuscripts as the Executive Director of the Helmerich Center for American Research and Gilcrease museum. He is missed.

8. Cushman, Ellen. "Decolonial Translation as Methodology for Learning to Unlearn." *Dartmouth Conference 50th Anniversary*. Ed. Christiane Donahue. Under contract.

9. The digital copy can be accessed at http://collections.si.edu/search/ by searching NAA MS 2590 (NMNH-2590a_vol2_49); Its translation appears in *The Sacred Formulas of the Cherokees Seventh Annual Report of the Bureau of Ethnology to the Secretary of the Smithsonian Institution, 1885–1886.* (Washington: Government Printing Office, 1891), 301–398.

10. Powell, "Protocols for the Treatment of Indigenous Materials."

11. Tejaswini Niranjana, *Siting Translation: History, Post-Structuralism, and the Colonial Context* (Berkeley: University of California Press), 3. See also, Rolando Vázquez, "Trans-lation as Erasure: Thoughts on Modernity's Epistemic Violence." *Journal of Historical Sociology* 24:1 (2011): 27–44.

12. James Mooney and George Ellison. *James Mooney's History, Myths, and Sacred Formulas of the Cherokees* (Asheville, NC: Bright Mountain Books), 12.

FOUR

Caretaking Around Collecting and the Digital Turn: Lessons in Ongoing Opportunities and Challenges from the Native Northeast

Christine DeLucia

Conversations about archives and digitization frequently center on interior and virtual spaces: the storage shelves of a special collections repository known intimately by archivists, the technological infrastructure that underpins glowing screens of desktop or mobile devices engaged by users. I wish to begin this set of reflections on digitization's possibilities for Native American and Indigenous Studies out on the land and water, because in my own thinking, research, collaboration, and writing about the Native Northeast, I am continuously drawn back to the very real places in which histories have taken shape and continue to unfold. I reflect from time to time on a specific waterway, often referred to in recent times as the Charles River, which winds eastward from Nipmuc-Massachusetts homelands to the saltwater of Boston Harbor and eventually the Atlantic Ocean.[1] Its flow is interrupted today by a series of modern dams, but even so, it powerfully manifests mobility, connection, flow, and replenishment — the kinds of conceptual keywords that often undergird discussions about practices of knowledge keeping. While the entire watershed is historically significant, a stretch of the river that passes through South Natick, Massachusetts encapsulates many dimensions of Indigenous history and the complexities involved in telling it. This section of the river has been a site of Indigenous removal and trauma as Native people navigating the maelstrom of the late seventeenth century were forcibly rounded up on boats by English authorities, then transported away from these home-grounds to a deadly island incarceration camp. It has also been a locus of Indigenous activism and re-gathering as descendants of some seventeenth-century survivors have returned, borne witness, and held ceremonies of remembrance here.[2] Perhaps most relevant for debates around knowledge systems, stewardship, and information transmission, it has long been — and in a sense continues to be — an uneasy site of "collecting" that has enacted obvious as well as subtle forms of violence and dispossession. The fine-grained particularities of this place, in other words, present serious challenges to using new technologies to translate exceedingly fraught Indigenous-colonial histories into alternate forms.

Before delving further into how Natick can help us perceive more sharply the complex dynamics involved in digitizing heritage collections, I offer a few critical touchstones pertaining to the larger contours of these issues, which span global geographies extending well beyond the Native Northeast. Amid exciting conversations about the constructive, forward-looking possibilities of digitization, it is worthwhile to reflect on *longue durée* developments in archiving and collecting that have shaped how, where, and why stories reside, move, and operate in the world. Indigenous forms of knowledge, the Maori scholar Linda Tuhiwai Smith contended in her foundational *Decolonizing Methodologies: Research and Indigenous Peoples*, have long been "regarded as 'new discoveries' by Western science. These discoveries were commodified as property belonging to the cultural archive and body of knowledge of the West."[3] As she and other Indigenous intellectuals and allies have stressed, collecting has recurrently been mobilized as a tool of colonization and an agent of conquest. In its Western and Euro-American expressions (which are intimately entangled with the origins and ongoing transits of settler colonialism), collecting has been predicated on logics of dispossession, appropriation, and repossession that have borne detrimental consequences for Indigenous communities: the deracination of knowledge from living communities, the claiming and sometimes attempted overwriting of heritage resources by entrepreneurial outsiders, the physical disconnection of Indigenous descendants from the still-vital materials created by their ancestors. These processes have unfolded in distinctive ways contingent on time and place, of course, and I do not presume to sum up the entirety of how collecting has been a friction point between many Indigenous peoples and Euro-Americans. It is essential to recognize, however, that the vibrant discourses arising from decolonizing methodologies present notable challenges to the digital turn and its sometimes under-theorized approaches to seemingly new forms of information use, which are almost always rooted, to one degree or another, in older and markedly problematic types of collecting. Tuhiwai Smith made her intervention before the digital humanities had taken off in a concerted fashion within academic settings, yet she cogently anticipated cautions and considerations that ought to figure prominently into any digital archiving endeavor, so long as it aspires to not simply replicate pre-existing colonialist practices of knowledge formation. In this chapter, I convey a selection of stories from my own research experiences across the Native Northeast to illustrate how the decolonizing advisements articulated by Tuhiwai Smith and a host of Native American and Indigenous Studies scholars can bear on localized situations.

How has collecting operated in the Native Northeast in ways that bolster — or push back against — the hegemonic power dynamics of New England settler colonialism? How have libraries, archives, museums, and associated repositories shaped the historical narratives, memories, and forms of knowledge that are present and meaningful among Tribal as well as Euro-American communities in this region, over multiple generations and into the twenty-first century? These were two questions that strongly inflected the research and writing of my first book, *Memory Lands: King Philip's War and the Place of Violence in the Northeast*. To pursue more Indigenous-centered understandings of multi-tribal resistances of the late seventeenth century and the multitude of ways in which this conflict (1675–1678) has been interpreted, commemorated, and at times profoundly misconstrued, I embarked on a far-ranging itinerary to locate alternative sources and narratives. An animating principle for my research was that it was incumbent on me to move beyond the handful of elite research libraries and archives that early Americanist scholars have conventionally used to develop their arguments about Native-colonial relations in the Northeast. Instead, I spent time in a series of "minor" repositories that are essential yet overwhelmingly overlooked nodes for studying the Native Northeast. These ranged from very small town historical societies (many established in the late eighteenth or nineteenth centuries by Euro-American antiquarians), to cultural heritage centers run by sovereign Tribal Nations (such as the Tantaquidgeon Museum of the Mohegan Tribal Nation and the Mashantucket Pequot Museum and Research Center), to anthropological museums housed at colleges and universities (filled with material culture items that were routinely acquired from Native communities through duress or coercion). By engaging with this sizable constellation of regional memory houses (over 160 to date), I aimed to gain deeper insights into patterns and structures of knowledge production, circulation, interpretation, and public memory formation.[4] These repositories have enabled me to better understand why collecting institutions have functioned in particular ways, and how seemingly mundane practices, such as the local classifying system used to organize vertical files of newspaper clippings, can illuminate underlying beliefs and ideologies about stewardship, access, and ownership in contexts of settler colonialism as well as persistent Indigenous sovereignty.

In addition to this sustained on-the-ground research over the past dozen years, I have also become involved with a range of digital humanities projects centered on Native American topics. They have arisen organically from acutely perceived needs to make Native heritage materials better accessible and more accurately contextualized for multiple constituencies: Tribal community members, undergraduate and graduate students, scholarly researchers, educators, and the public.[5] Through varied roles I have gained familiarity with multi-year efforts to build up these projects, endeavors that have required substantial investments of time, energy, and technological expertise. These projects have spanned a period of tremendous transformation and capacity building in the digital humanities (ca. 2006 to the present), and their evolution has helped me recognize the opportunities as well as challenges that such initiatives present as they attempt to transmute paper records, artifacts, and other heritage sources of high importance to Native descendant communities into digital formats.[6] I am grateful to scores of curators, librarians, archivists, technology staff members, and learning specialists for conversations that contributed to new understandings, helped navigate obstacles, and worked toward development of appropriate processes rather than over-focusing on completed end products. All of these experiences inform the comments I make below about the promises but also pitfalls of seeking to connect the Native Northeast more robustly with digital futures.

Given these broader, ever-shifting contexts of projects that often move at dizzying speeds, and in response to perceived pressures to meet deadlines and funding expectations, how can a locality such as Natick shed light on the need for additional sensitivities and caretaking around digitization in the Native Northeast? If you visit South Natick today and travel down by the river dam, you will encounter a local library (the Bacon Free Library) that also contains an historical society encompassing archival, print, and material culture collections. Given the centrality of the Natick area to Native Algonquian communities during the so-called Praying Town era and its aftermath — Protestant missionary efforts to Christianize Natives, and continuous Indigenous reshaping of these bids, extensively documented by historian Jean O'Brien (White Earth Ojibwe) — this might seem a vital place for research as well as community-engaged projects, with digitization as a logical next step to make these holdings more widely visible and usable.[7] Yet the historical backstory of this repository casts its collections in a different light. When Euro-American town residents underwrote construction of this building in the late nineteenth century, they selected a site in the midst of a well-known Native burial area. Native ancestral remains and funerary objects were disturbed during the building process. Some of them appear to have been added to the collections, part of a much wider trend of antiquarian collecting that was rampant throughout New England and the emerging United States. History itself, to put it more starkly, along with the extractive and entitled mentalities around collecting that motivated Euro-American antiquarians convinced that New England Natives had vanished, or would imminently do so, have made this repository into a deeply troubling place.[8]

Institutions and their supporters change over time, and the Natick Historical Society has seen a number of important developments pertaining to Native subjects and materials in recent decades. In the late twentieth century, the historical society undertook the ethically and legally notable process of a repatriation review (following passage by US Congress of the Native American Graves Protection and Repatriation Act in 1990), and engaged in a number of returns of sensitive materials to descendant communities. Its collection and exhibition spaces contain sources that speak in enormously compelling ways about Native presence, survivance, and adaptation in this region, and staff members are desirous of connecting with more diverse publics. Yet the attractive stone repository standing today is part and parcel of a long history of painful dispossessions and dislocations, making it a potentially difficult venue for research by, with, and for Native communities.[9] When I think about the potential for digitizing its collections, it is not immediately clear to me how this complex past of settler-colonial disturbances ought to inflect the discussion. Would digitization be an asset, making materials available in a manner that does not require in-person presence at a site imbued with sensitivities? Could a web-based resource encompassing digital surrogates of the historical society's holdings allow users to focus on the materials themselves, without having to subject themselves to the unease or even trauma of entering into a fraught space? Moreover, traveling to Natick can be cost- and time-prohibitive for scholars and community members, so being able to remotely access documents, maps, and artifacts could conceivably be a useful change that helps address issues of equity and the political economies of knowledge production. On the other hand, is it not possible to so neatly dissociate materials from their holding contexts? The items presently contained in the historical society's glass cases and storage areas persist atop a real place that arguably should be treated in dramatically different ways out of respect for Indigenous ancestors and descendants. The Natick situation invites us to reflect more closely upon how collecting sites' unique histories need to be understood and reckoned with: their imbrication within contested histories involving Indigenous homelands, settler-colonial territorial dispossessions, and practices of acquiring materials that involved violations of many kinds. Sources under consideration for digitization need to be reckoned with not in abstract or dissociated ways, but instead assessed in the context of specific historical locales, networks, and relationships.

The complicated dynamics around collecting and access that Natick foregrounds may be pronounced at this site, but they are not unique to this location. Many Tribal community members, historians, genealogists, and other researchers have "archive tales," personal accounts of experiences related to collection spaces that trenchantly convey the challenging terrain involved in seeking out historical and heritage resources.[10] In one corner of southern New England, for example, there are multiple stories about a town repository's having discarded important historical documents in a dumpster. It was no coincidence, certain storytellers assert, that documents were being surreptitiously destroyed in the midst of an active Tribal legal battle involving matters of sovereignty, recognition, and land. Euro-American town residents and officials may maintain alternate versions of these events, of course. What these stories indubitably reflect is that both the Tribe and surrounding municipalities had become keenly aware of the roles played by documents in US legal arenas, and of the political significance of being able to reference a cohesive archive. Given the centrality of written documentation to US systems of adjudication, historical knowledge production, and pursuit of so-called objectivity in historical representation, compromising that archive could make Tribal members' very abilities to present certain historical truths more difficult.[11] As a number of Native scholars have noted, written documentation has long occupied a paramount place in how Euro-American practitioners define acceptable sources for understanding the past. "How does one confront the demands of the discipline of history regarding particular kinds of written documentation, and the continued marginalization of particular kinds of sources — oral histories, for example?" Jean O'Brien asks. "Who gets to decide what history matters, and what counts as reliable evidence?"[12] She goes on to challenge the purported scarcity of documentation pertaining to Indigenous pasts (there is in fact an abundance), and draws attention to ongoing contestations about recognizing and redefining the very nature, scope, and contents of what the archive for Indigenous histories is, has been, and can be.

Taking into account such reflections on the contested nature of the archive itself, if accounts of intentionally disruptive deaccessioning accurately characterize this area's collections landscape, how should they inform potential digitization projects? What would it mean to begin digitizing, and thereby conferring certain legibility as an "authoritative" archive, upon collections that have been winnowed and transformed in highly uneven (even potentially illegal) ways? Even setting aside matters of blatant discarding, Euro-American repositories across the Northeast and United States have for generations kept, preserved, valued, and rendered findable certain historical resources — often those that speak most directly to colonialist versions of the past — while allowing others to disintegrate, become lost or misplaced, or simply become treated as marginal, effectively rendering them as understories to the "official" archive. Archive tales like the one recounted here offer valuable qualitative insights into how real people, including Indigenous community members who continue to experience history being mobilized against them in distressing ways within settler-colonial legal and policy domains, make sense of the nature of information circulation. They urge us to reflect upon foundational issues of presence/absence in any collection being considered for digitization, and to consider how sources that are tangibly, visibly present today may conceal histories of attempted destruction, removal, and erasure.[13]

Two other examples convey additional complexities that ought to be under discussion when framing digitization projects. Consider the historical society that holds a corpus of vital seventeenth-century manuscripts by and about leading Native figures in the region, with potential to shed light on formative land negotiations that laid the foundation for historical and ongoing contestations over land and sovereignty. While this society has pursued an open philosophy about certain portions of its collection (which includes rich materials about Euro-American, African American, and other experiences), it has enforced a policy that precludes researchers from consulting or even touching these specific manuscripts. Instead, readers are referred to photocopy reproductions of poor quality, making accurate interpretation of their contents very difficult. This policy was ostensibly designed for protective reasons, evidencing a narrowly defined preservationist logic that values the physical integrity and longevity of the manuscripts above other considerations. However well intentioned, this policy has had the effect of foreclosing substantive inquiries about a pivotal series of interactions between Native people and Euro-American colonizers. Moreover, the policy presents a form of gatekeeping that makes it difficult or impossible for present-day Tribal community members to directly engage with ancestors' documents. Given that the value of a manuscript is arguably not only about content, but also about the artifactual uniqueness of it — the inky traces left by ancestors' hands, the pictorial marks used in the place of signatures to attest to Indigenous affirmations, albeit in often coercive settings — this is a non-trivial consideration around access.[14] Should this repository one day become interested in scanning the manuscripts and making them digitally available, such a project, unless carefully conceived, would still not address underlying considerations around who can or cannot have in-person contact with original resources, matters that involve deep-seated assumptions around privilege, status, credentials, custodianship, and perceived legitimacy as an archive user.

If this example presents a contentious situation around the use of surrogates (broadly understood here as stand-ins for original materials, whether in paper or digital forms), a final case gestures at different complications attending the recourse to copies. There is a certain state library in the Northeast that holds an important historical treaty with numerous Tribal signatories. In the twentieth century, this treaty was removed from Tribal custody under questionable circumstances. It eventually came into state hands, and in light of its contested provenance and trajectory the library agreed, following consultations with the Tribe, to not make the original treaty available to non-Tribal researchers, except with express permission from Tribal authorities. When I called up this treaty to view in the library's reading room one summer day, I fully expected to receive the copy of it. To my surprise and dismay, staff members handed me the original, evidently unaware of these previously negotiated restrictions. (Staff turnover throughout the years may have contributed to this breach in protocol, as well as various forms of institutional amnesia.) When I think about a repository such as this becoming invested in digitization endeavors, a primary reaction is concern, given its prior track record in dealing appropriately with ownership, stewardship, and differential accessibility. The status of the original treaty as a unique artifact matters intensely, and there are significant implications entwined in the (selective) recourse to reproductions. I recognize that the two preceding examples can present apparently contradictory calls for action: in the first case, a desire for more direct access to original materials; in the second, a desire for less, at least among certain constituencies of readers. What I aim to convey is that the very ability for users to encounter or not encounter original materials involves embedded politics that are highly specific to each location and historical context, and arises from long-term negotiations between Native people and Nations, and the non-Native institutions that have laid claim to heritage resources. These dynamics may not be evident at a first glance, but can become known through research into the histories of the collections themselves, and through conversations with staff members, users, and others about their evolving management over time. Without fundamental reckoning with these dynamics, any bids for creating digital surrogates or devising new forms of classification and connection will likely only push the problems down the road.

I share these vignettes not to imply that all Euro-American collecting institutions in the Northeast engage in colonialist tactics of appropriation and exclusion, nor to suggest that the practices and policies described are intentional acts of continuing marginalization. Indeed, there is a wide spectrum of protocols that influence in minute yet consequential ways how particular historical documents and material culture objects are handled and made legible to multiple publics. But it is important to underscore that many of the region's cultural heritage venues still present obstacles and even affronts to Tribal community members, scholars working in Native American and Indigenous Studies, and others who seek to use these collections for transformative purposes. A large number of repositories containing significant materials pertaining to Indigenous pasts and presents are severely under-resourced (especially in an era of continuing fiscal austerity that has limited state and federal funding), and disengaged from conversations about decolonizing methodologies that have gained traction in academia. Even if these repositories' staff members were inclined to promote positive change within their institutions, they would need to undertake time-intensive labor to self-educate about pertinent concepts and practices, and to initiate the important forms of relationship building with present-day Tribal communities and knowledge keepers that undergird ethically attuned projects. Yet sometimes all it would take to set in motion alternative approaches is a single conversation or interaction.

By way of conclusion, I would build upon these cautions to gesture toward future possibilities for leveraging digital tools to enable more holistic, even restorative, approaches to history and memory. In my daily research and teaching practices, I routinely engage with digital resources that serve laudable ends:

zoom-able historical maps that repositories have scanned at high resolution and made available to assist scrutiny of details about Indigenous homelands and colonial territorial claims; transcriptions of previously obscure manuscripts about Indigenous rights, petitions, and related legal resistances that editorial teams have produced through paleographic decipherment; digital photographs of material objects that speak to the everyday lives of Indigenous people who survived and thrived amid daunting colonial pressures, now viewable and searchable through online museum databases; oral traditions relayed by Native language speakers, now recorded and made available on cultural resource websites developed by Tribal Nations.[15] When carefully constructed and mindful of underlying structures of power, authority, and responsibility, digital tools that engage Indigenous resources and subjects can foster new types of scholarly practice, pedagogy, and outreach that can enact positive influences on the world.

My current research has taken me into Northeastern material culture and the ways that tangible Indigenous objects such as burl bowls, stone pestles, furniture, and scores of other items were frequently acquired and/or seized from Native people and homelands, then classified according to Euro-American schemas and held, as well as interpreted, alongside textual sources such as manuscripts and imprints. Yet as professional norms shifted and museum collections became separated in many instances from libraries and archives, many of these important heritage objects are now housed in utterly disparate places from the provenance information required to make appropriate sense of them. These dislocations bear significant consequences for repatriation endeavors, culturally informed public history interpretation, and scholarly investigations. The connective, integrative capacities of digitization — which allow multiple points of entry, flexible interpretive pathways, and alternative renditions of temporality that are difficult to achieve in conventional, linearly structured textual monographs[16] — could assist with relinking now-dispersed objects and texts, helping regather them (at least virtually, for the moment) into webs of relations that better speak to their meanings for communities.[17] Equally important, such digital tools can help reconnect heritage objects presently held in non-Native repositories with the internal collections maintained and stewarded by Tribal communities themselves, which employ community-informed systems of organization, preservation, and interpretation.[18] While the end-goal for some, many, or even all of these externally held objects may eventually be their return to home communities, there are en route vital ways that digitization can ease their transit back into more appropriate contexts and relationships.

Notes

1. These place names reflect contested histories of Indigenous and colonial placemaking that over several centuries have resulted in multiple, shifting toponyms across the Native Northeast. On conceptualizing and naming these geographies (and cultural as well as political implications), and possibilities for using analog and digital cartographies to convey alternate senses of place, see Lisa T. Brooks, *The Common Pot: The Recovery of Native Space in the Northeast* (Minneapolis: University of Minnesota Press, 2008); Brooks, "About the Project," in *Our Beloved Kin: Remapping a New History of King Philip's War,* digital resource http://ourbelovedkin.com/awikhigan/about?path=index; George Neptune, "Naming the Dawnland: Wabanaki Place Names on Mount Desert Island," *Chebacco: The Magazine of the Mount Desert Island Historical Society XVI* (2015): 92–108; David Sanger, Micah A. Pawling, and Donald G. Soctomah, "Passamaquoddy Homeland and Language: The Importance of Place," in *Cross-Cultural Collaboration: Native Peoples and Archaeology in the Northeastern United States*, ed. Jordan E. Kerber (Lincoln: University of Nebraska Press, 2006), 314–328; J.B. Harley, "New England Cartography and the Native Americans," in J.B. Harley, *The New Nature of Maps: Essays in the History of Cartography*, ed. Paul Laxton (Baltimore: Johns Hopkins University Press, 2002), 169–196.

2. These histories, and contested processes of memorialization around them, are related in Part I: The Way to Deer Island, in Christine M. DeLucia, *Memory Lands: King Philip's War and the Place of Violence in the Northeast,* The Henry Roe Cloud Series on American Indians and Modernity (New Haven, CT: Yale University Press, 2018). I recognize conversations around the Deer Island Memorial with Pam Ellis, Rick Pouliot, Kristen Wyman, Marcus Hendricks, and others that have influenced my understandings of this place and its continuing resonances.

3. Linda Tuhiwai Smith, *Decolonizing Methodologies: Research and Indigenous Peoples* (New York: Zed Books, 2004), 61.

4. Howard Mansfield developed the concept of "memory houses" — institutions that actively shape which forms of the past are maintained and valued within communities, often in exclusionary or sanitized ways — in his book *In the Memory House* (Golden, CO: Fulcrum Publishing, 1993). I explore the functions of such sites in more detail, and with attention to the agency of Indigenous visitors and interlocutors, in a recent essay about collecting in the Northeast: Christine DeLucia, "Fugitive Collections in New England Indian Country: Indigenous Material Culture and Early American History Making at Ezra Stiles's Yale Museum," *The William and Mary Quarterly* 3rd ser., 75:1 (Jan. 2018): 109–150.

5. My introduction to using digital tools for Native American Studies came while I was an undergraduate at Harvard College, where I assisted Malinda Maynor Lowery (Lumbee), then a faculty member in the Harvard History Department, in building course websites for her classes on Native American topics. This work was facilitated by the

Harvard Instructional Technology Group and the Presidential Instructional Technology Fellows program https://pitf.harvard.edu/quotes/testimonials. As a doctoral student at Yale University, I assisted Alyssa Mt. Pleasant (Tuscarora), then a faculty member in the Yale American Studies Program and History Department, with developing an American Indian Studies Resources Portal https://web.archive.org/web/20101222140011 /http://aisresources.commons.yale.edu/home. This portal helped make visible the sizable array of materials pertinent to Native subjects spread across the university's many libraries, archives, museums, and related repositories. This work was facilitated by the Yale Instructional Technology Group and its Instructional Innovation program. I have also been connected, primarily in a user and/or consultant role, with the *Yale Indian Papers Project* https://yipp.yale.edu based at Yale University, which aims to digitize, transcribe, interpret, and connect documents pertinent to New England Native histories. Finally, as a faculty member at Mount Holyoke College I have participated in planning discussions around the emerging Digital Archive of Native American Intellectual Traditions http:// danait.wordpress.amherst.edu, an initiative supported by Amherst College, especially archivist Michael Kelly and American Studies faculty members Lisa Brooks (Abenaki) and Kiara Vigil (Dakota/Apache heritage). I also worked with the John Carter Brown Library at Brown University to convene a gathering on "Digital Futures of Indigenous Studies" (March 2016) https://www.brown.edu/academics/libraries/john-carter-brown /event/2016/03/04/roundtable as part of the library's ongoing Indigenous Studies initiative.

6. For a useful overview of the historical trajectory of digital humanities projects that have engaged Native American and Indigenous topics and communities, see Siobhan Senier, "Digitizing Indigenous History: Trends and Challenges," *Journal of Victorian Culture* 19:3 (2014): 396–402. Senier's critique of how "the most visible and best-funded digital archives have tended to privilege colonial collections over those stewarded, often for centuries, by tribal communities themselves" (397) is well-warranted and raises important considerations around resources and institutional homes that are somewhat beyond the scope of my own essay.

7. Jean M. O'Brien, *Dispossession by Degrees: Indian Land and Identity in Natick, Massachusetts, 1650–1790* (New York: Cambridge University Press, 1997). O'Brien extensively discusses disruptive antiquarian history-making practices in *Firsting and Lasting: Writing Indians Out of Existence in New England* (Minneapolis: University of Minnesota Press, 2010).

8. On these fraught histories, see my discussion of Natick in Christine DeLucia, "Antiquarian Collecting and the Transits of Indigenous Material Culture: Rethinking 'Indian Relics' and Tribal Histories," Object Lessons column, *Common-place: The Journal of Early American Life,* 17:2 (Winter 2017), http://common-place.org/book/antiquarian -collecting-and-the-transits-of-indigenous-material-culture-rethinking-indian-relics -and-tribal-histories. See also discussion of the Bacon Free Library's origins and location

in Natick Historical Society, "Our History," https://www.natickhistoricalsociety.org/our -history; *Natick History* brochure (available at Natick Historical Society); and Rev. J.P. Sheafe, Jr., "The Indian Burying Ground," *A Review of the First Fourteen Years of the Historical, Natural History and Library Society of South Natick, Mass.* (South Natick, MA: Printed for the Society, 1884), 29–32. Part of my understanding of the historical collection development at Natick comes from a site visit in June 2016. I recognize staff members for sharing information about institutional and local histories.

9. For a concise discussion of what doing history "with communities" can entail, from a scholar with extensive collaborative and consultative ties to Northeastern Tribal communities, see Amy E. Den Ouden, "Histories with Communities: Struggles, Collaborations, Transformations," in *Sources and Methods in Indigenous Studies*, ed. Chris Andersen and Jean M. O'Brien (New York: Routledge, 2017), 143–151.

10. I have not identified by name the places, institutions, or individuals in this section in order to maintain a degree of anonymity for those who might be put at risk through these stories' public discussion and analysis. In several cases, there is potential for constructive change to take root at the institutions in question, and I do not wish to impede those processes by singling the sites out for critique, especially since practices like the ones mentioned herein are undoubtedly widespread throughout New England and the United States. All of the instances described in this section came to my attention through research, fieldwork, and informal conversations, ca. 2006–2017.

11. For critique of the ways in which History as a discipline and set of methods has exercised influence on Native American lives and politics in the present, with attention to the selective manner in which "objectivity" has been defined by Euro-American practitioners, see Angela Cavender Wilson, "American Indian History or Non-Indian Perceptions of American Indian History?" in *Natives and Academics: Researching and Writing About American Indians,* ed. Devon A. Mihesuah (Lincoln: University of Nebraska Press, 1998), 23–26.

12. Jean M. O'Brien, "Historical Sources and Methods in Indigenous Studies: Touching on the Past, Looking to the Future," in *Sources and Methods in Indigenous Studies*, 17–18.

13. My thinking on archives, erasures, and the historical power dynamics of settler colonialism have been shaped by a number of critiques, including assessments of how the archive of race-based transatlantic slavery contains important yet often under-scrutinized silences. See, for example, Brian Connolly and Marisa Fuentes, "Introduction: From Archives of Slavery to Liberated Futures?" *History of the Present,* 6:2 (Fall 2016): 105–116, which discusses how the "archives of slavery and the oppressive power structures they represent and reproduce, left uninterrogated, contributes to a system of racial denigration that has persisted in slavery's afterlife" (115).

14. A Native community member featured in a recent documentary film about the Wôpanâak Language Reclamation Project http://www.wlrp.org describes the emotional

impact and social value of directly encountering texts handwritten by Algonquian ancestors; see Anne Makepeace, prod., *We Still Live Here: Âs Nutayuneân* (2011), http://www
.pbs.org/independentlens/films/we-still-live-here.

15. The resources described here come from digital initiatives such as the Map Collection at the John Carter Brown Library, accessible through the LUNA Imaging database https://www.brown.edu/academics/libraries/john-carter-brown/jcb-online/image
-collections/map-collection; the documentary editing products of the *Yale Indian Papers
Project* http://findit.library.yale.edu/yipp; the Collections Database of the Five Colleges
and Historic Deerfield Museum Consortium http://museums.fivecolleges.edu; and the
Language Resources shared by the Penobscot Nation's Cultural and Historic Preservation
website http://www.penobscotculture.com/index.php/language-resources.

16. On such interventions, see Lisa Brooks, "The Primacy of the Present, The Primary
of Place: Navigating the Spiral of History in the Digital World," *PMLA* 127:2 (March 2012):
308–316.

17. For one example of ongoing restorative research involving material culture currently dispersed in multiple locations, see Margaret Bruchac et al., *On the Wampum
Trail: Restorative Research in North American Museums* https://wampumtrail.wordpress
.com. Debate has arisen around collecting institutions such as the Smithsonian Institution about 3D digitization of Indigenous heritage objects, and the ways that such un-
dertakings can help reconnect communities to important items, while also potentially
causing difficulties around what constitutes full repatriation. See for instance R. Eric
Hollinger et al., "Tlingit-Smithsonian Collaborations with 3D digitization of Cultural
Objects," *Museum Anthropology Review*, 7:1–2 (Spring-Fall 2013): 201–253; Gwyneira
Isaac, "Perclusive Alliances: Digital 3-D, Museums, and the Reconciling of Culturally
Diverse Knowledges," *Current Anthropology* 56:S12 (December 2015): S286–S296.

18. On Tribal involvement in and exercise of sovereignty over archaeological work
and collection formation in the Northeast, see Brian D. Jones and Kevin A. McBride,
"Indigenous Archaeology in Southern New England: Case Studies from the Mashantucket
Pequot Reservation," in *Cross-Cultural Collaboration*, 265–280; Craig N. Cipolla and
James Quinn, "Field School Archaeology the Mohegan Way: Reflections on Twenty Years
of Community-Based Research and Teaching," *Journal of Community Archaeology and
Heritage* 3:2 (2016): 118–134; Stephen W. Silliman, "Collaborative Indigenous Archaeology:
Troweling at the Edges, Eyeing the Center," in *Collaborating at the Trowel's Edge: Teaching
and Learning in Indigenous Archaeology,* ed. Stephen W. Silliman, Amerind Studies in
Archaeology #2 (Tucson: University of Arizona Press, 2008): 1–21.

PART II   *Methods*

FIVE

New Methods, New Schools, New Stories:

Digital Archives and Dartmouth's Institutional Legacy

Thomas Peace

> To reclaim, reshape, and transform the archives to meet the needs
> of Indigenous peoples requires an honest and blunt engagement with the
> bureaucratic and arcane structures that govern and shape research today.
> Church, State, and Corporate archives must be acknowledged as enmeshed
> in the specific nation- and history-making endeavors they foment.[1]
> *Crystal Fraser and Zoe Todd, "Decolonial Sensibilities"*

Across North America, the removal of monuments, and related contestation over
place names, rages as popular memory is contested; similar transformation is
taking place within academic histories. Informed by scholars working in critical Indigenous, Feminist, and Black Studies (among others), it is increasingly
common for historians to listen and respond to the descendants of the peoples
about whom we write; as a result, the stories told about the past have begun to
shift and the hegemony of the white settler nation-state in determining them is
weakening. In light of these historiographical openings, it is increasingly apparent that historians and the general public have misinterpreted and, perhaps on
some topics, understand very little about what took place in the past. Recently,
scholars such as Michael Witgen and Drew Lopenzina have demonstrated the
intentional nature of this historiographical myopia. For them, earlier North
American historiographies have entrenched a "false history created by the idea of

European discovery" and "repeated acts of colonial unwitnessing."[2] In deploying this language of deliberate misremembering, Witgen and Lopenzina suggest that historians (among other academic disciplines) have fostered a specific, selective — and simplistic — settler-national narrative that refused to acknowledge contrary and contesting voices.

My depiction of this recent historiographical change is, of course, in itself somewhat simplistic; it ignores important continuities of contrary and contesting voices outside of, but also within, academia.[3] Nonetheless, when brought into conversation with Crystal Fraser and Zoe Todd's observations about the colonialist rigidities of the archive, we can see how institutional repositories have been literally stacked against historical interpretations that challenge the nation-state. Rodney G. S. Carter put this a little more directly in his reflection on power and archival silences: "Those marginalized by the state are marginalized by the archive," Rodney writes, "Archival violence is found in the use of documents to enforce and naturalize the state's power and in the active silencing of the disenfranchised."[4]

In drawing out his idea about "unwitnessing," Lopenzina builds on these observations. Framing his thinking around Jacques Derrida's concept of the "House of the Archive," where the word "archive" is understood through its Greek roots in "government" and "rule," Lopenzina argues that the structures of this important institution have encouraged the selective curation of North America's past to favor some stories over others. In order to overcome the archive's potential for violence and function as a tool of control, Lopenzina suggests we must revisit how historical evidence has been organized and constructed; for those of us working with historical records by and about Indigenous peoples, he calls for the building of a "Longhouse of the Archive."[5]

The tension between these potentially fresh histories and the acknowledged colonialist nature of the archive offers an important moment for reflection on both emerging historiographical practices and the stories that can emerge from them. Revisiting the early history of Dartmouth College, specifically the biography of one of its earliest Indigenous students, Louis Vincent Sawatanen, points to a need for broader reconceptualization of historical research methods and archival navigation. This will provide a clearer sense of the College's regional influence at the turn of the nineteenth century, and perhaps some new areas of research for scholars interested in studying eighteenth- and early nineteenth-century Indigenous intellectual networks. This type of re-envisioning is already well underway in projects like the *Yale Indian Papers Project* (YIPP), the *Great*

Lakes Research Alliance for the Study of Aboriginal Arts and Culture (GRASAC) and *The Occom Circle*.[6] In this chapter, though, I want to use this smaller case study, with its focus on Dartmouth College, to point to the promise of these projects, but also to highlight some of the challenges presented by archival reordering in a digital space. Creating Lopenzina's "longhouse of the archive" in a digital space has great potential to re-envision the past, helping us push beyond national and institutional boundaries to better represent the relationships and networks that were meaningful to the people we study. If not treated carefully, however, this approach also risks reifying those interpretations, reinforcing some of the power structures such revisionism aims to replace.

Revisiting Dartmouth's Early History

Over the course of the 1810s and 1820s, Dartmouth alumnus and non-sectarian Christian evangelist Thaddeus Osgood travelled the Canadas arguing for non-denominational free schooling. Though his interests were broadly focused on educating the poor, Osgood spent considerable time thinking about and visiting Indigenous communities in the colonies. He was highly mobile and, as a result, fairly well connected to likeminded allies. His travels brought him into contact with people likely familiar with his alma mater, specifically the Mississauga schoolteacher Thayendanegea (John Jones) — whose Kanyen'kehá:ka (Mohawk) father-in-law, Jacob Brant, attended Eleazar Wheelock's Moor's Indian Charity School at the same time as Osgood studied at Dartmouth, the colonial college that developed from it — and Louis Vincent Sawatanen, a Wendat schoolteacher and diplomat, who graduated from Dartmouth in 1781.[7] Though Osgood makes only limited reference to these men in his accounts, the connections between them are noteworthy, as they help us develop a better understanding of Wheelock's influence, the charity school and Dartmouth College in early nineteenth century British North America, while pointing towards the need for a broader research infrastructure that works against the colonial biases of the archive.

Some might find this an odd starting point. By the early 1770s in most studies of these institutions, Wheelock's efforts to school First Peoples are generally regarded as a failure.[8] With some exceptions, this argument suggests that Mohegan community activist and Presbyterian minister Samson Occom was one of Wheelock's few "successful" students, a claim that varies among historians.[9] Regardless of how one defines success, Occom formally broke with Wheelock in 1771 after nearly two decades of working closely together, lamenting to him somewhat famously "that instead of your Semenary Becoming alma Mater, She will be too *alba* mater."[10] This damning play on words, between alma mater (nourishing mother) and alba mater (white mother), points to a broader shift identified by historians: Dartmouth's 1769 founding and move to Hanover, New Hampshire, on the banks of the Upper Connecticut River, marked a redirection in the institution's emphasis away from Indigenous students and toward educating colonists. In the words of some historians, by this time Wheelock's efforts to evangelize among Indigenous populations were in "shambles"; the school's founder turned his attention therefore to educating colonists.[11] Though some, like Jean Barman, Colin Calloway, and Jean-Pierre Sawaya, have pushed beyond this temporal framing, histories of Indigenous engagement with the college mostly end here.[12] Much of the college's history during this period confirms this historiographical decision, keeping the focus on the late eighteenth century.

The problem with this narrative is that it fails to explain Osgood's encounters with Dartmouth- and Charity School-educated Indigenous teachers and their relations two generations later. Indeed, Thayendaneaga and Sawantanen were not unique in their ties to Wheelock's schools. In the sixty years that followed Occom's rupture with Wheelock, forty Abenaki, Haudenosaunee, and Wendat boys attended classes at one of the two institutions; a handful of them (as was the case in the earlier period) became teachers in their home communities or elsewhere. Indeed, Michael Oberg's recent book *Professional Indian: The American Odyssey of Eleazar Williams* and Barman's *Abenaki Daring: The Life and Writings of Noel Annance* provide two biographical studies of students who attended the institutions during this period. Though Williams attended the school for only a couple of weeks, Annance was part of a multi-generational Abenaki engagement with Wheelock's schools.

Williams, from Kahnawake and the grandson of the well-known New England captive Eunice Williams, was drawn to the charity school following eight years of study under Nathaniel Ely and his wife in Longmeadow, Massachusetts; a connection that reflected the Kahnawake family's continued connection to their New England kin.[13] Though more-or-less comfortable with the Elys, Williams did not feel the same support at the Charity School. There, Oberg argues, he felt humiliated and poorly cared for.[14] Within weeks he left, eventually coming to serve as an Anglican missionary to the Oneidas. Claiming to work on their behalf, he was deeply involved in their removal to Wisconsin in the 1820s. In 1835 he returned to the St. Lawrence Valley to teach school and served the Anglican

Church at Akwesasne, where he was mostly unsuccessful and somewhat isolated. He died in 1858 after having made a name for himself later in life claiming to be the lost son of Louis XVI.[15]

Annance had a very different experience. He came to the school through family connections, specifically through his father, François Annance, who attended the Charity School and college in the late 1770s. Alongside his older brother, Noel Annance attended both Moor's Indian Charity School and Dartmouth College between 1808 and 1813, when the War of 1812 interrupted his schooling. He then went on to have an extensive career in the western fur trade, specifically in the Oregon Country, before returning to Odanak in 1845 where, like Williams, he was caught between Catholic-Protestant tensions and was therefore somewhat unsuccessful in his desire to become a schoolteacher.

Both Williams and Annance were third-generation descendants of New England captives, the legacy of which was important to them and their connections to the school. Ultimately, though, they identified more closely with their Indigenous kin. Their careers after leaving Wheelock's schools share some similar qualities, using diverse strategies often built around their earlier education in response to the westward expansion of settler colonial hegemony. What we see by looking at these recent biographies, covering as they do students' motivations for attending the school, is a much more student-focused approach. Rather than placing attention on Eleazar Wheelock's motivations for recruiting students, and his overall purpose in offering them an education, Oberg and Barman have instead begun to ask why — or why not, in Williams's case — students attended these institutions.

Their approach resonates strongly with Hilary Wyss's differentiation between "readerly" and "writerly" Indians at these types of school; the difference between these two categories of student behavior, in her opinion, being the image of Indigenous students white educators and missionaries desired (the "readerly" Indian) and the students' actual desire for, and strategic deployment of, skills that they learned at the school (the "writerly" Indian). Framed within Scott Lyons's concept of "rhetorical sovereignty," Wyss emphasizes the agency deployed by students as they failed to conform to white missionaries and teachers' desires for them.[16] From this vantage point, the question of whether Wheelock and his colleagues succeeded in their mandate becomes less important, replaced instead by an analysis of the diverse student, community, and national motivations for sending students to the school. Motivations for coming down to Hanover and the relationships forged or broken at the charity school and college become much more central to the questions we ask about these students' experiences.

Taking a more student-centered approach to the charity school and college frames the history of these institutions in a somewhat different light. In addition to Williams and Annance, we might add earlier alumni, such as Samson Occom, Thayendanegea (Joseph Brant), Joseph Johnson, and Louis Vincent Sawatanen. Similarly, we could look at contemporaries of Williams and Annance such as Thayendanegea's sons Joseph and Jacob Brant, another Vincent (possibly Sawatanen's son), or the Abenaki minister Peter Paul Wzokhilain. In this list of eight alumni, we can see people who made a substantive impact, often asserting Indigenous rights and autonomy to colonial and imperial governments in northeastern North America. Occom, for example, championed the well-known Mohegan Land Case as his community faced mounting pressure for expanding settler society. Johnson, Occom's son-in-law, worked with his father-in-law to create a new space for his people at Brotherton among the Oneidas in response to similar pressures. Likewise, Joseph Brant, a contemporary of Johnson's, negotiated the migration of his people to the Grand River, and fought tirelessly against both the emerging United States and British North America for Mohawk independence and sovereignty. Sawatanen, who attended the charity school a decade after Johnson and Brant, played a similar role in his community, facilitating a series of petitions for Wendat land and resources in response to settler migration onto their lands. Likewise, we might point to the Abenaki Congregational minister Wzokhilain's publication of Abenaki-language texts as fitting within a similar vein (though the limited amount of material on Wzokhilain's life prevents us reaching too firm a conclusion here).[17]

Though we could split this list down the middle along the Canadian-US border line, what becomes clear is that aside from Occom, Johnson, and Williams, most of these men lived their lives in what were emerging as the colonies of Lower and Upper Canada rather than the United States. The relationship between Moor's Indian Charity School and the northern British settler colonies developing on Wendat, Abenaki, Anishinaabe, and Haudenosaunee Lands (among others) remains poorly understood. Only two historians, Sawaya and Barman, have addressed it in much detail.[18] Their conclusions suggest that descendants of captive New Englanders living in Laurentian Indigenous communities, such as the Kanyen'kehá:ka community at Kahnawake and Abenakis at Odanak, forged relationships across the region. What Osgood's story and the connections that spin out from it demonstrate, however, is that there is more here; we cannot understand the history of Moor's Indian Charity School and the early history of Dartmouth College without adequately taking into account its Great Lakes and Laurentian context.

There are many reasons why connections between the college and peoples who lived in what would become Canada have been poorly chronicled by historians and archivists. First, the specific and local historical and historiographical ruptures caused by the departure of most of Wheelock's Indigenous students and Samson Occom during the late 1760s and early 1770s have shaped our inquiries about Indigenous engagement with Wheelock's institutions, restricting interest to the earlier period. Second, the coincidence of the American Revolution has framed research questions nationally, rather than around much more important socio-political structures such as Indigenous nations and lands. From this latter vantage point, continuities have prevailed despite this significant Eurocentric political rupture. It should be no surprise, for example, that most of the Indigenous students who attended the college after 1770 were Abenaki from Odanak on whose homeland Dartmouth College now stands.[19] Third, the linguistic skills necessary to research in this period requires familiarity with both English and French, as well as support from experts in Latin, Iroquoian, and Algonquian linguistics. Unfamiliarity with these languages has led many to overlook a crucial segment of the material record and reinforced these national divisions. And finally, extending Fraser and Todd, Carter, and Lopenzina's observations about the "House of the Archive," these questions have been hampered by the nature of the archive itself.

National, institutional, and biographical archives have shaped how we think and discuss Indigenous engagement with the college and its central personalities. Reflection upon the limitations and constraints that determine how we navigate the historical record is a subject about which we need to be much more explicit. As a consequence of these barriers to research, historians have tended to focus upon key individuals and institutions with which they engage, rather than the broader cultures and networks within which they were embedded; of course, there are a number of exceptions.[20] What emerged between the 1760s and 1830s in the Northeast was a regional Indigenous intellectual network that spanned the nascent national border, within which we must locate Moor's Indian Charity School and Dartmouth College as an important, but not the only, node.

Resituating Samson Occom and Kahkewaquonaby: From Writing to Schooling

To illustrate this point, let's examine two well-known figures in each nation's history, Samson Occom and Kahkewaquonaby (Peter Jones). Seen in their respective national framing, the records left by Occom and Kahkewaquonaby help us to better understand how historians have constructed the Northeastern past. Contrasting their lives and the material traces that have been preserved in archival collections demonstrates how both Occom and Kahkewaquonaby's prolific writing has drawn scholarly attention to their lives, and how the collection and curation of their writings has shaped our understanding of their influence on their home communities and settler societies more broadly.[21]

In the United States, Samson Occom is perhaps the best known Indigenous Christian missionary of the eighteenth century. Over a fifty-year career, Occom worked tirelessly for his faith, his people, and the promise of schooling for Northeastern Indigenous peoples. In addition to his published texts, such as *Sermon at the Execution of Moses Paul* (1772) and *A Choice Collection of Hymns and Spiritual Songs* (1774), his perspective on the events of his day are clearly expressed in seventy-six letters, twenty sermons, and twenty-four diaries. In total, Occom's archives extend for over 1,000 manuscript pages, held primarily by the Connecticut Historical Society and Dartmouth College.[22] As a result of this documentary legacy, there is a fairly extensive historiography written about this man, perhaps best encapsulated by Joanna Brooks's *The Collected Writings of Samson Occom* and the recently launched *The Occom Circle* project, which motivated this publication.

Kahkewaquonaby, the brother of Thayendanegea (John Jones) discussed in the introduction, is, in Canada, perhaps the best known Mississauga Christian missionary of the nineteenth century. Over a thirty-year career, Kahkewaquonaby worked tirelessly for his faith and his people, arguing strongly for the promises of schooling and Christianity as tools through which the Mississauga could survive the rapid social and political changes taking place in the early-to-mid nineteenth century. In addition to two books, his perspectives on the world around him are clearly expressed in numerous published articles, sermons, and personal papers, which, at the University of Toronto, measure three feet in length. As a result of this documentary legacy, there is a fairly extensive historiography about this man, perhaps best encapsulated in Donald Smith's two books, *Sacred Feathers* and *Mississauga Portraits*.[23]

If we shift our focus somewhat, however, away from writing and archives, to better incorporate the broader context of schooling and settler colonialism, a somewhat different image of the past begins to emerge. To a certain extent, Marisa Fuentes takes this approach in *Dispossessed Lives: Enslaved Women, Violence and the Archive*. Much like Fraser and Todd, Carter, and Lopenzina, Fuentes worries about the consequences of "historical methods that search for archival veracity, statistical substantiation, and empiricism" for the enslaved women she studies.[24] Though the historical actors discussed in this chapter lived lives quite different from those Fuentes seeks to redress, the argument about archives is similar. To use Fuentes's argument, what I am suggesting here is that "paying attention to these archival imbalances illuminates systems of power and deconstructs the influences of colonial constructions of race, gender, and sexuality on the sources that inform this work."[25] The proliferation of scholarly attention drawn to men like Occom and Kahkewaquonaby is a reflection of the nature of the archive. Fuentes calls for us to "fill out" the occasional archival appearances (and even complete absence) of historical actors from the documentary record with greater attention placed on spatial and historical context.[26] In this case, it involves shifting our perspective slightly, away from writing, towards historically contextualized systems of power such as schooling.

The richness of archival holdings about Occom and Kahkewaquonaby's lives has meant that their life stories are often told in such a way as to make their experiences seemingly unique. Though situated within a context of widespread dispossession, that setting is seldom adequately foregrounded or discussed as a phenomenon requiring greater interrogation.[27] As a consequence, scholars have tended to emphasize Indigenous writers and the act of writing against colonialism (Wyss's "writerly" Indian) without adequately grappling with its implications related to education and schooling.[28] How and why did these men learn to write? What was the place of the school within this process? And to what extent were the experiences of these men unique or determined by gender? Asking these questions about schooling need not privilege the school as an important institution in Indigenous communities, nor render these men complicit in the spread of colonial institutions that may have developed from this early history, such as residential/boarding schools. Rather, such an analysis helps us understand the degree to which these people grappled with the institutions of settler society as they were developing on the land.

If we want to answer these questions, we need to situate Occom and Kahkewaquonaby's experiences within the late eighteenth and early nineteenth century colonial resettling and widespread dispossession of Indigenous peoples from the land. For both men, their lives were defined by radical geo-political transformation as British, and then American, expansion increasingly made it impossible for Northeastern peoples to ignore the growing presence of settlers and their colonial institutions. This experience was viscerally felt following the Seven Years' War as New England planters, American loyalists and patriots, and then trans-Atlantic British migrants flooded onto Mohegan, Haudenosaunee, and Anishinaabe Homelands in numbers never before seen.[29]

Historians have well demonstrated a correlation between schooling and dispossession. Linford Fisher's work on Indigenous Christianity in New England demonstrates, for example, that Mohican, Pequot, and Narragansett schools in the 1740s and 1750s had greater institutional importance in comparison to Wheelock's relatively poorly attended charity school.[30] Elizabeth Elbourne makes similar correlations in her work on the Kanyen'kehá:ka-British alliance in the 1760s and 1770s.[31] My own work has suggested that we revisit the eighteenth-century history of Indigenous education and schooling in the St. Lawrence Valley, specifically New France, with an eye towards more tightly linking schooling and European expressions of colonialism in North America.[32] Though sharing much with scholars whose work addresses writing and printing, by expanding the focus towards the history of schooling, I think we arrive at a much more complex set of relationships and deeper history of settler colonialism than many biographical narratives suggest. This is the context — the rising hegemony of settler colonialism in the northeast — within which we must consider Occom and Kahkewaquonaby's biographies.

To understand schooling as a strategy some people within Indigenous communities used to engage this changing context we must turn to another, better known Thayendanegea: the Kanyen'kehá:ka Pine Tree chief, Joseph Brant. Brant was John Jones's wife's grandfather and, I think we can safely state, was somewhat interested in the model of schooling Eleazar Wheelock provided. In addition to attending the charity school himself in the 1760s, in the opening years of the nineteenth century, Brant sent to the school his eldest two sons from his third marriage, Joseph and Jacob; they both attended for about three years.

Brant's decision-making process to both engage with the charity school and champion schooling more generally must be contextualized within the long history of Kanyen'kehá:ka schooling and its association with Britain's westward expansion onto their land. Dating to at least the mid-1750s, when the well-known schoolteacher and diplomat Paulus Sahonwagy began working with the Society for the Propagation of the Gospel, Brant's people had schools taught by one of their own.[33] On and off, depending on the diplomatic needs of his community, Sahonwagy taught school until the end of his life, ending his work along the Grand River in the late 1780s. Though a teacher and sometimes employee of the Anglican Society for the Propagation of the Gospel, he was also active militarily during the Seven Years' War and occasionally served in a diplomatic capacity for his people with the British and other member nations of the Haudenosaunee Confederacy.[34]

Building on the work of Daniel Richter, Elbourne emphasizes how these schools, and personalities like Sahonwagy and Thayendanegea, negotiated British Christian influence as a strategy of alliance. She argues that schools and missionaries in the community, whose presence had just as much to do with the politics of alliance as religion, were controlled and maintained by the communities themselves. From within this context, Elbourne and others demonstrate that there were clearly undocumented members of these communities who maintained Anglican traditions and colonial skills beyond the purview of missionaries and archives; their lives are poorly recorded and therefore difficult to take into account when we think about this period.[35]

In her 1993 doctoral dissertation, Jean Fittz Hankins traced some of these Indigenous missionaries and teachers working in New England and New York between 1700 and 1775. She estimates that at least 180 Indigenous men served as preachers and 150 men and women served as teachers for one of the four Protestant missionary societies active in the colonies.[36] If we frame these activities as an index of responses to settler imposition, rather than Indigenous assimilation, we can begin to see how these lives teach us about broader patterns afoot in eighteenth-century northeastern North America.

By looking more broadly at the context of schooling in the Northeast, it becomes apparent that there was much more engagement with schooling than historians often emphasize. Rather than there just being a handful of people like Occom or Kahkewaquonaby, who selectively engaged with mission schools, it appears from Fisher and Hankins's work that many boys and girls interacted with this form of education. Neither were these schools completely tied to missionary endeavors. The longstanding place of schooling in the Kanyen'kehá:ka history of education, for example, is illustrative of how these institutions were not merely tools of European evangelism, but also important sites of alliance and tools shaping community responses to settler encroachment.[37] As we think about what it means to build Lopenzina's "longhouse[s] of the archive," it is important that we consider broader institutional apparatuses related to the creation of these historical records, adequately embedding the archive within this context.

Sawatanen, Traces from the Past, and Intellectual currents of the Northeast

Sawatanen's life illustrates this point.[38] Though not entirely obscure — he is often noted by historians as being one of Dartmouth's few pre-twentieth-century Indigenous graduates — much of his life is difficult to recover through the archival record. Unlike Occom and Kahkewaquonaby, he did not publish his writings, though he was certainly capable of doing so if he had been so inclined, and he made little direct effort to ensure his life was remembered within the library or archive. Nonetheless, he taught school at both the Kanyen'kehá:ka community on the Bay of Quinte and in his home community of Lorette, as well as serving as a key instigator for Wendat claims against the emerging settler state in 1790s and early 1800s.[39] In focusing on his life, we can see how potential archival reorganization made possible through emerging digital technologies presents an opportunity to expand our understanding of the dozens, if not hundreds of men and women like him, who lived in the seventeenth- and eighteenth-century Northeast.

Over the past decade, I have spent a considerable amount of time piecing together Sawatanen's life. In doing so, I have drawn together sources spread throughout the Atlantic World. His time at Dartmouth is well documented in the college's Rauner Library and Special Collections. This collection of documents outlines some of his roles during the American Revolution, serving in Timothy Bedel's regiment as an interpreter for the Continental Congress in negotiations with the Penobscots, and some of his experiences as a student.[40] Other documents about Sawatanen's military service are found in his service file at the US National Archives and in the published *Papers of George Washington*.[41] The archives of the Conseil de la Nation huronne-wendat near Quebec City hold several photocopied documents from Dartmouth's collection that I have not been able to track down in the college's collection, but clearly originated from within this archive.[42] One of those documents, a letter sent back to Wheelock's son John in 1784, indicated that Sawatanen was at that time teaching school at Montreal with a Mr. Stuart.[43] After a little bit of digging, this reference to Stuart turns out to be John Stuart, an Anglican missionary who worked with Thayendanegea and Sahonwagy in Canajoharie, moving with the Kanyen'kehá:kas to Montreal and then the north shore of Lake Ontario, on the Bay of Quinte, during and after the American Revolution. Anglican records in the Quebec provincial archives, as well as records from Dartmouth's collection, demonstrate that Sawatanen accompanied these people on this second move.[44] In 1791, Sawatanen returned to his home at

Lorette and began teaching school, which is where, nearly three decades later, he likely encountered Osgood.

Much like Sahonwagy's role as both teacher and diplomat, Sawatanen was an active participant, for nearly four decades, in petitioning the crown for Wendat rights in the region. Here, just nine miles from Quebec City, the connection to the Stuart family also continued, whereby John's fifth son Andrew, a member of the legislative assembly by the late 1810s, championed the Wendat cause.[45] Stuart's close business and political ally, John Neilson, a prominent printer in the colony, also maintained a fairly close relationship with the community, corresponding periodically with Sawatanen and Thaddeus Osgood, with whose story I began.[46] Sawatanen died in 1825; his obituary, the only copy I have been able to find, appeared in the *Salem Gazette*.[47] In tracking down the documents detailing Sawatanen's life, the breadth of his social and political networks become clear. Here we can see how over the course of his life Sawatanen was connected to Kanyen'kehá:ka, Penobscot and Abenaki peoples, affiliated with the Catholic, Congregational, and Anglican colonial churches, while maintaining a strong commitment to his people at Lorette.

In his introduction to Brooks's anthology of Samson Occom's writings, Robert Warrior laments: "one reason that recent readings of Occom have been so impoverished, I would offer, is that he has been considered as a lone figure rather than as someone standing amid an extensive social network."[48] Though works like Brooks's anthology as well as Lisa Brooks's *The Common Pot* and Lopenzina's *Red Ink*, among others, have responded to this critique, the fragmentary traces remaining from Sawatanen's life provide another opportunity, and a differing vantage point, for us to understand what this extensive social network might have looked like.

It is tempting in framing this context to situate the charity school and Dartmouth College as a central node shaping how Sawatanen lived his life. The charity school and college were undoubtedly important to him. But to frame his story entirely around the school would be to ignore the context laid out above, specifically, how schools emerged as sites of contest as settler geographies imposed themselves on Indigenous landscapes at the end of the eighteenth century. From this perspective, we might use Sawatanen's life not just to focus on the history of schooling, but also to look at important nodes within his network — the places where his story overlaps with many others.

One of those places is the Kanyen'kehá:ka community on the Bay of Quinte, the present-day community of Tyendinaga, where Sawatanen taught school in the mid-1780s. As the birthplace of the Peacemaker, this is a significant Homeland for Haudenosaunee peoples. It also has a deep history of confronting European colonialism. In the 1670s, it was an important fur trading site and home to a Gayogo hó:no' (Cayuga) community likely comprised of Wendat and Attawandaron descendants whose ancestors had lived on this land before integrating with neighboring peoples such as the Haudenosaunee.[49] For a handful of years, Sulpician missionaries Claude Trouvé and François de Salignac de la Mothe-Fénelon, then Recollet missionary Louis Hennepin, also lived near the community. Contemporaries observed that missionary efforts were fraught, but as agents of the French empire, they were vanguards of the kingdom's expansion into the Great Lakes: the French built militarized posts at both Quinte and present-day Kingston by the turn of the eighteenth century.[50] Though fighting for their own reasons, Anishinaabe and politically sovereign Wendat allies, whose interests in returning to their Homelands were not unlike the Haudenosaunee-affiliated Wendat and Attawandaron peoples, facilitated this colonial expansion onto the north shore of Lake Ontario, pushing the Haudenosaunee south of the lake. In the decades following the Haudenosaunee departure, Anishinaabe peoples, with whom the British negotiated problematic treaties over the fifty years between 1780 and 1830, came to call these shores home.[51]

This is the context within which we might situate the Bay of Quinte as a critical node in a late eighteenth and early nineteenth century Indigenous intellectual network.[52] The bay, situated between the Kanyen'kehá:ka community on the north shore and Mississauga on the islands, drew in many prominent Indigenous leaders of the time. Not only was Sawatanen there for a short time in the 1780s, but he was followed by the fairly well-schooled Cherokee-Scot John Norton, who, upon leaving his teaching post and a short stint with the Indian Department, became a Pine Tree chief at Grand River and close ally of Thayendanegea (Joseph Brant).[53] After that time, British men, who routinely complained about the community's disinterest, taught at a school funded by the Society for the Propagation of the Gospel.[54] Just over two decades later, the well-known Pequot historian William Apess spent the winter on the Bay of Quinte, likely with the Kanyen'kehá:ka.[55] Apess described the bay as "alive with its [the forest's] sons and daughters."[56] It was here that Barry O'Connell, one of his biographers, suggests that Apess "gained some positive sense of himself as an Indian," as a result of the intellectual currents circulating in the region; Abenaki historian Lisa Brooks has labelled this the "scene of his rebirth."[57]

Though he likely stayed at Tyendinaga, by the time he over-wintered there, Apess had begun to identify as a Methodist, a confession he would formalize with ordination in 1829. Methodism was quite influential among the Mississaugas in the 1820s, 1830s, and 1840s. Though at the time of Apess's visit, the Mississaugas on the Bay of Quinte had not yet allied with the Methodists, they did so shortly thereafter, receiving visits from both Kahkewaquonaby in 1826 and Osgood in 1829, tying the community into the networks underpinning this chapter.[58] The central point here is that tracing Sawatanen's life and the history of schooling points us away from Dartmouth and towards a place like the Bay of Quinte as a site of importance for many of the key figures involved in Dartmouth's latter history and in broader histories of Indigenous writing and schooling.

If we take Dartmouth as one node, Mohegan and Brotherton as two others, and the Bay of Quinte as a fourth, perhaps we can begin to trace what this late eighteenth and early nineteenth century Northeastern Indigenous intellectual network might have looked like. Doing so enables us to cut across national and cultural borders, decentering the discussion away from Wheelock, the charity school and the college itself. On the Bay of Quinte we can see the careful ways that Anishinaabe and Haudenosaunee peoples, as well as semi-outsiders like Sawatanen (Wendat) and Apess (Pequot), engaged with each other, as well as with colonial English and French, Protestant, and Catholic influences.

The extent of these inter-relationships remains to be researched, but, importantly, they point to robust international diplomacy and networks that often elude the "House of the Archive." The documentary traces of Sawatanen's life help frame our research in a fundamentally different manner. Instead of placing educational institutions, missionary work, and specific individuals in the foreground, reorganizing archives in ways that facilitate the recovery and better representation of Indigenous lives presents opportunities to focus more on broader patterns of experience and relationship. From this perspective, we might better understand the interconnections between writing, schooling, and settler colonialism while also better giving voice to people like Sawatanen without access to the press and archival memory.

The Promises and Pitfalls of the Digital Archive

Digital archives hold promise for this type of substantive historiographical revision. In drawing our attention to the possibility of a "Longhouse of the Archive," Lopenzina calls for such a reorientation, emphasizing the need to cultivate new archival and historiographic strategies.[59] This is no easy task. In describing the *Yale Indian Papers Project*, which attempts just this type of reorganization, the creators clearly outline the challenge. In their view, the variety, geographic spread, and scope of more traditional archival collections addressing the history of Indigenous communities and nations forms a barrier to research.[60] Further, archives and libraries with large holdings direct our attention toward some subjects over others. Fraser and Todd frame this challenge well in their reflection on decolonizing archives:

> A fundamental challenge lies in the fact that the majority of archival documents in Canadian archives have been produced by non-Indigenous people: namely white men who dominated exploration, political, and other "great men" tropes of Canadian history . . . Archival records produced by Indigenous people prove to be far and few between. We know very little about the lives of Indigenous women, apart from a few celebrated heroines, such as Thanadelthur, Kateri Tekakwitha, and E. Pauline Johnson. Even less is known about Indigenous children, two-spirited individuals, and liminal figures such as medicine men and women.[61]

We could use the abundance of military and missionary histories about Indigenous peoples as further examples of this historiographical and archival bias. I also think, however, that the flourishing of biographies, such as those of Occom and Kahkewaquonaby, is a related consequence, encouraging our scholarly gaze upon seemingly unique individuals (usually men) rather than the contexts in which they lived.[62]

Sawantanen's story, however, points towards an opportunity for change. My encounter with this man occurred because I began my research at a moment when the archive and the nature of historical research shifted. In the digital age, the archive has been decoupled from its institutional frame, allowing for what Wolfgang Ernst has called the enacting of repeatable "different aggregations of the past."[63] To put it differently, Ernst suggests that the digital archive presents an opportunity for a "non-narrative alternative to historiography."[64] Under these conditions, there is significant potential for re-envisioning the past and the development of more complicated and challenging historical interpretations. This has been the argument I have tried to put forward in this chapter. The promise of the digital archive lies in the creation of new archival relationships in order to recover historical interconnections by bringing together material related to people, places, communities, or cultures not envisioned by any single archive's organizational structure.

We must be careful, however, in blazing this path forward. Such restructuring must also be accompanied by a questioning of the digital archive itself. Fuentes argues that this type of archival recovery may in fact be impossible. "The very call to 'find more sources' about people who left few if any of their own," she writes, "reproduces the same erasures and silences they experienced in the late eighteenth century."[65] Suggesting that we can recover the past simply by reorganizing the archive is naïve. Alongside reorganization, Fuentes calls for a shift in how we approach historical records. For her, scholars must interrogate archival silences by moving beyond disciplinary boundaries to include their subjects' "historical or historiographical representations, . . . the theoretical significance of colonial [systems of power]," and the framing of archival languages and perspectives.[66] Digital archives can help recover voices from the past; they do not, however, recover the perspectives of those peoples deliberately left out of the documentary record or archive. If we are to follow Lopenzina's idea of building a "Longhouse of the Archive," we must call attention, and listen, to those archival silences, situating them within their broader historical, historiographical, and theoretical contexts.[67]

As we reflect upon these archival silences, we must also consider their relationship to power, not only taking into consideration how Indigenous (and other) voices have been excluded from the archive by those people holding power in colonial society, but also the fact that silence can be an intentional strategy for resistance and autonomy. Carter draws this out well in his work, emphasizing that although the act of invoking silence seeks to intervene in relational power dynamics, it is not enacted in an effort to achieve dominance:

> This power is not "power over" where power is exerted by one group over another. Rather, this type of power may be seen as being "power with," "power as capacity," or "power to," that as opposed to focusing on controlling others, deals with personal empowerment and control over the individual's thoughts, feelings, and behaviors. It seeks not to diminish the power of others in order to increase the power of the individual, but rather it may be democratic and co-operative, seeking to increase the power of others at the same time as asserting and increasing their own power.[68]

Drawing on feminist theory, Carter labels this strategic deployment of silence as natural, while the silences identified in this paper he would define as unnatural. "Unnatural silences must be combatted by the archivist," Carter writes, "but natural silences, those where the marginalized can assert their own power, must be respected."[69] In rethinking and perhaps restructuring archival collections in a digital environment, the ethics of digitally reproducing texts and making them widely accessible needs to be carefully navigated. The potential intentionality of archival silence must be taken seriously. The work of determining how new digital archives are to be constructed requires careful navigation and involvement of the peoples it is most likely to affect.

In thinking about these issues, Ernst raises a third methodological consideration. He asks an important question about conducting historical research in the first decades of the twenty-first century: "what if the public will prefer to use Google rather than institutional Internet portals to get access and information on national, academic, and cultural memory?"[70] In asking this question, Ernst has hit upon a critical methodological problem for historians in the digital age. Indeed, many of the documents about Sawatanen cited above were found using Google and Google Books rather than through more traditional historical methods. Though crucial for understanding Sawatanen's life, this type of historical research is problematic if not addressed openly. In a persuasive article on scholarly newspaper use in Canada, Ian Milligan demonstrates how the digital turn has in some ways compromised scholarly conventions. Examining the citations in Canadian history doctoral dissertations, he noted that once the *Toronto Star* and *Globe and Mail*, the two largest newspapers in the country, made it easy to keyword search their archives, putatively national studies overwhelmingly drew on this digital material from Toronto-centric newspapers in favor of analog newspaper collections from elsewhere in Canada. Furthermore, most scholars had little understanding of how the software worked, meaning that they could not critically engage with its outcomes.[71] Milligan's work warns that our navigation of easily available digital tools, especially Google, but also digital databases available through university libraries, can lead to misunderstanding and selective interpretations of the past, presenting just as much inherent bias as the institutional challenges it seeks to overcome.

Expanding on Milligan's arguments, Lara Putnam calls our attention to the broader methodological prospects and problems of finding research material through this type of armchair digital research. Much like in the case study I outlined, Putnam succinctly interconnects the transnational and digital turn, demonstrating both the important benefits brought to transnational study by digital reproduction of primary and secondary sources, but also the pitfalls of relying on this material without studying the provenance behind the images. By decoupling archival research practices from physical location and local culture, the people and context that can guide our understanding of archival silences, historians embracing digital archives risk producing work that perpetuates structures of oppression. Putnam cautions historians about the perils of uncritically drawing upon digitally reproduced source material. "The risk," she writes, "is that digitally enabled transnational history can let us think we are speaking of the world and to the world while actually insulating us from it."[72] Though Putnam's observations might be interpreted as leading us back to an entrenchment of the institutional and colonial nature of the archive, her comments share with Fraser and Todd, Carter, Lopenzina, and Fuentes the critical need to understand the workings of the archive and the communities we study. We must heed these warnings carefully if we want to direct our attention towards building Lopenzina's "Longhouse of the Archive."

Conclusion

"Longhouses of the Archive" are already under construction. Projects like the *Yale Indian Papers Project*, GRASAC, and *The Occom Circle* provide important models for librarians, archivists, and historians interested in creating digital archives for Indigenous materials. Attention to Sawatanen and Dartmouth's nineteenth-century legacy helps to demonstrate the potential benefits of this type of archival reorientation. In bringing together the disparate traces left from Sawatanen's life, we can see how we might revise Northeastern histories to focus more regionally on common experiences of settler colonialism. From this regional (rather than national) perspective, this case study points towards the importance of student experiences of, and community motivations for, schooling as well as the development of Indigenous intellectual networks within the region. In pointing to the promise digital archives hold for this type of historical revisionism, however, there are also important cautions. Foremost in this context is the continued emphasis on Christian missions and colonial institutions such as schools. Reframing the archive, as Lopenzina and Ernst well articulate, does not abdicate the need for continued critical engagement, interrogating the relationship of these new archival structures to colonial systems of power past and present.

Notes

The author would like to acknowledge the Social Sciences and Humanities Research Council of Canada for funding this research through their post-doctoral and Insight Development research programs as well as thank the faculty and students in the Native American Studies Program at Dartmouth College where the seeds for several of the ideas explored in this chapter were planted.

1. Crystal Fraser and Zoe Todd, "Decolonial Sensibilities: Indigenous Research and Engaging with Archives in Contemporary Colonial Canada," in *Decolonising Archives* (L'Internationale Online, 2016), 37. http://www.internationaleonline.org/bookshelves /decolonising_archives accessed November 19, 2018.

2. Michael Witgen, *Infinity of Nations: How the Native New World Shaped Early North America* (Philadelphia: University of Pennsylvania Press, 2013), 18; Drew Lopenzina, *Red Ink: Native Americans Picking Up the Pen in the Colonial Period* (Albany: State University of New York Press, 2012), 5.

3. From a historical perspective we might point to the longstanding practice of Indigenous peoples petitioning the crown. See Maxime Gohier, *La Pratique Pétitionnaire des Amérindiens de la Vallée du Saint-Laurent sous le Régime Britannique: Pouvoir, Représentation et Légitimité (1760–1860)* (PhD diss., Université du Québec à Montréal, 2014); Lopenzina frames nineteenth-century Pequot writer William Apess's writings in a similar vein, writing against colonial oppressions. See Lopenzina, *Red Ink* and *Through an Indian's Looking-Glass: A Cultural Biography of William Apess, Pequot* (Boston: University of Massachusetts Press, 2017). These perspectives on the past have continued to be voiced from within Indigenous nations. See for example Lisa Brooks, *The Common Pot: The Recovery of Native Space in the Northeast* (Minneapolis: University of Minnesota Press, 2008); Siobhan Senier, *Dawnland Voices: An Anthology of Indigenous Writing from New England* (Lincoln and London: University of Nebraska Press, 2014); Marie Battiste, ed. *Living Treaties: Narrating Mi'kmaw Treaty Relations* (Sydney: Cape Breton University Press, 2016); From a historiographic perspective scholars like Georges Sioui and Daniel Paul led the way in writing autohistory. See Georges E. Sioui, *Pour une Autohistoire Amrindienne* (Quebec: Les Presses de l'Université Laval, 1989) and Daniel N. Paul, *We Were Not the Savages: A Micmac Perspective on the Collision of European and Aboriginal Civilization* (Halifax: Nimbus Publishing, 1993).

4. Rodney G.S. Carter, "Of Things Said and Unsaid: Power, Archival Silences, and Power in Silence" *Archivaria* 61 (Spring 2006): 219.

5. Lopenzina, *Red Ink*, 16.

6. Though all structured somewhat differently, each of these projects focuses on bringing together disparate collections and resources to transcend archival limitations. YIPP and GRASAC are particularly focused on digitally collecting documents and objects produced by specific Indigenous nations but held in disparate colonial institutions. Importantly, each of these projects was framed in consultation with the present-day communities whose ancestors produced the material they have gathered together. GRASAC has a governance structure that includes provisions for Indigenous control over the material in their database. For more on these projects visit YIPP at http://yipp.yale.edu; GRASAC at http://grasac .org; and *The Occom Circle* at http://www.dartmouth.edu/~occom.

7. Jacob Brant was the son of John Jones's namesake, an earlier Thayendanegea, the well-known Kanyen'kehá:ka Pine Tree Chief Joseph Brant. See Donald B. Smith, "John Jones," *Dictionary of Canadian Biography (DCB)*, http://www.biographi.ca/en/bio/jones _john_1798_1847_7E.html accessed October 2017.

8. James Axtell, "The Little Red School," in *The Invasion Within: The Contest of Cultures in Colonial North America* (New York: Oxford University Press, 1985); Alan Taylor, *The Divided Ground: Indians, Settlers, and the Northern Borderland of the American Revolution* (Toronto: Vintage, 2006), 369; Margaret Connell Szasz, "Indian Schoolmasters to the Iroquois, from the 1760s to the 1770s," in *Indian Education in the American Colonies*, 2nd ed. (Lincoln: University of Nebraska Press, 2007); Linford Fisher, *The Indian Great Awakening: Religion and the Shaping of Native Cultures in Early America* (New York: Oxford University Press, 2012); Hilary E. Wyss, *English Letters and Indian Literacies: Reading, Writing, and New England Missionary Schools* (Philadelphia: University of Pennsylvania Press, 2012), 39. Many of these scholars point to limited presence of Indigenous peoples from the St. Lawrence.

9. On the various interpretations of "success" see Axtell, "The Little Red School," 204, 213–215; Taylor, *The Divided Ground*, 58; Szasz, "Indian Schoolmasters," 199–200; Fisher, *The Indian Great Awakening*, 122–126, 158; Wyss, *English Letters and Indian Literacies*, 11–12.

10. Samson Occom to Eleazar Wheelock, July 24, 1771, Dartmouth College Archives (DCA), 771424.

11. Fisher, *The Indian Great Awakening*, 163.

12. Jean Barman, *Abenaki Daring: The Life and Writings of Noel Annance* (Montreal and Kingston: McGill-Queen's University Press, 2016); Colin Calloway, *The Indian History of an American Institution: Native Americans and Dartmouth* (Hanover: University Press of New England, 2010); Jean-Pierre Sawaya, "Les Amérindiens domiciliés et le protestantisme au XVIIIe siècle: Eleazar Wheelock et le Dartmouth College," *Historical Studies in Education* 22:2 (Fall 2010): 18–38.

13. John Demos, *The Unredeemed Captive: A Family Story from Early America* (New York: Vintage, 1994); Evan Haefeli and Kevin Sweeney, *Captors and Captives: The 1704 French and Indian Raid on Deerfield* (Amherst and Boston: University of Massachusetts Press, 2003).

14. Michael Oberg, *Professional Indian: The American Odyssey of Eleazar Williams* (Philadelphia: University of Pennsylvania Press, 2015), 33.

15. Phillipe Sylvain, "Eleazar Williams," *DCB*, http://www.biographi.ca/en/bio/williams _eleazar_8E.html accessed October 2017.

16. Wyss, *English Letters and Indian Literacies*, 6–8.

17. On the lives of these men see Brooks, *The Common Pot*; Lopenzina, *Red Ink*; Rick Monture, *We Share our Matters: Two Centuries of Writing and Resistance at Six Nations*

of the Grand River (Winnipeg: University of Manitoba Press, 2014); Jonathan Lainey and Thomas Peace, "Louis Vincent Sawantanan, premier bachelier autochtone canadien," in Gaston Deschênes and Denis Vaugeois, *Vivre la Conquête* , vol. 1 (Sillery: Septentrion, 2013), 204–214. A modified English version of this essay appears as "Louis Vincent Sawatanen: A Life Forged by Warfare and Migration," in Kristin Burnett and Geoff Read, *Aboriginal History: A Reader* (Toronto: Oxford University Press, 2016), 106–116.

18. Sawaya, "Les Amérindiens domiciliés"; Barman, *Abenaki Daring*.

19. Colin Calloway has an excellent map that well illustrates this point in *The Indian History of an American Institution: Native Americans and Dartmouth* (Hanover, NH: University Press of New England, 2010), see pp. xvi–xvii.

20. See for example Maureen Konkle, *Writing Indian Nations: Native Intellectuals and the Politics of Historiography, 1827–1863* (Chapel Hill: University of North Carolina Press, 2004); Brooks, *The Common Pot*; Fisher, *Indian Great Awakening*; Wyss, *English Letters*.

21. I have chosen to focus on Kahkewaquonaby because of my greater familiarity with his life. Other scholars, however, have pointed to the well-known Anishinaabe author Kahgegagahbowh (George Copway), and often both men, in their work on this subject. See Bernd C. Peyer, *The Tutor'd Mind: Indian Missionary-Writers in Antebellum America* (Amherst: University of Massachusetts Press, 1997); Konkle, *Writing Indian Nations*; Donald Smith, *Mississauga Portraits: Ojibwe Voices from Nineteenth-Century Canada* (Toronto: University of Toronto Press).

22. Joanna Brooks, *The Collected Writings of Samson Occom, Mohegan* (Toronto: Oxford University Press, 2006), introduction.

23. See for example Peter Jones, *Life and Journals of Kah-ke-wa-quo-na-by* (Toronto: Anson Green, 1860); Peter Jones, *History of the Ojebway Indians* (London: Houlston and Wright, 1861); Peter Jones Fonds, E.J. Pratt Library, University of Toronto; Donald Smith, *Sacred Feathers: The Reverend Peter Jones (Kahkewaquonaby) and the Mississauga Indians* (Toronto: University of Toronto Press, 1987); Smith, *Mississauga Portraits*.

24. Marisa Fuentes, *Dispossessed Lives: Enslaved Women, Violence and the Archive* (Philadelphia: University of Pennsylvania, 2016), 6.

25. Fuentes, *Dispossessed Lives*, 6.

26. Fuentes, *Dispossessed Lives*, 4.

27. Lisa Brooks's *The Common Pot* is an important exception to this claim.

28. For example see Lopenzina, *Red Ink*; Phillip Round, *Removable Type: Histories of the Book in Indian Country, 1663–1880* (Chapel Hill: University of North Carolina Press, 2010); Brooks, *The Common Pot*; Konkle, *Writing Indian Nations*; Hilary Wyss, *Writing Indians: Literacy, Christianity, and Native Community in Early America* (Amherst: University of Massachusetts Press, 2000); Peyer, *The Tutor'd Mind*. Exceptions are Wyss, *English Letters and Indian Literacies* and Fisher, *The Indian Great Awakening*.

29. On the significance of this transition see James Belich, *Replenishing the Earth: The Settler Revolution and the Rise of the Anglo-World, 1783–1939* (New York: Oxford University Press, 2009).

30. Fisher, *The Indian Great Awakening*, chap. 6.

31. Elizabeth Elbourne, "Managing Alliance, Negotiating Christianity: Haudenosaunee Uses of Anglicanism in Northeastern North America, 1760s-1830s" in Tolly Bradford and Chelsea Horton, eds., *Mixed Blessings: Indigenous Encounters with Christianity in Canada* (Vancouver: University of British Columbia Press, 2016), 38–60.

32. Thomas Peace, "Borderlands, Primary Sources, and the Longue Durée: Contextualizing Colonial Schooling at Odanak, Lorette, and Kahnawake, 1600–1850," *Historical Studies in Education* 29:1 (Spring 2017): 8–31.

33. Elbourne, "Managing Alliance, Negotiating Christianity," 48.

34. Gus Richardson, "Sahonwagy," *DCB* http://www.biographi.ca/en/bio/sahonwagy _4E.html accessed October 2017.

35. This point has been made about southern New England in Fisher, *The Indian Great Awakening*; the lower Great Lakes and Mohawk Valley by Elbourne, "Managing Alliance, Negotiating Christianity"; and the St. Lawrence Valley by Peace, "Borderlands, Primary Sources, and the Longue Durée."

36. Jean Fittz Hankins, "Bringing the Good News: Protestant Missionaries to the Indians of New England and New York, 1700–1775" (PhD diss., University of Connecticut, 1993), 3–4; 171, n17; 204–214; appendices 2, 3, and 14. The missionary societies Hankins studied were the New England Company, the Scottish Society, the Society for the Propagation of the Gospel, and the Moravians.

37. For more on Haudenosaunee schooling see Keith Jamieson, *History of Six Nations Education* (Brantford, ON: Woodland Indian Cultural Educational Centre, 1987); Keith Jamieson and Michelle Hamilton, *Dr. Oronhyatekha: Security, Justice, and Equality* (Toronto: Dundurn Press, 2016); Alyssa Mt. Pleasant, "Guiding Principles: Guswenta and the Debate over Formal Schooling at Buffalo Creek, 1800–1811," in *Indian Subjects: Hemispheric Perspectives on the History of Indigenous Education*, ed., Brenda J. Child and Brian Klopotek (Santa Fe, NM: School for Advanced Research, 2014), chap. 6.

38. Lainey and Peace, "Louis Vincent Sawantanan, premier bachelier autochtone canadien" and "Louis Vincent Sawatanen: A Life Forged by Warfare and Migration."

39. House of Assembly, Committee Room, Jan 29, 1819. *Eighth Report of the Committee of the House of Assembly, on that Part of the Speech of His Excellency the Governor in Chief Which Relates to the Settlement of the Crown Lands with the Minutes of Evidence Taken before the Committee* (Quebec: Neilson & Cowen, 1824), 11–12; See also 'Timeline of the Huron community,' n.d., Archives du Conseil de la nation huronne-wendat (ACNHW), Collection Francois Vincent, FV/104/6/b6; see also Georges Boiteau, "Les chasseurs hurons de Lorette," (MA thesis: Université Laval, 1954), 56–57, 61; Denis Vaugeois, *The*

Last French and Indian War: An Inquiry into a Safe-Conduct Issued in 1760 that Acquired the Value of a Treaty in 1990 (Montreal and Kingston: McGill-Queen's University Press, 2002), 74.

40. On his service in the American Revolution see DCA 776156; 778326; 780103.1; On his time at the college see 775290; 778327; 818576.

41. US National Archives and Records, Military Service Records, Louis Vincent, Bedel's New Hampshire Regiment; To the Rev. John Wheelock, June 9, 1781, *The Papers of George Washington*, series 3c, Varick Transcripts, Letterbook 4, p. 153; To General Bayley, June 9, 1781, *The Papers of George Washington*, series 3b, Varick Transcripts, Letterbook 13, p. 424.

42. ACNHW: FV/32/3/f.3; FV/34/3/b.4; FV/36/3/j; FV/37/3/k.1

43. ACNHW: FV/37/3/k.1

44. *Église d'Angleterre, Bibliothèque et Archives Nationales du Québec à Québec* (BANQ-QUE), P1000, s3, d2735, p. 30; *State of Religion in Canada*, n.d., LAC, Colonial Office 42, vol. 72, p. 234; John Wheelock to John Forrest, June 15, 1785, DCA, 785365; "From Quebec to Niagara in 1794: Diary of Bishop Jacob Mountain," in *Rapport de l'archiviste de la province de Québec* (Roch Lefebvre, Imprimeur de Sa Majesté la Reine, 1959–1960), 164–165; John Wheelock to Jedidiah Morse, Feb 25, 1811, DCA, 811175.1.

45. Ginette Bernatchez, "Andrew Stuart," *DCB*, http://www.biographi.ca/en/bio/stuart_andrew_7E.html accessed October 2017.

46. Correspondence seems to have been greater with Neilson than Stuart, though this may reflect the provenance of each collection. For letters from Louis Vincent Sawatanen see BANQ-QUE Fonds John Neilson P 192 1972-00-002/22; Louis Vincent to John Neilson, 1820, LAC Neilson Collection, vol. 190, 5012–5014.

47. "Death Notices," *Salem Gazette* 39:39 (May 17, 1825): 3.

48. Joanna Brooks, *The Collected Writings of Samson Occo*m, vii.

49. Jon Parmenter, *The Edge of the Woods: Iroquoia, 1534–1701* (Winnipeg: University of Manitoba Press, 2010), 134.

50. Daniel Richter, *The Ordeal of the Longhouse: The Peoples of the Iroquois League in the Era of European Colonization* (Chapel Hill: University of North Carolina Press, 1992), 121.

51. Smith, *Mississauga Portraits*, 214–220.

52. For more on this intellectual network see: Thomas Peace, "Indigenous Intellectual Traditions & Biography in the Northeast: A Historiographical Reflection," *History Compass* (April 2018) https://doi.org/10.1111/hic3.12445

53. Carl F. Klinck, "John Norton," *DCB* http://biographi.ca/en/bio/norton_john_6E.html accessed October 2017.

54. George Hodgins, *Documentary History of Education in Upper Canada* (Toronto: Warwick Bros & Rutter, 1894), 35–40.

55. Lopenzina, *Through an Indian's Looking Glass*, 126–136.

56. William Apess, *On Our Own Ground: The Complete Writings of William Apess, A Pequot*, Barry O'Connll, ed. (Boston: University of Massachusetts Press, 1992), 33. The quotation is from Apess's 1829 autobiography *A Son of the Forest* (New York: self-published, 1829).

57. Apess, *On Our Own Ground*, xxxiii; Brooks, *The Common Pot*, 173–174.

58. Smith, *Mississauga Portraits*, 221–222; Thaddeus Osgood, *The Canadian Visitor Communicating Important Facts and Interesting Anecdotes Respecting the Indians and Destitute Settlers in Canada and the United States of America.* (London: Hamilton and Adams, [1829?]), 64.

59. Lopenzina, *Red Ink*, 13.

60. *Yale Indian Papers Project*, http://yipp.yale.edu/about accessed October 2017.

61. Fraser and Todd, "Decolonial Sensibilities," 35.

62. For recent examples of biographies on Indigenous intellectuals from this period see Allan Sherwin, *Bridging Two Peoples: Chief Peter E. Jones, 1843–1909* (Waterloo: Wilfrid Laurier Press, 2012); Smith, *Mississauga Portraits*; Oberg, *Professional Indian*; Jamieson and Hamilton, *Dr. Oronhyatekha*; and Lopenzina, *Through an Indian's Looking-Glass*.

63. Wolfgang Ernst, "Radically De-Historicising the Archive: Decolonising Archival Memory from the Supremacy of Historical Discourse" in *Decolonising Archives*, 12.

64. Ernst, "Radically De-Hisoricising the Archive," 12.

65. Fuentes, *Dispossessed Lives*, 6.

66. Fuentes, *Dispossessed Lives*, 146.

67. The idea of listening to silences comes from Carter, "Of Things Said and Unsaid," 223. Carter's work does an excellent job at demonstrating just how complicated this listening can be, pointing to how, if done poorly, it can reinforce processes of marginalization. See especially 226.

68. Carter, "Of Things Said and Unsaid," 227.

69. Carter, "Of Things Said and Unsaid," 227.

70. Ernst, "Radically De-Historicising the Archive," 16.

71. Ian Milligan, "Illusionary Order: Online Databases, Optical Character Recognition, and Canadian History, 1997–2010," *Canadian Historical Review* 94:4 (2013): 540–569.

72. Lara Putnam, "The Transnational and the Text-Searchable: Digitized Sources and the Shadows They Cast," *American Historical Review* 121:2 (April 2016): 399.

SIX

Entangled Archives: Cherokee Interventions in Language Collecting

Kelly Wisecup

In this chapter, I consider the deep, interconnected, and ongoing histories of two archival collections. One collection currently resides in — or is entangled with — the other, but despite their shared material space, these collections have separate origins and divergent futures. The first was created by Cherokee John Ridge in 1826 in response to a request from Albert Gallatin, a diplomat and statesman with longstanding interests in Native linguistics, and it is held among Gallatin's papers at the New-York Historical Society (NYHS). A spokesman for the Cherokees, Ridge was the son of one of the tribe's key leaders in the eighteenth and early nineteenth centuries and cousin to Elias Boudinot, editor of the bilingual newspaper the *Cherokee Phoenix*. In 1825, Ridge traveled with several Muskogee Creek men to Washington, DC, where they hoped to renegotiate the illicit Treaty of Indian Springs. Ridge served as an amanuensis for the negotiations. During this time, Superintendent of Indian Affairs Thomas McKenney passed along to Ridge several requests from Gallatin, one a request for word lists and translations in Southeastern Indigenous languages and the other for cultural and historical information about the Cherokees. After multiple letters from Gallatin to McKenney and what seem to have been repeated demands from the latter to Ridge, Ridge created word lists for five Southeastern Indigenous languages, a translation of the Lord's Prayer in Cherokee, and brief reports on Southeastern Native history. The materials feature Ridge's own knowledge of the Cherokee language as well as historical and linguistic information he obtained from the Muskogee leaders he had accompanied to the US capitol.[1]

The second collection encompasses the first: starting in 1825, Gallatin, with the support of the Department of War, solicited manuscript and printed word lists from government agents, missionaries, and Native people. These word lists formed the basis for his linguistic map, later published in 1836 by the American Antiquarian Society.[2] Also in 1836, and in collaboration with the Society, Gallatin published a lengthy "Synopsis" of North American tribes in the Society's *Transactions*.[3] Gallatin and his frequent correspondent Peter Du Ponceau, chair of the American Philosophical Society's Historical and Literary Committee, envisioned their collections and publications as continuing Thomas Jefferson's call in *Notes on the State of Virginia* to collect and study Native languages as a means of discovering Indigenous people's origins. Yet Gallatin also expanded Jefferson's project, for he sought not primarily to study origins, but to "discover[. . .] the affinities which may exist between the several Indian languages, or between them and other languages."[4] But for Gallatin and other US collectors, linguistic collection was not simply an activity that would provide insight into North America's past; it formed the foundation for creating theories about the relations between language and land, theories that, in the hands of the Department of War, supported efforts to remove Native nations like the Cherokees from their ancestral homelands. At the same time, Gallatin's linguistic collecting helped to form the basis of several historical and philosophical societies, such as the American Philosophical Society (APS) and the NYHS, by generating committees and requiring the creation of new collections and physical spaces to hold word lists, maps, and tables.[5]

In contrast to Gallatin's large collection at the NYHS and his multiple publications, Ridge's collection does not exist on its own, but is filed within a folder within Gallatin's papers. His lists are unpublished, uncatalogued, and unsearchable via subject headings or finding aids, practically invisible within the larger Gallatin collection unless one knows where to look in the voluminous collection, composed of both unattributed and attributed word lists, on all sizes of paper, in bound books, and in scattered leaflets. While a 1981 article by William Sturtevant in the *Journal of Cherokee Studies* identifies and analyzes a letter from Ridge to Gallatin, which is held in the same set of folders as the vocabularies, the word lists have received virtually no attention.[6] This oversight is perhaps due not only to their archival location within Gallatin's collection, but also to their non-narrative form, which contrasts with the autobiographies, sermons, novels, and poems on which scholars interested in pre-1900 Native writing have focused. The oversight of Ridge's word lists may also be a result of the fact that he was one of the signers of the Treaty of New Echota, the 1835 treaty that ceded Cherokee lands in the Southeast to the United States and facilitated the removal of Cherokee people west of the Mississippi River.[7] In addition to writing in genres that have received little critical attention and publishing anonymously at times, Ridge has been seen less as someone who contributed to remembering Cherokee histories than as an agent of removal, dispossession, and loss.

Ridge's collection has thus not been regarded as contributing to the founding archives of early American history, literature, and philology in the ways that Gallatin's has. Yet his linguistic work cannot be so easily folded into colonial collections, for it exists in tension with Gallatin's lists, tables, and publications. Unlike US collections, Ridge's linguistic work does not attempt to fix Indigenous nations in archival or geographic place. Instead, it participates in a different set of memory practices grounded in the Southeast. In this chapter, I take up the word lists he created in 1825, a decade before the Treaty of New Echota and five years before the passage of the Indian Removal Act, a moment when Cherokee and other Southeastern people had strategically adopted elements of "civilization" in order to obtain US protections of their lands against the states and settlers.[8] This was also a time when Ridge strongly opposed any removal of Southeastern people from their ancestral homelands, a position he publicized through his work to renegotiate treaties like Indian Springs, and through his speeches and letters.

In focusing on the word lists, this chapter also reorients the scholarly attention on Gallatin and the collecting projects of historical and philosophical societies.[9] I ask how scholars might define and analyze materials that, like Ridge's word lists, are encompassed by larger collections created by Euro-Americans, but that differ from those larger collections in their origins and purposes. I also ask how the lists and their place in Gallatin's collection help us to reconsider the role of digital archives.

Unlike many Native American cultural materials, Ridge's word lists were not taken without his knowledge, but created on purpose for Gallatin. Yet they also cannot be folded seamlessly into Gallatin's collections or into the archives of the NYHS. And if Ridge's word lists are perhaps unusual objects of study, given the focus in Native American Studies on more familiar genres, their archival position nonetheless represents that of many writings by Native people: they are held within the papers of Euro-American collectors and, thus, often invisible in finding aids or search catalogs. As a result of this arrangement — often based on the collections as the archives received them — Native writings are often not held in material proximity to materials by other Native writers or to topics that have relevance based on their content.

A number of digital archive projects have worked to return digital copies of materials created by Native people but held within non-Native archives to their Native communities of origin.[10] These forms of "respectful repatriation" revise conceptions of texts, access, ownership, and knowledge.[11] This chapter builds on this work while also taking a closer look at questions of archival arrangements and their effects on how scholars locate, select, digitize, and analyze texts. It asks how digital archive and repatriation projects might revise the current physical location of Native writings, even while also acknowledging some of the contexts that shaped their production and continue to shape their circulation. To begin to answer this question, I ask how the content of Ridge's word lists might help us to envision readings of and different locations for the lists. While Gallatin aimed to transform Indigenous words into objects that he could manipulate and compare to develop theories about Indigenous languages and homelands, Ridge disrupts the relationships between language and land that Gallatin and others sought to posit. Instead, he recontextualizes linguistic collections by locating his word lists in specific Southeastern language practices, relations to land, and tribal relations. In what follows, I first show that if Indian removal and settler-colonialism took place in particular communities and on the ground, it was imagined and justified in archives and in the material forms that collectors employed to arrange their materials. Then, I explain how, in opposition to these archival imaginings, Ridge develops an alternate practice of and outcome for collection and linguistic translation, one grounded in Southeastern spaces and histories.

Making Linguistic Relations, Linking Language and Land

To understand how the NYHS and other archives aim to shape the significance and meanings of Ridge's word lists, it is necessary to examine Gallatin's linguistic collecting project and the material practices connected to it. For nineteenth-century Euro-American collectors, the processes of archiving and the spaces made for those processes created meaning out of the assembled documents. In their formative years, US archives were spaces not only where materials were stored, but also where the work of correlating language and geography occurred — and, thus, where the work of imagining how Native nations might be attached to discrete and diminishing areas of land occurred. For Gallatin at the NYHS and Du Ponceau at the APS, collecting was only the first step in the project to understand the relationships between language and land. The longer and allegedly more intellectually difficult task involved transferring words from spoken exchanges and collectors' notes to word lists, tables, and comparative columns. For example, acts of cataloging and filing Ridge's word lists and copying them into a master file of words from multiple Native languages helped to give them a place in the archive and define their meaning. Adapting Linnaean and natural historical methodologies of arranging objects in tables and cabinets to discover the similarities and differences among them, Du Ponceau and Gallatin utilized material forms such as blanks, lists, and tables to organize the words spoken and recorded in exchanges with linguistic collectors. Collectors described their gathering and arrangement of entities as diverse as Indigenous words, cultural materials, human remains, histories, images, and "hieroglyphics" with the language of natural history, by referencing the "Linneus [sic] of languages," who would classify "idioms and dialects,"[12] and by calling artifacts "fragments of history, as Bacon would say."[13]

Such collecting and archival processes transformed words into material objects that collectors could place in various configurations, experimenting with these arrangements to uncover linguistic similarities and, ideally, groupings. This work took place at multiple archives, but also in letters between men like Du Ponceau and Gallatin, as they shared information, incorporated data sent by the other into new forms, and debated the meanings of their findings. For example, Du Ponceau's manuscript book *Indian Vocabularies* assembles word lists that he collected, borrowed, and then copied into a repurposed book that had previously listed "continuance dockets." In the book, he transcribes manuscript lists donated by Jefferson, explorers and surveyors such as Stephen Long and Thomas Say, and missionary John Heckewelder, alongside those in printed books. This collection of "Indian vocabularies" creates what Du Ponceau calls a "bird's eye view of the whole": it assembles the disparate lists into one space, while also placing the vocabularies in proximity to one another.[14] The neatly copied lists encourage readers to compare the features of various languages by flipping back and forth from one page to another, and these acts of comparative observation would ideally illuminate shared or different attributes among various languages. Studying such lists and tables would, ideally, allow observers to arrive at conclusions that exceeded the sum of their parts.[15] Accordingly, this epistemology privileged a "specific type of observation in which objects were always seen against one another," a comparative practice that relied on material forms

FIGURE 6.1. Peter Du Ponceau, *Indian Vocabularies, 1820–1844.* The American Philosophical Society, Philadelphia, PA. Mss.497.In2.

of compilation such as lists in order to assemble objects in various configurations.[16] These forms of organization were key to attempts to classify, standardize, and correlate objects and, thus, to tabulate a picture of the entire world, one that envisioned all living things within a table that would transform them, through classification, into known types.[17]

For Du Ponceau, looking at and comparing linguistic features was key not only to arranging languages, but also to interpreting the significance of these language groups. He wrote to missionary Daniel Butrick that, "It is from the languages, principally that we can judge whether those nations are connected with each other, or are altogether separate Tribes or Races. [. . .] how many such *head nations* (if I can so express myself) there are between the Carolinas & the Mississippi we do not know & we can only obtain that knowledge by Grammars & Vocabularies, (but principally, *Grammars* of their respective languages)."[18] This knowledge was achieved only after one had trained the eye to recognize linguistic features and their similarities to and differences from other languages, a process of the archive, facilitated by catalogs like Du Ponceau's. As Du Ponceau insisted, it was after a reader became "tolerably conversant with Indian languages, and is familiarized, as it were, with their physiognomy," that one "acquires a greater degree of perception, which enables him to judge with more or less certainty, sometimes by a single insulated word, of their general construction and grammatical forms."[19]

Du Ponceau's reference to physiognomy emphasized the importance of *seeing* (rather than hearing or speaking) words, as well as the ways that acts of seeing in the archive allowed him to imagine various relationships among languages. The term "physiognomy" aligned linguistic collection and study with sciences of the body, which focused on physical appearance to draw conclusions about character. "Physiognomy" was also employed in botanical contexts to describe the appearance, form, and characteristics of a plant, and when used in a linguistic context, the term suggested that Du Ponceau aimed to make linguistic characteristics visible, so that their grammars and structures could be observed and compared. Like uses of physiognomy in the human and botanical sciences, linguistic observation also relied on the assumption that observable features had a direct relation to invisible ones. Such research also depended on a stable orthography, requiring that all collectors, from Indian agents to ministers to soldiers to Native sources, represented sounds in the same way. While US collectors attempted to guard against inconsistent orthographies by distributing printed word lists for agents in the field to complete, not all of their correspondents used the same orthographies, and not all made their orthographies transparent.

If collectors relied on the physical space of the archive and on material objects like paper and books to render words into objects of study, they also envisioned that these archival acts would have consequences that went beyond the archive to illuminate the relations between Native languages and land. Du Ponceau discussed his view of these connections in a letter to Heckewelder, writing, "If the Naudowesies (or Sioux) should be as what you say about the name would be lead to suppose, a kindred race with the Hurons, they must also be a kin to the Iroquois or the Six nations, and this would help me to understand, how these handfuls of men the Iroquois & Hurons, came to be planted in the middle of the multitude of Algonquin tribes, apparently unconnected by language with any other nation."[20] Gallatin developed these assumptions that language revealed geographic location in his own work, even while drawing on incomplete evidence. In his 1826 *Table of Indian Tribes of the United States, East of the Stony Mountains: Arranged According to Languages* and *Dialects, Furnished by Albert Gallatin*, Gallatin arranged Native people in what he aimed to position as two mutually enforcing categories. The table's first column ordered tribes by language families, while the second situated them in place by identifying their "State or Territory, and Place of Residence."[21] However, Gallatin lacked linguistic information for some tribes, so he shifted his mode of classification accordingly: "The divisions of the tribes that follow are purely geographical, the information obtained respecting their languages being insufficient."[22] The dual columns do not represent wholly separate categories, but forms of classification that Gallatin saw as interrelated, and his shift from linguistic to geographic organizations relies on his assumption that these categories are also interchangeable, that language corresponds to land and vice versa. Thus, geographic knowledge would also enable one to make claims about language, while information about a tribe's language could enable Gallatin to speculate about the geographic location of their homelands. His map drew on linguistic collections to imagine where to place Native people in North America — on maps and in geographic space.

Collectors aimed to build upon the relations they discovered in archives to develop policies for arranging Native people in actual space and in relation to the United States. Indeed, collecting words and enacting polices regarding land use often went hand in hand: in the Southeast, the Indian agents tasked with the responsibility of transforming Native sustenance practices as part of the so-called civilization policy were also the men on whom Jefferson and, by extension, Du Ponceau and Gallatin relied for word lists. In particular, Benjamin Hawkins, the Indian agent to the Muskogees or Creeks who also worked extensively with the Cherokees and Choctaws, played a key role in these tribes' adoption of Western agricultural practices. US politicians hoped that these shifts would decrease the land tribes "needed" and attach people to individual plots of land, thus opening up "excess" land to US settlers.[23] At the same time that he aimed to dispossess Native peoples of their lands, Hawkins drew on his familiarity with and proximity to these tribes to create several word lists for Jefferson's collection.[24] The work of Hawkins and other Indian agents allowed the United States to imagine Indian Country as a series of discrete areas possessed by individual tribes or even individuals with whom the United States could negotiate about purchase or removal. This reframing of Native people in geographic categories on maps was directly supported by — and sometimes interchangeable with — the archival reframing of Native people in supposedly overlapping geographic and linguistic categories.[25]

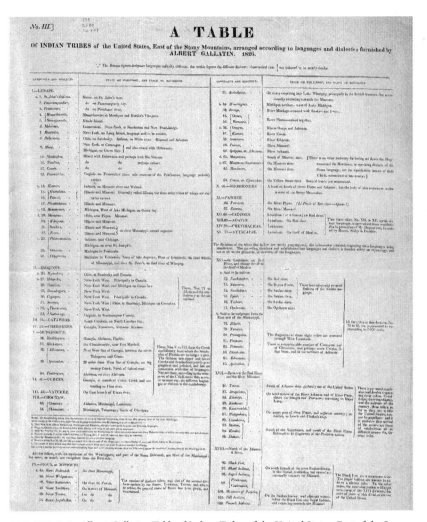

FIGURE 6.2. Albert Gallatin, *Table of Indian Tribes of the United States, East of the Stony Mountains: Arranged According to Languages and Dialects, Furnished by Albert Gallatin.* 1826. The American Philosophical Society, Philadelphia, PA.

Recontextualizing Colonial Collections, Translating Cherokee Relations

By 1825, John Ridge was hardly unfamiliar with these connections among linguistic collecting and archives, the imposition of Western practices under the name of "civilization," and US demands for land. Europeans and US Americans had been collecting natural specimens and objects belonging to Native people in the Southeast for decades, due to the work of Indian agents like Hawkins, to the collecting of traders and botanists such as James Adair and William Bartram, and the botanical projects of missionaries like Anna Maria Gambold, a Moravian teacher at Spring Place, the school Ridge attended from 1810–1815.[26] Ridge was also familiar with the ways that these projects supported what US Americans called improvement. He explicitly states in commentary that accompanies his word lists that "Agent Col. Hawkins" attempted to disperse Creek families "far from their original towns [. . .] by convincing them of the advantages to be derived from separate & individual townships."[27] Arranging Creek and, for that matter, Cherokee lands into private property was supposed to encourage other civilized actions, such as farming rather than hunting and practices of inheritance that ran through men rather than the matrilineal structures that characterized Southeastern Native nations.[28]

Ridge's own encounter with US linguistic collection likewise occurred in the context of negotiations about land claims. He received several requests from Gallatin for linguistic, geographic, and cultural information about Southeastern Native people while in Washington, DC serving as an amanuensis for Creek leaders, who were renegotiating the Treaty of Indian Springs (1825).[29] The United States's spurious claims to land made in that treaty would likely have been foremost on his mind when, in return to Gallatin's request, Ridge sent twelve pages of word lists in Cherokee, Muskogee Creek, Yuchi, Natchez, and Hitchittee and nine additional pages describing these tribes' recent histories and geographic locations.[30] While Ridge discusses both land and language, as Gallatin requested, he frustrates the modes of comparison on which Euro-American collectors relied to connect these two categories, and he posits instead a different, ongoing set of relations to land and to community that precede the existence of the United States.

Ridge states that he had compiled the vocabularies "as well as my time would admit & as far as the English orthography can convey the Indian sounds. It is impossible, without the aid of characters purposely made, to write the Indian words correctly in the English."[31] He may have been referring here to the Cherokee syllabary, which was in widespread use by 1821, and which the Cherokee Nation had officially adopted instead of several proposed English orthographies, including one created by linguistic John Pickering. The Cherokees explicitly rejected orthographies that privileged English and the Roman alphabet in favor of the syllabary, which relied on Cherokee sounds, perspectives, and lived experience.[32] As Ridge emphasizes the limitations he confronted when compiling word lists in English, rather than with "characters purposely made," he indicates to Gallatin that he should not read the lists as transparent representations of "Indian sounds." Instead, the lists are approximations of those sounds made with a system that distorted and misrepresented them. Ridge's attention to English's inadequacies cast doubt on Gallatin's collecting projects, which relied on the assumption that representing Indigenous words in English would offer a trustworthy basis for comparison and categorization.

Ridge's word lists also visually represent the inadequacy of English transcriptions. He frequently annotates his word lists in ways that highlight the failures of those lists as translations and, more broadly, of Gallatin's translation, comparison, and categorization project. For example, Ridge provides a literal translation of Indigenous words for the cardinal directions, noting when some languages (such as Natchez) lack words for western concepts such as heaven, and he adds pronouns to Cherokee names for family members to show that Cherokee speakers included a relational pronoun with such nouns. These annotations often run up against or across the hand drawn columns dividing each language, thus, visually demonstrating how Southeastern Indigenous words disrupt English-language categories. What might appear simply to be a messy list actually reflects the limitations and insufficiencies of the English language and corresponding orthographies as a framework or set of comparisons through which to translate and study Native languages. Ridge's word lists do not simply align words for comparison and contrast; they indicate how Southeastern languages exceed and contest the categories in which linguists attempted to place them. Ridge's annotations remind Gallatin that his word lists are not complete, transparent representations of Native languages, but approximations based on an inadequate orthography. In doing so, Ridge's lists also disrupt the relations between language and geography that Gallatin and other collectors sought to imagine by showing that they rested on faulty assumptions. Language, Ridge's lists suggest, offers no satisfactory basis for mapping the similarities or differences among tribal nations and, thus, for geographical charts and Indian policy.

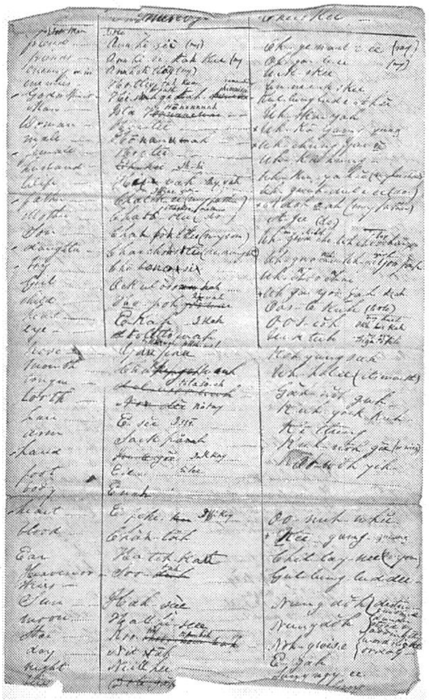

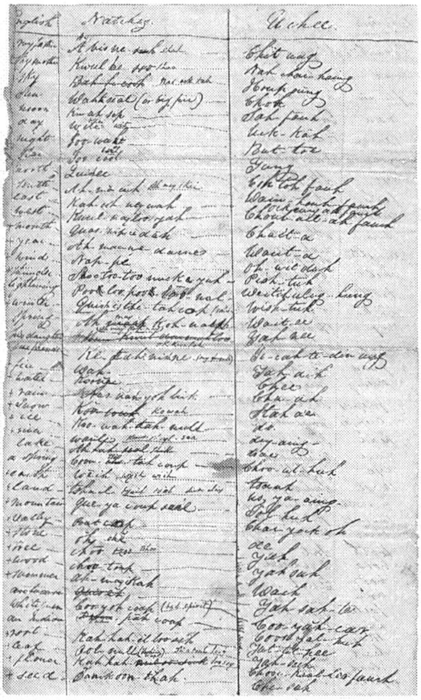

FIGURES 6.3 and 6.4. John Ridge, "Comparative Vocabulary," no date, Gallatin Papers, Box 64-3, Indian Languages. New York Historical Society. New York, NY.

Instead, Ridge offers an alternate account of the relations between Native people and land. He details a set of relations among Southeastern peoples, relations grounded in tribal lands and in communal practices that preceded the creation of the United States. In some cases, such relations are realized through families who lived in places that had long been their homelands or at important ceremonial sites, despite US attempts to move them onto individual farms. In other cases, people maintained these through practices that had long oriented them in specific lands, even if colonial violence and removal meant that they had been displaced. For example, Ridge explains that Uchee people retained their presence at their original town, near the mouth of the "famous Uchee brook." Several families remain there, where, as Ridge notes, "there is still a Square & Council house [. . .] in which their Council fire was once kindled." Similarly, he explains that Natchez people came east from the Mississippi valley to escape colonial violence, and that they "still retain their own Language & have respect for fire which was perpetually kindled as an object of worship in their prosperous days on the banks of the Mississippi." Finally, Ridge points out that "strangers" suppose that the tribes in the Creek confederacy have their own territorial limits and that they are dispersed far from their original towns, thanks to Hawkins's influence. But while some Creek families might hold individual plots of land, the law of the Creek nation "reaches to each town," and the tribes rebuilt "their Town houses & other public works," continue to hold "Ball plays with other towns," and to call on "individuals even at the distance of eighty miles to contribute to their portion of aid." Ridge concludes his description by stating that "The Towns in the Nation have their annual festivals or Green Corn Ceremonies, which are punctually attended, by the people at their own respective towns, to feast and rejoice with their own Kindred Tribes."[33]

In each of these cases, Ridge describes linguistic, ceremonial, and everyday practices that link people to one another, to their histories, and to specific lands, while also maintaining these practices for the future. These descriptions are particularly significant given the particular histories to which he referred: both the Natchez and the Creeks had experienced colonial violence and pressure to leave or cede their homelands and to adopt Western practices. After their defeat by French colonial forces in 1731, Natchez survivors fled west to live among other Indigenous communities. While, as George E. Milne points out, the Natchez did not operate as a united military force after this war, they did not disappear but maintained their identity as a separate people (and, as Ridge points out, their respect for fire and related practices).[34] Despite losing "their homeland, and by extension, access to those sites from which they drew their political and spiritual power," Natchez people, Ridge argues, maintained the ceremonies that continued to help define them as a people in a new land.[35] Moreover, Ridge's account of Creek law and ceremonies was likely obtained, just as his word lists were, from the Creek leaders he had accompanied to Washington, DC. Once again, this account emphasizes the durability and continued enactment of Creek practices, as well as the significance of central, communal, and ceremonial places to which people traveled at certain times of the year.[36] While Hawkins's reports on the Creeks had emphasized their increasing Westernization, as some Creek people adopted private property and Western views of inheritance, Ridge's report points to the continuing importance of the Green Corn ceremony and the town squares where these ceremonies took place.[37] For Ridge and his Creek sources, elements of the civilization policy did not eradicate Creek practices but existed alongside them.

Moreover, by describing the Natchez's respect for fire and the Uchees' and Creeks' participation in ceremonies that began with the lighting of a sacred or council fire, Ridge contextualizes language in practices involving key material and symbolic entities for the Cherokees and other Southeastern Native peoples. Ridge's primary reference for his description of fire would likely have been the Cherokee practice of building a fire for each of their six major ceremonies. In these cases, the peoples' maintenance of the fire enacted and renewed their relations to one another.[38] As the keepers of the sacred fire, the Cherokees made fire a central metaphor of their survival and ability to be reborn as a people in the face of challenges. As Daniel Heath Justice writes, keeping council fires lit was both a key metaphor and a practice: "The survival of the People — of the nation itself — is thus directly linked to their thoughtful attention to their responsibilities as keepers of the sacred fire."[39] Meanwhile, for the Creeks, Green Corn Ceremonies and other seasonal ceremonies began with the lighting of a ceremonial or sacred fire into which the year's old harvest was put as a celebration of and purification for the new year.[40] As the new fire was kindled each year, it also offered the context in which to celebrate the harvest, heal "broken human relationships," and "bring people back together and strengthen their ties to each other and to the square ground."[41]

In the place of relations constructed through archival observations, arrangements, and comparisons, Ridge posits Southeastern Indigenous peoples' practices for forming and renewing relations as a basis for understanding language and peoples. Moreover, he makes clear that these practices continued to form an obstacle for US archival, collection, and, by extension, removal projects; he does so by imitating the material forms of those projects even as he showed how Indigenous languages and relationships exceed US categories. In doing so, Ridge redefines the relations among words, land, and peoples that collectors aimed to construct in archives, and he posits instead a set of relations that relies on participatory action, shared resources, and towns or other specific lands made important through ceremony. His project is less to produce entirely new relations than to compile the materials — metaphors, practices, stories, objects — that had long composed relations in the Southeast and to posit their survival even in the context of so-called improvement. In doing so, he assembles some of the elements that compose what Justice calls peoplehood: the "relational system that keeps the people in balance with one another, with other peoples and realities, and with the world."[42] The fact that these materials take various forms — word lists, metaphors of fire, ethnographic descriptions — attests to the ways that these practices remained vibrant and central even as they adapted to colonialist pressures and tribal changes. Unlike the lists, comparative tables, and maps that US collectors generated as they attempted to translate languages and then to fix Native people in linguistic and geographic frames, Ridge's lists and contemporary Cherokee linguistic materials alike avoid stabilizing words or people in static categories. Instead, Ridge's lists allow for some of the changes that treaties with the United States had brought about while also acknowledging that these changes happened alongside the continuation of long-standing relations and practices.

Digital archives and scholarship have worked to develop new ways of arranging and circulating archival materials created by Native people, in order to place them in new digital spaces that might restore them to the tribal contexts in which they had their origins. Indeed, this scholarship has helped researchers to think more carefully about archival arrangements and categories and their shaping of texts. Ridge's own engagement with Gallatin and his archival project raises a number of further questions for future scholarship on archives, both paper and digital. Gallatin's archive shows that, contrary to much scholarship claiming that Western archives decontextualize materials, the act of *recontextualizing* collected materials in the space of the archive and then connecting them to another set of outside contexts (in this case, land and language) was key to settler-colonial processes of removal and dispossession.[43] The material form of Ridge's lists — the hand-drawn lines for words for different languages and the words that exceed those lines — are the basis on which he challenges Gallatin's processes of collecting and arranging and related observations. Ridge's "messy" lists help him point to contexts outside of the archive altogether, thus also challenging the ways Gallatin relied on arrangements of word lists to speculate about how to assign land in North America to individual tribal nations. His archival intervention, while held within Gallatin's collection, rejects the ways that the physical space of the archive produced categories that sought to order Ridge's work and the peoples he represented.

If, then, both colonial and Indigenous archival projects are reliant on or turn to external contexts, how might digital archives acknowledge those contexts as key to the texts' significance while also remaining cognizant of their own embeddedness in particular material and temporal contexts? How might they acknowledge the colonialist ends of archives like Gallatin's by way of ensuring that they do not erase histories of colonialism and violence?[44] And how might they do so without losing sight of the alternate sets of contexts evoked by Native writers like Ridge, who placed their work into conversation with colonial collecting projects, but did so in ways that complicated, rather than furthered, those projects? Given the importance in Ridge's lists of tribal national spaces and practices that created and renewed relationships among people, how might archives — digital and physical — acknowledge and represent those practices? While Ridge's word lists are not digitized — and indeed remain largely unknown and still encompassed within Gallatin's papers — their content and material form offer new ways to conceptualize the relationships among collections and between collections and geographic places, tribal homelands, and archival processes. In this way, they show that scholars have much to learn from studying archival arrangements, from questioning the relationship among various collections now grouped together, and from analyzing the relationship between material and archival forms.

Notes

1. See Albert Gallatin Papers, Indian Languages, Box 64–3. New-York Historical Society, New York, NY.

2. See Gallatin Papers, Indian Languages, Boxes 64–67.

3. See Albert Gallatin, "A Synopsis of the Indian Tribes of North America," in *Archaeologia Americana, Transactions and Collections of the American Antiquarian Society*, vol. II. (Cambridge: Printed for the Society at the University Press, 1836).

4. James Barbour, Circular, Department of War, May 15, 1826. American Indian Vocabulary Collection. American Philosophical Society. Philadelphia, PA.

5. At the NYHS, see the Gallatin Papers, especially the Indian Languages sections and 1820s correspondence with collectors like Peter Du Ponceau, and at the APS, see the copy of Gallatin's *Table of the Indian Tribes of the United States, East of the Stony Mountains Arranged According to Languages and Dialects, Furnished by Albert Gallatin* (1826) and Gallatin's letters to Peter Du Ponceau in the Historical and Literary Committee Letter Books. Volume III, American Philosophical Society, Philadelphia, PA.

6. William Sturtevant, "John Ridge on Cherokee Civilization in 1826," *Journal of Cherokee Studies* 6 (1981): 79–91.

7. On Ridge's actions in the 1830s, see Daniel Heath Justice, *Our Fire Survives the Storm: A Cherokee Literary History* (Minneapolis: University of Minnesota Press, 2006), chapter 2; William G. McLoughlin, *Cherokee Renascence in the New Republic* (Princeton, NJ: Princeton University Press, 1986), chapter 20–22; Kelly Wisecup, "Practicing Sovereignty: Colonial Temporalities, Cherokee Justice, and the 'Socrates' Writings of John Ridge," *NAIS: Journal of the Native American and Indigenous Studies Association* 4:1 (Spring 2017): 30–60.

8. On the Treaty of New Echota and Cherokee strategic responses to "civilization" programs, see Justice, *Our Fire Survives the Storm*; McLoughlin, *Cherokee Renascence*; Tiya Miles, *The House on Diamond Hill: A Cherokee Plantation Story* (Chapel Hill: University

of North Carolina Press, 2010); Theda Perdue, *Slavery and the Evolution of Cherokee Society, 1540–1866* (Knoxville: University of Tennessee Press, 1979). For the few studies of Ridge's writings — a commonplace book from his time at Cornwall Mission School and his anti-removal speeches — see Hilary E. Wyss, *English Letters and Indian Literacies: Reading, Writing, and New England Missionary Schools, 1750–1830* (Philadelphia: University of Pennsylvania Press, 2012), especially chap. 4; Maureen Konkle, *Writing Indian Nations: Native Intellectuals and the Politics of Historiography, 1827–1863* (Chapel Hill: University of North Carolina Press, 2004), chap. 1.

9. For two recent studies of such projects, see Sean Harvey, *Native Tongues: Colonialism and Race from Encounter to the Reservation* (Cambridge, MA: Harvard University Press, 2015); Robert Lawrence Gunn, *Ethnology and Empire: Languages Literature, and the Making of the North American Borderlands* (New York: New York University Press, 2015).

10. See especially the work of Kim Christen and Jane Anderson, represented by Murkutu http://mukurtu.org, the Plateau People's Web Portal http://plateauportal.libraries.wsu.edu, and Kimberly Christen, "Opening Archives: Respectful Repatriation," *The American Archivist* 74 (2011): 185–210. In addition, see Ellen Cushman, "Wampum, Sequoyan, and Story: Decolonizing the Digital Archive," *College English* 76:2 (2013): 115–35 and the work of the Center for Native American and Indigenous Research (CNAIR) at the APS.

11. Christen, "Opening Archives."

12. Historical and Literary Committee, *Transactions of the Historical & Literary Committee of the American Philosophical Society, Held at Philadelphia, for Promoting Useful Knowledge*, vol. I (Philadelphia: Abraham Small, 1819), xxxvi.

13. Caleb Atwater, "Description of the Antiquities Discovered in the State of Ohio and Other Western States," in *Transactions and Collections of the American Antiquarian Society* (Worcester, MA: Printed for the American Antiquarian Society, 1820), 195.

14. *Transactions of the Historical & Literary Committee*, xviii.

15. Daniela Bleichmar, *Visible Empire: Botanical Expeditions & Visual Culture in the Hispanic Enlightenment* (Chicago: University of Chicago Press, 2012), 48.

16. Bleichmar, *Visible Empire*, 52.

17. Lorraine Daston and Elizabeth Lunbeck, *Histories of Scientific Observation* (Chicago: University of Chicago Press, 2011), 88–91.

18. Peter Du Ponceau to Daniel Butrick, September 7, 1818, Historical and Literary Committee Letter Books. American Philosophical Society, Philadelphia, PA.

19. *Transactions of the Historical & Literary Committee*, xxxvii. On linguistic collecting and its relation to histories of race, see Harvey, *Native Tongues*; for a reading of Du Ponceau's anatomical metaphors Gunn, *Ethnology*, especially 37–39.

20. Peter Du Ponceau to John Heckwelder, August 3, 1816, Historical and Literary Committee Letter Book.

21. Albert Gallatin, *Table of Indian Tribes of the United States, East of the Stony Mountains: Arranged According to Languages and Dialects, Furnished by Albert Gallatin*. 1826.

22. Gallatin, *Table*.

23. For just two books on Hawkins's work in and effect on the Creeks, see Robbie Ethridge, *Creek Country: The Creek Indians and their World* (Chapel Hill: University of North Carolina Press, 2003); Claudio Saunt, *A New Order of Things: Property, Power, and the Transformation of the Creek Indians, 1733–1816* (Cambridge: Cambridge University Press, 1999), especially chap. 7.

24. See Benjamin Hawkins, "Vocabulary of the Cherokee and Choctaw and A Comparative Vocabulary of the Muskoges, or Creek, Chickasaw, Choctaw, and Cherokee Languages," *American Indian Vocabulary Collection*, American Philosophical Society.

25. See Mark Rifkin, *Manifesting America: The Imperial Construction of U.S. National Space* (New York: Oxford University Press, 2009), 14: Linda Tuhiwai Smith, *Decolonizing Methodologies: Research and Indigenous Peoples* (London: Zed Books, 1999).

26. Anna Maria Gambold's list of plants found near Spring Place was published in *The American Journal of Science*, vol. 1. (1818), 245–51. For more on the Moravian mission, see Rowena McClinton, ed., *The Moravian Springplace Mission to the Cherokees, Abridged Edition* (Lincoln: University of Nebraska Press, 2010).

27. John Ridge, "Comparative Vocabulary," n.d., Gallatin Papers, Box 64–3, Indian Languages. New-York Historical Society. New York, NY.

28. See Miles, *House*; McLoughlin, *Cherokee Renascence*.

29. As William G. McLoughlin points out, this treaty was signed by only eight Creek leaders; it led to leader William McIntosh's execution on the grounds that he had sold the land for his personal gain. See McLoughlin, *Cherokee Renascence*, 372–73.

30. I use Ridge's spellings here and throughout.

31. Ridge, "Comparative Vocabulary."

32. See Ellen Cushman, *The Cherokee Syllabary: Writing the People's Perseverance* (Norman: University of Oklahoma Press, 2011), 8.

33. Ridge, "Comparative Vocabulary."

34. See George E. Milne, *Natchez Country: Indians, Colonists, and the Landscapes of Race in French Louisiana* (Athens: University of Georgia Press, 2015), especially 207–08.

35. Milne, *Natchez Country*, 197.

36. On Creek practices of the Green Corn Ceremony and of *poskita* (annual celebrations and purifications in which new fires were kindled that women carried to each town), see Saunt, *New Order*, 22, 84, and 259.

37. Ethridge, *Creek Country*, 94–95.

38. Justice, *Our Fire Survives*, 26.

39. Justice, *Our Fire Survives*, 26.

40. See Joel W. Martin, *Sacred Revolt: The Muskogees' Struggle for a New World* (Boston: Beacon Press, 1991), 36–42; Joshua Piker, *Okfuskee: A Creek Indian Town in Colonial America* (Cambridge, MA: Harvard University Press, 2004), 9–10.

41. Martin, *Sacred Revolt*, 38.

42. Justice, *Our Fire Survives*, 24.

43. See Cushman, "Wampum, Sequoyan, and Story"; Bleichmar, *Visible Empire*; Malea Powell, "Dreaming Charles Eastman: Cultural Memory, Autobiography, and Geography in Indigenous Rhetorical Histories," in *Beyond the Archives: Research as a Lived Process*, eds. Gesa E Kirsch and Liz Rohan (Carbondale: Southern Illinois University, 2008), 115–27; Timothy B. Powell, William Weems, and Freeman Owle, "Native/American Digital Storytelling: Situating the Cherokee Oral Tradition within American Literary History," *Literature Compass* 4:1 (2007): 1–23.

44. For the importance of focusing not only on Indigenous survival and resilience but also on settler-colonialism and its violence, see Amy Lonetree, *Decolonizing Museums: Representing Native America in National and Tribal Museums* (Chapel Hill: University of North Carolina Press, 2012).

SEVEN

Recovering Indigenous Kinship:

Community, Conversion, and the Digital Turn

Marie Balsley Taylor

When discussing strategies for relocating early American literature within Native space, Abenaki scholar Lisa Brooks encourages scholars to move beyond what is written in order to consider the stories, people, and places that have been obscured or left out. The problem, she argues, is that "[t]oo often, we privilege what is known — New England — over what many do not know, the networks of kinship and waterways that constitute Native space." For Brooks, a broader approach requires specificity. By focusing on the details of Indigenous practices, systems, and relationships, we can expand the background against which we locate texts written within Indigenous spaces. This attention to detail, Brooks argues, allows us to create "an unfamiliar reading of a familiar narrative" which in turn "provide[s] a lens to [a text's] multiple interpretive possibilities."[1] Inspired by Brooks and others, scholars of early America have begun to relocate American literature within Native space. Using literary analysis to think about Indigenous diplomacy, performance, and relationships to land, scholars are productively creating a growing body of work that offers new methodological models that broaden the interpretive possibilities for early American texts. Here, I add another methodological possibility to this growing list — that offered by kinship. More specifically, I show how kinship ties can be productively reconstructed using digital tools that allow us to synthesize early American genealogical writings and records that have previously been scattered or overlooked.

While there are clear limits to using kinship as a methodology, when used cautiously, the reconstruction of Indigenous familial and social relationships allows us to imagine potentially new motivations for many of the Native people described in early American literature, about whom we have little to no information. In this chapter, I focus on using kinship to shed new light on the words and actions of the first Indigenous convert described in seventeenth-century New England missionary writings, the Pequot Indian Wequash. Because the archival sources on early converts like Wequash are sparse and the records that we do have are often heavily implicated with the aims of the missionary authors, it is hard to separate the lives of the converts from the colonial rhetoric through which they are represented. Reconstructing kinship, I argue, offers a way of thinking more concretely about how an Indigenous convert's familial relationships, or what Brooks terms one's "network of relations," can serve as a potential framework for contextualizing Christian conversion.[2]

In turning to kinship as a methodological guide for organizing and interpreting colonial documents, I am following the lead of Brooks and others, including the creators of *The Occom Circle*. As Brooks writes in her well-known work, *The Common Pot: The Recovery of Native Space in the Northeast*, by focusing on Indigenous networks of relations we can move analysis away from Indigenous-settler relationships and instead consider Indigenous authors as acting "within Native space." For example, when we focus on Samson Occom as a "leader at Mohegan," rather than a pupil of the Congregational minister Eleazar Wheelock, "a very different picture emerges." As Brooks notes, Occom's interactions with Wheelock make up only a small part of an "extensive network" of relations.[3] Taking Brooks's methodology and applying it to the digital realm, the creators of *The Occom Circle* have digitized Occom's writings and facilitated search tools to "place Occom at the center of a broad network of historical relations."[4] The tools of digitization allow us to reconnect kinship references that have been separated across space and time in order to bring previously obscured kinship ties to the fore. As I illustrate in what follows, a methodology that prioritizes kinship and employs the tools of digitization not only provides us with a means of productively repositioning and reinterpreting the existing writings of Indigenous authors, but can also be used to recreate the lives of Indigenous people who left their marks outside of the written archives.

Erasing Kinship

Employing kinship as a methodological guide to the archives requires more than simply an acknowledgment that Native people existed, and continue to exist, within a network of relations. Rather, it necessitates that we take Indigenous kinship seriously. More than merely a means of organizing society, kinship was at the heart of an Indigenous person's identity. Kinship ties not only defined one's familial relationships, but they also determined one's place in society, one's relationship to land, and one's responsibility to their community. Among the Southern New England Algonquians who figure largely in early American writings, kinship was a means of both defining and maintaining community. An Indigenous community, or sachemship, was comprised of a few hundred people who were affiliated by kinship networks. As anthropologist Kathleen Bragdon explains, "Loyalty . . . rested with the sachemship as an ongoing social grouping, to whom one's ancestors had belonged and to which one's own posterity would be loyal."[5] These kinship networks were not limited to one's face-to-face community, but extended to other communities as well. The result being that the Indigenous people of southern New England were connected across large expanses of land by intricate webs of kinship ties.

Kinship also determined an individual's place in society. The leader of the sachemship, the sachem, maintained their authority through their kinship networks. Other communal roles were also determined by familial ties.[6] As Brooks points out, kinship not only guided human interaction, it also guided one's affiliation with land. A community's land tenure system was "dependent on the relationship between a sachem and his village."[7] Communal land claims were asserted by the sachem, who worked in consultation with other members of the community to establish land use for both individuals and groups. The community's effective use of land was paramount to its survival. As a guide for one's social, political, and spiritual actions, an Indigenous person's networks of relations made up their understanding of what it meant to be human.[8]

Kinship not only defined life within Indigenous communities, it also governed the ways in which Native people in southern New England interacted with the arriving English settlers. Kinship was at the heart of southern New England Algonquian diplomatic practices. As historian Colin Calloway explains: "Dealing with other peoples as trade partners required making alliances and turning strangers who were potential enemies into friends and even relatives. Native peoples extended or replicated kinship . . . to include people with whom they were not related by birth or marriage, bringing them into their community by adoption, alliance, and ritual."[9] As Brooks explains in her oft-cited metaphor of the common pot, New England's Native people conceived of themselves as existing within a network of relations that was both cooperative and interdependent. This interdependence extended to the arriving Europeans. "As soon as Europeans settled on the coast, they became inhabitants in Native space. In the common pot, shared space means shared consequences and shared pain. The actions of the newcomers would affect the whole."[10] Indigenous diplomacy was thus performed through the lens of kinship. Native communities extended kinship to settlers in order to "incorporate the 'beings' from Europe into Native space" and protect the whole.[11]

Importantly, the arriving English recognized the significance of Indigenous kinship networks from the start. When describing Indigenous "relations of consangunitie and affinite, or, Blood *and* Marriage" for his English readers, Separatist minister Roger Williams explained that the Narragansetts "hold the band of brother-hood so deare, that when one had commited a murther and fled, they executed his brother; and 'tis common for a brother to pay the debt of a brother deceased."[12] Puritan missionary John Eliot also appreciated the importance of kinship ties and he strategically observed Indigenous familial and social relationships. As Ojibwe historian Jean O'Brien points out, Eliot "quickly grasped that persuading Indians to listen would be most effectively achieved by working through the Indian social order."[13] Eliot explained his strategy in the 1649 missionary tract *The Glorious Progress of the Gospel* writing: "I doe endeavour to engage the Sachems of greatest note to accept the Gospel, because that doth greatly animate and encourage such as are well-affected, and is a dampening to those that are scoffers and opposers."[14] Not only were English settlers aware of Indigenous kinship networks, but they also worked within these networks to advance their colonial aims.

Given the central role that Indigenous kinship ties played in guiding the actions of both Native people and New England settlers, it is significant that many colonial authors crafted their writings in such a way as to obscure or erase kinship ties. Colonial authors omitted kinship for a number of multifaceted reasons; however, at its core, erasing kinship provided a means for settlers to claim ownership over Indigenous bodies and lands. By sidestepping references to kinship in their legal documents and treaties, English settlers concomitantly ignored the mutually recognized rights that kinship accorded Indigenous people in terms of sovereignty and land claims. At the same time, English authors erased documentary evidence of kinship in their reports and letters back to England as a way of concealing their own failure to uphold Indigenous rights. Portraying Indigenous people as isolated from their homes and communities provided English authors with the ability to textually recreate Native people in their own image — as willing and eager English subjects.

The erasure of kinship is particularly evident in Early American missionary narratives — a collection of documents containing some of the most detailed descriptions of Indigenous people in colonial New England. Indeed, the writings of Early American missionaries form the basis of much of our contemporary scholarship about Indigenous people in Colonial New England. These missionary archives, like other documents of colonialism, are, as anthropologist and historian Ann Stoler writes, "both transparencies on which power relations were inscribed and intricate technologies of rule in themselves."[15] Ostensibly written to document the settlement of New England, seventeenth-century missionary texts were also deliberately crafted to legitimize colonial rule. When circulated among an English readership, these accounts worked to proclaim the successful conversion and subsequent transformation of New England's Native people. As part of their attempts to represent the English colonial venture as a benevolent one, missionary authors painstakingly depicted conversion as a dualistic choice in which the Indigenous convert is so eager to join the English community that he or she willingly abandons their Indigenous one. By defining Indigenous converts almost exclusively in terms of their relationships to English people and practices, missionary narratives effectively masked a convert's network of relations. In emphasizing that converts were eagerly turning to Christian practices (or more precisely English ones) and away from Indigenous practices, the Bay Colony leaders endeavored to assure their English supporters that they were (finally) fulfilling the aims of their 1628 charter to "win and incite the Natives of Country, to the knowledge and Obedience of the only true God and Saviour of mankind" which was the "principal end of this Plantation."[16]

The project of erasing kinship began early. In 1643, members of the Bay Colony began producing missionary literature in earnest with the publication of *New Englands First Fruits*, the first of several tracts describing Indigenous conversion in New England. These tracts, collectively known as *The Eliot Tracts*, recorded the words and actions of Indigenous people to provide evidence to English supporters that the New England missionary project was having an effect. The first convert proclaimed by the Bay Colony was Wequash, a Pequot warrior who had aligned with the Narragansetts and subsequently served as a guide for the English during the Mystic Massacre (1637) — the deadliest battle of the Pequot War. Following the Pequot War, Wequash developed ties with the Puritan missionaries who eventually oversaw his conversion to Christianity. In *New Englands First Fruits*, Bay Colony authors Thomas Weld and Hugh Peter proclaim Wequash's conversion as indisputable evidence that God had clearly "begun to gather" his "*first Fruits*" among "those poore *Indians*."[17]

Only a few months after the publication of *New Englands First Fruits*, Roger Williams also penned an account of Wequash's conversion in his Indigenous language primer, *A Key into the Language of America*. Like *New Englands First Fruits*, *A Key Into the Language of America* recorded the words and deeds of New England's Native people for English readers. However, Williams, who had been ousted by the Bay Colony in 1635, took a different stance on the state of colonial missions than the Bay Colony authors. As literary scholar Jeffrey Glover explains, "*A Key* reported to an English reading public that the governors of the Massachusetts Bay Colony had left behind records of untrustworthy dealings with Algonquian groups . . ."[18] Among these "untrustworthy" accounts, Williams claims, was their description of Wequash's conversion. As Williams writes, he was "not so confident as the others" regarding the state of Wequash's soul.[19] Recounting a visit Williams himself had made to the Pequot man as he was dying, Williams describes Wequash as maintaining a "sence of inward hardnesse and unbrokennesse" until his final breath.[20] For the Bay Colony authors, the missionary project is a burgeoning success story evidenced by the pious conversion of their first convert. For Williams, the project is lackluster and fraught with confusion illustrated by the uncertain state of Wequash's soul.[21]

Despite their differing perspectives, both *New Englands First Fruits* and *A Key Into the Language of America* inaugurate the missionary project's erasure of kinship ties by depicting Wequash as deliberately isolating himself from his tribal community in order to join an English Christian one. In *New Englands First Fruits*, Weld and Peter showcase Wequash's potential for conversion by emphasizing his decision to move away from his tribal homelands. As they explain, in the aftermath of the Pequot War, Wequash came to "dwell amongst the English at *Connecticut*" where he eventually converted to Christianity.[22] Similarly, in *A Key Into the Language of America*, Williams portrays Wequash's readiness for Christian salvation by characterizing the Pequot man's most significant relationships as those he has with English leaders. As Williams recounts, on his deathbed Wequash is surrounded only by his English community, which is comprised of Williams himself and George Fenwick, the Connecticut leader and later parliamentarian. Williams and Fenwick serve as Wequash's surrogate family, and it is Fenwick, not his tribal community, to whom Wequash wills his son Wenamoag.[23] For the English authors, Wequash's isolation from his lands and his community indicate to English readers that the Pequot man is ready for both English conversion and colonialism.

It is important to note that the English claims of Wequash's isolation were not solely rhetorical, but had some basis in the actual conditions of seventeenth-century Native people. As a survivor of the Mystic Massacre, Wequash was at the center of one of the deadliest battles in the early years of English settlement — a battle made even more difficult by the fact that he was a Pequot. In *New Englands First Fruits*, Weld and Peter present colonial violence as evidence supporting the sincerity of Wequash's conversion. As they argue, it was the devastation of the Pequot War and the Mystic Massacre in particular that drove Wequash to the English. After Wequash "beh[eld] the mighty power of God in our English Forces, how they fell upon the *Pegans*, where divers hundreds of them were slain in an houre; The Lord, as a God of glory in great terrour did appeare unto the Soule and Conscience of this poore Wretch."[24] While the Pequot War was devastating to the Pequot Nation, its effects were exacerbated because it came on the heels of a series of imported diseases that had decimated other Native communities up and down the coast. There is clear evidence to suggest that the chaos and disruption wrought by the arriving colonists strained Native kinship ties.[25] Facing isolation, Wequash may have been left with no choice but to forge new alliances after the shattering losses sustained during the war. In the face of desolation, he may have established ties with the English as part of his attempts at survival.

However, to claim that Indigenous isolation in the colonial period was solely the result of the material conditions of colonialism is to both ignore the rhetorical function of isolation and to underestimate the foundational role that kinship played in shaping Indigenous identity. When we look closer at the accounts of Wequash, we can see that the obfuscation of kinship ties in these early conversion accounts is rooted in the generic conventions anchoring the narratives — conventions that must be acknowledged if we want to fully understand the colonial aims that undergird these accounts. When describing some of the methodological considerations necessary for analyzing archival documents, literary theorist Charles Bazerman reminds us that "Making sense of a single claim, sentence, or even datum requires an understanding of what kind of text it appears in, engaged in what sort of inquiry using what methods, and where it stands within the evolving intertextual discussion of the field."[26] Both *New Englands First Fruits* and *A Key into the Language of America* translate Wequash's conversion to their English readers using the generic conventions of the conversion narrative — a genre that was used throughout Puritan New England to record conversion, first for English converts and later for Indigenous ones. As part of a larger Protestant reform movement that prioritized *personal* salvation, the Bay Colony missionaries and Williams were keen to ascertain whether or not Wequash, their potential convert, had made an *individual* choice to accept Christian salvation.

The conventions of the conversion narrative developed in conjunction with the formation of the Puritan church in colonial New England. Separated from the ecclesiastical structures in England, the New England settlers developed their own means of vetting potential members. To illustrate one's readiness for church membership, New England Protestants employed a codified narrative form recited by all church members — the conversion narrative. As literary scholar Patricia Caldwell explains, prior to joining the church, potential members were required to give a "relation before the entire congregation of . . . a genuine experience of conversion (not doctrinal 'knowledge' or 'belief')."[27] Existing church members assessed the potential member's narrative in order to determine its authenticity. In a belief system where only some were chosen by God, the conversion narrative was an attempt to give evidence that one had been chosen — or, as Caldwell terms it, to "merge . . . the visible with the invisible church."[28] The result was a narrative form in which one attempted to publicly display the personal workings of one's soul in order to prove the authenticity of one's individual salvation.

When New England missionaries began actively proselytizing Native people, they adapted the conversion narrative for use by Indigenous converts. Deployed among Native converts, the conversion narrative took on new resonances. Not only were English observers interested in ascertaining the state of an Indigenous convert's soul for spiritual reasons, they were also fascinated by the words and deeds of the seemingly inscrutable and foreign "poor Indians."[29] As literary scholar Sarah Rivett writes, "the testimonies of faith spoken [by the Praying Indians] . . . conjoined the enigma of grace and Baconian procedures of natural science such that a holy empiricism of sorts became a hallmark of Puritan practices of faith."[30] In recording Wequash's words and deeds, Williams and the Bay Colony leaders emphasize the Pequot warrior's distance from his "savage" community as part of their efforts to confirm his readiness to perform Christian civility. For the English authors, Wequash's isolation from his tribal community — his changed cultural performance — is what makes the Pequot man's profession of faith plausible.

While the material conditions of colonialism may have contributed to English conceptions of Wequash as isolated from his Indigenous community, a close look at the archival documents shows that isolation was the product of colonial aims facilitated by generic conventions. By looking at the ways Wequash has been recorded over time, we can see a marked difference in references to Wequash before and after the 1643 conversion accounts. Prior to the publication of the conversion narratives, Wequash is referred to as part of the Narragansett community. He is described by Williams as a "valiant man" living among the Narragansetts who also happens to be a Pequot.[31] During the Pequot war, Wequash is a referenced as a "Pequot guide, a man of great use" or simply as "an Indean called Wequash."[32] Even after his conversion, before the publication of the conversion narratives, Governor John Winthrop refers to Wequash merely as "an Indian."[33] These pre-1643 accounts position Wequash as an integrated member of his Indigenous community — as one Indian among many.

It is only following the publication of the 1643 conversion narratives that Wequash is marked as exceptional. After his death, the story of the Pequot warrior becomes a rhetorical tool for advancing the colonial missionary narrative. From my research, it seems that the Puritan minister Increase Mather is the first to take up the designation of isolation conferred on Wequash by the conversion narrative. In 1677, during King Philip's War, or Metacom's Rebellion, Mather wrote a history *A Relation of the Troubles Which Have Hapned in New-England, By Reason of the Indians There*, which was a history of Indigenous-English relations. When retelling the story of the Pequot War, Mather includes a reference to Wequash. As Mather recounts, Wequash was "a Pequot Captain, who was revolted from the Pequots."[34] Echoing the logic of the conversion narrative, Mather emphasizes Wequash's isolation from the Pequots in order to establish his trustworthiness. It is precisely because Wequash has left the Pequots that the English can rely on him to serve as their guide. Subsequent historians continue to use Mather's designation of Wequash as having "revolted from the Pequot," giving Mather's statement cumulative credibility as historical fact. In the nineteenth century, antiquarian Samuel Drake repeated Mather's designation in *The Book of the Indians*, claiming the Wequash had revolted from the Pequots "upon some disgust received."[35] In the twentieth century, Alfred Cave turned back to this earlier history in his well-known work, *The Pequot War*, in which he defines Wequash as a "renegade Pequot" — a phrase that remains the primary shorthand designation scholars use to refer to the Pequot Captain.[36] For the past 300 years, post-1643 observers of Wequash repeat the logic of the conversion accounts — namely that Wequash's association with the English, be it as a soldier or a convert, is one that inevitably required disassociation from the Algonquians.

Recovering Kinship

While the differences in historical treatment of Wequash over time illuminate the rhetorical aims of the colonial archives, restoring Wequash's kinship ties necessitates that we employ new methodologies to rearrange the archival documents. It is here that the process of digitization comes into play. As historian James Opp points out in his article, "The Colonial Legacies of the Digital Archive" digitization not only allows us to disseminate information to a larger body of readers, it also "produces new relationships and associations through the power of relational databases."[37] In the case of Wequash, the archives and tools made available by digitization have allowed me to position the Pequot man and his conversion in a new light by providing the means to reconnect him to his fellow Algonquians. By taking kinship as my primary organizational premise, I found evidence indicating that Wequash's conversion did not produced isolation, but was rather the outcome of Wequash's desire to restore his Indigenous community.

As several scholars have reminded us, digitization comes with its own methodological aims. The displacement of documents from collections and curatorial influence removes the benefits that come from accumulated archival knowledge. The result is that individual scholars must be exceedingly careful in their interpretative practices. As literary scholar Tanya Clement writes, "The computer's ability to sort and illustrate quantified data helps identify patterns, but understanding why a pattern occurs and determining whether it is one that offers insight into a text requires technologies of self-reflective inquiry."[38] In rearranging the documentary references to New England's first proclaimed Indigenous convert, I am keenly aware of the need to interrogate the underpinnings behind my own methodological approach. My own archive of references to Wequash was guided by my interpretation of seventeenth-century kinship ties — an interpretation created through the close reading of historical documents, ethnographic studies, and conversations with contemporary Indigenous people who challenged me to approach Indigenous kinship as more encompassing and influential than I had previously thought. While my reading of kinship clearly has its limitations, my hope is that in creating an alternative archival history for Wequash, I can complicate the existing narrative of the Pequot man as isolated — a complication which in itself provides a means of enacting Brooks's charge to produce "unfamiliar readings of familiar texts."

When searching for archival references to Wequash, I was guided by the premise that the Pequot man was, by definition, a product of kinship, and that for him to completely break all his kinship ties would be almost antithetical to what it meant to be both Pequot and Algonquian. I started my search for Wequash's kinship ties by looking for seventeenth-century references to the Pequot guide by mining databases like *Early English Books Online*, the *Yale Indian Papers Project*, and *Sabine Americana*. Though the references in those databases were few and far between, they painted a picture of Wequash as deeply inculcated into the networks of kinship that constituted southern New England Algonquian society. While Wequash is often cited as a Pequot, I discovered that his brother, Wequashcook, is often referred to as a Nayantic sachem.[39] Both brothers were the sons of the eastern Nayantic sachem, Wepitamock (brother of Ninigret).[40] As a member of the Nayantic sachemship, Wequash had kinship ties with the Narragansett sachems and close affiliations with Uncas, the Mohegan sachem. As these ties began to come together, a new story started to emerge. For example, Wequash's decision to align himself with the Narragansett during the Pequot War was not treacherous, but was rather the result of his kinship ties to his Narragansett uncle and cousin, Canonicus and Miantonomi — ties that seem to have been shored up after Wequash had a falling out with a specific Pequot leader, the newly appointed Pequot sachem Sassacus, and not the entire tribe.[41] After mapping and tracing these kinship ties, I found that Wequash's network of relations, and indeed Algonquian kinship ties in general, were much broader and sustained than either Williams or the Bay Colony authors had allowed for in their conversion narrative accounts.

To further develop my portrait of Wequash, I turned to later sources, particularly eighteenth- and nineteenth-century ethnographies and the New England town annuals that mapped out the particular settler histories of New England communities. Once housed in county courthouses and local archives, many of the town annuals are increasingly available via Google Books, making them accessible to a much larger readership.

Like the seventeenth-century conversion narratives, these later sources come with their own set of aims and conventions. Eighteenth-century New England settlers spent a substantial amount of time and energy mapping out the genealogical lines of earlier Indigenous people as part of the logic of dispossession. Settler preoccupation with Indigenous genealogy was a way of sanctioning land transactions made by their ancestors. By tracing the lineage of a specific sachem with whom earlier English settlers had some form of a treaty, questionable though it may have been, the settlers attempted to prove that their land claims were just — or that the Indigenous person with whom they had treated indeed had the right to "sell" the land. Nineteenth-century New England town histories likewise worked to recreate Indigenous genealogies as part of settler colonialism's entanglement with blood claims. As O'Brien explains in *Firsting and Lasting*, non-Native New Englanders focused on documenting Indigenous blood lines as a means of illustrating that all the "pure-blooded" Indians had disappeared — a sentiment that allowed them to further justify their dispossession of Native lands.[42]

Yet, when read in a new light, New England town histories can provide us with a rich context for understanding Indigenous lives. These histories are an example of what O'Brien terms "'unexpected' archives," which she defines as archives "that have been underutilized and unappreciated, many of them stemming directly from the relationship of tribal peoples within settler colonialism." To make new use of these archives, O'Brien explains that they "must be appreciated from Indigenous perspectives."[43] When using the Indigenous genealogies recorded in New England settler archives, we must also recognize the differences between genealogy and kinship. Genealogies, or recorded lines of familial descent, only give us a limited picture of kinship as the lines of kinship expand beyond genealogical affiliations. Settler genealogies of Indigenous families were selectively recorded to advance a particular narrative of Indigenous disappearance, meaning they must be read with cautious skepticism. Despite these caveats, genealogies still suggest relational connections among Indigenous people and point to kinship ties that may otherwise be overlooked.

When used to search for information about New England's first convert, digitized New England town histories provided me with a means of further mapping Wequash's kinship ties. In J. Hammond Trumbull's 1852 *History of Connecticut*, I found more details confirming Wequash's ties to the Nayantic. The 1852 history also clarified my suspicions that Wequash was likely a sachem. While the first reference to Wequash as a sachem was made by Williams in an offhand remark, the later histories provide additional details that attest to the fact that Wequash was a sachem among the Pequot who later moved himself and his followers to the Narragansett after his dispute with Sassacus.[44] Knowing Wequash's kinship affiliations and his status as a sachem provided me with the background knowledge to make conjectures about Wequash's relationship to land.

Within Indigenous Studies scholarship, land not only functions as a physical place, but the study of a community's relationship to land serves as its own methodology, in that it provides a means of interpreting and assessing Indigenous communities and their texts. As literary scholars Stephanie Fitzgerald (Cree) and Hilary Wyss explain, Native literary studies strategies rely on a "network of relationships: intellectual, geographical, and textual, all of which gesture toward land as the glue that binds Native communities."[45] Focus on an Indigenous community's relationship to land is not only important because of its significance to Native communal identity, but because arriving settlers sought to obscure Indigenous land rights in their rush to name and claim Indigenous lands for themselves. Given this preoccupation with land, it is not surprising that many local New England histories carefully documented the history of settler land ownership in New England. In an 1877 *History of Guilford, Connecticut*, I discovered information regarding the history of land ownership around Saybrook Fort — the location to which Wequash moved after his conversion to Christianity. As the missionary authors claim in *New Englands First Fruits*, Wequash moved to Saybrook Fort sometime after the end of the Pequot War — likely in 1637 or 1638.[46] According to the 1877 Connecticut history, at the time of Wequash's move, the lands around Saybrook Fort were recognized by Indigenous people and settlers alike as belonging to Wequash and Uncas, the Mohegan sachem who, like Wequash, had kinship ties among the Pequots. In 1639, Uncas treated with George Fenwick and allowed him usage of the land. Later, in 1640 or 1641, Wequash made a similar treaty with the missionary Henry Whitfield.[47]

Together with knowledge of Wequash's kinship ties and his status as a sachem, the land records provide us with the final piece needed to defamiliarize the missionary explanation for Wequash's decision to "dwell among the English at Connecticut." Though Wequash's desire for close ties with the English missionaries may have been one factor motivating his move, the Pequot leader was also moving back to his familial lands after the devastation of the Pequot War. Two seventeenth-century references to Wequash give us insight into the specific ways that kinship guided Wequash's move back to Connecticut. These two references are often overlooked in scholarly analysis of Wequash's conversion. In an October 1637 letter, Williams wrote to Governor Winthrop informing him that "there are many of the scattered Pequot rendezvoused with Uncas the Mohegan Sachem and Wequash the Pequot, who being employed as one of the guides to the English in their late wars, is grown rich, and a Sachem with the Pequots . . ."[48] Six months later, in April 1638, Williams again wrote to Winthrop, this time warning him that, "The Pequots are gathering into one, and plant their old fields, Wequash and Uncas are carrying away the people and their treasure, which belong to yourselves."[49] Significantly, Williams's letters were penned at the same time as the Puritan missionaries claimed that the Pequot man was beginning his journey towards Christian salvation. In the context of kinship, the Pequot sachem moved to the lands around Saybrook Fort to aid Uncas, his relative, as they worked to regather the scattered Pequots.

My study of Wequash as a product of kinship opens several new interpretive possibilities for understanding the Bay Colony's first convert. At the same time as the English leaders crafted their conversion accounts with particular spiritual, political, and social motivations, Wequash performed conversion with a number of other possible motivations — most prominent among them his kinship ties to the Pequots. Kinship also opens up new avenues for understanding English literary forms from a Native point of view. The 1643 accounts of Wequash's conversion helped to fuel a distinct genre of Indigenous conversion narratives. The fact that the first recorded Indigenous conversion narrative in New England was performed by a convert acting out of his kinship ties requires us to continue to rethink the hybrid nature of Puritan literary forms. While the English held the pen, their writings remained grounded in the lives of the actual Algonquians that they encountered upon New England's soil.

As my work with Wequash illustrates, Indigenous kinship ties are not absent or obscure, however, accessing them requires new ways of organizing and reading documents. As we continue to advance in digitization, we need to deeply interrogate our organizational practices to bring kinship to the forefront. Arranging digital archives by early sachems, tribes, and kinship webs would result in a defamiliarization of familiar archives. In archives structured by kinship, Winthrop and Williams would not serve as central organizational nodes, but would rather be part of larger, more expansive networks of relationships. Prioriiizing Native networks also opens up new backgrounds within which to locate early American texts. When we no longer see Wequash as an isolated convert first, but rather as a Pequot who is also a convert, we can rethink the impetus behind Indigenous conversion and reimagine the process of colonial textual production, resulting in a whole host of unfamiliar readings of familiar narratives.

Notes

1. Lisa Brooks, "Turning the Looking Glass on King Philip's War: Locating American Literature in Native Space," *American Literary History* 25:4 (2013): 729.

2. Lisa Brooks, *The Common Pot: The Recovery of Native Space in the Northeast* (Minneapolis: University of Minnesota Press, 2008), 6.

3. Brooks, *Common Pot*, xli.

4. "Project History," *The Occom Circle* (Hanover, NH: Dartmouth College). Last modified 8/16/16, http://www.dartmouth.edu/~occom/project-history accessed May 8, 2017.

5. Kathleen Bragdon, *Native People of Southern New England, 1500–1650* (Norman: University of Oklahoma Press, 1996), 141.

6. William Cronan, *Changes in the Land: Indians, Colonists, and the Ecology of New England: 20th Anniversary Edition* (New York: Farrar, Straus and Giroux, 2003), 59.

7. Brooks, *Common Pot*, 68.

8. Brooks, *Common Pot*, 2.

9. Colin Calloway, *Pen and Ink Witchcraft: Treaties and Treaty Making in American Indian History* (New York: Oxford University Press, 2012), 12.

10. Brooks, *Common Pot*, 5.

11. Brooks, *Common Pot*, 7.

12. Roger Williams, *A Key into the Language of America* (1643) (Bedford, MA: Applewood Books, 1997), 28–29.

13. Jean O'Brien, *Dispossession by Degrees: Indian Land and Identity in Natick, Massachusetts, 1650–1790* (Lincoln: University of Nebraska Press, 1997), 28.

14. Edward Winslow, "The Glorious Progress of the Gospel amongst the Indians in New England," in *The Eliot Tracts with Letters from John Eliot to Thomas Thorowgood and Richard Baxter*, ed. Michael P. Clark (Westport, CT: Praeger Press, 2003), 153–154.

15. Ann Laura Stoler, "Colonial Archives and the Arts of Governance," *Archival Science* 2 (2002): 87.

16. Charles I, *A Copy of the Kings Majesties Charter for Incorporating the Company of the Massachusetts Bay in New-England in America, 1628* (Boston: Printed for S. Green, for Benj. Harris at the London Coffee House, 1689), 22.

17. Hugh Peter and Thomas Weld, "New Englands First Fruits," in *The Eliot Tracts: With Letters from John Eliot to Thomas Thorowgood and Richard Baxter*, 58, 62.

18. Jeffrey Glover, "Wunnaumwáyean: Roger Williams, English Credibility, and the Colonial Land Market," *Early American Literature* 41:3 (2006): 431.

19. Williams, *A Key*, x.

20. Williams, *A Key*, xi.

21. Several scholars have discussed the competing accounts of Wequash in *New Englands First Fruits* and *A Key into the Language of America*. For example, see Kristina Bross, *Dry Bones and Indian Sermons: Praying Indians in Colonial America* (Ithaca: Cornell University Press, 2004), 190–192; Laura Stevens, *The Poor Indians: British Missionaries, Native Americans, and Colonial Sensibility* (Philadelphia: University of Pennsylvania Press, 2004), 185–186; Drew Lopenzina, *Red Ink: Native Americans Picking Up the Pen in the Colonial Period* (Albany: State University of New York Press, 2012), 80–84.

22. Peter and Weld, "New Englands First Fruits," 62.

23. John William De Forest, *History of the Indians of Connecticut from the Earliest Known Period to 1850* (Hartford, CT: WM. JAS. Hamersley, 1853), 179–180.

24. Peter and Weld, "New Englands First Fruits," 61.

25. Alfred Cave, *The Pequot War* (Boston: University of Massachusetts Press, 1996), 49.

26. Charles Bazerman, "The Orders of Documents, the Orders of Activity, and the Orders of Information," *Archival Science* 12 (2012): 385.

27. Patricia Caldwell, *The Puritan Conversion Narrative: The Beginnings of American Expression* (New York: Cambridge University Press, 1985), 45.

28. Caldwell, *The Puritan Conversion Narrative*, 47.

29. Thomas Shepard, "The Clear Sun-Shine of the Gospel Breaking Forth Upon the Indians in New-England," in *The Eliot Tracts: With Letters from John Eliot to Thomas Thorowgood and Richard Baxter*, 110.

30. Sarah Rivett, *The Science of the Soul in Colonial New England* (Chapel Hill: University of North Carolina Press, 2011), 128.

31. Roger Williams, *Letters of Roger Williams 1632–1682*, ed. John Russell Bartlett (Providence: Printed for the Narragansett Club, 1874, 2012 reprint), 18.

32. Williams, *Letters*, 26. Lion Gardiner, *Relation of the Pequot Warres*, ed. Andrew Newman, *Early American Studies* 9:2 (2011): 480.

33. John Winthrop, *The Journal of John Winthrop, 1630–1649*, ed. by Richard S. Dunn, James Savage and Laetitia Yeandle (Cambridge, MA: Harvard University Press, 1996), 69.

34. Increase Mather, *A Relation of the Troubles Which Have Hapned in New-England, By Reason of the Indians There; From the Year 1614. To the Year 1675* (Boston: John Foster, 1677), 31.

35. Samuel Gardner Drake, *The Book of the Indians, Or, Biography and History of the Indians of North America from Its First Discovery to the Year 1841* Book II (Boston: Benjamin B. Mussey, 1841), notes to page 96.

36. Cave, *The Pequot War*, 146, 148. For examples of scholarship repeating Cave's designation of Wequash as a "renegade Pequot," see Lion Gardiner, "Relation of the Pequot Warres," ed. Andrew Neuman, *Early American Studies* 9:2 (2011): 480, n28; Nabil Matar, *Turks, Moors, and Englishmen in the Age of Discovery* (New York: Columbia University Press, 1999), 104; Scott Weidensaul, *The First Frontier: The Forgotten History of Struggle, Savagery and Endurance in Early America* (New York: Houghton Mifflin Harcourt Publishing Company, 2012), 140.

37. James Opp, "The Colonial Legacies of the Digital Archive: The Arnold Lupson Photographic Collection," *Archivaria* 65 (2008): 12.

38. Tanya Clement, "Text Analysis, Data Mining, and Visualizations in Literary Scholarship," in *Literary Studies in the Digital Age: An Evolving Anthology* (New York: Modern Language Association of America, 2013). https://dlsanthology.mla.hcommons.org accessed May 6, 2017.

39. Harman Garrett, "The Humble Declaration of Harman Garrett," (1678). *Yale Indian Papers Project*, New Haven: Yale University, http://hdl.handle.net/10079/digcoll/4062 accessed May 9, 2017.

40. Williams, *Letters*, 170.

41. Michael Leroy Oberg, *Uncas: First of the Mohegans*, (Ithaca, NY: Cornell University Press, 2003), 47.

42. Jean O'Brien, *Firsting and Lasting: Writing Indians Out of Existence in New England* (Minneapolis: University of Minnesota Press, 2010), xxi–xxii.

43. Jean O'Brien, "Historical Sources and Methods in Indigenous Studies: Touching on the Past, Looking to the Future," in *Sources and Methods in Indigenous Studies*, ed. Chris Andersen and Jean O'Brien (New York: Routledge, 2016), 18

44. J. Hammond Trumbull, *The Public Records of The Colony of Connecticut from 1666 to 1678: With the Journal of the Council of War, 1675 to 1678: Transcribed and Edited, In accordance with a Resolution of the General Assembly, with notes and an appendix* (Hartford: F.A. Brown, 1852), note on p. 57. For Williams' reference to Wequash as a sachem, see Williams, *Letters*, 67.

45. Stephanie Fitzgerald and Hilary Wyss, "Land and Literacy: The Textualities of Native Studies," *Early American Literature: Special Joint Issue: Projecting Early American Literary Studies* 45:2 (2010): 241.

46. Peter and Weld, "New Englands First Fruits," 62. Governor Winthrop's journal confirms that Wequash was residing at Saybrook Fort at the time of his death, though he may have lived in other areas around Connecticut. In 1642, Winthrop writes that Wequash, "an Indian, living about Connecticut river's mouth, and keeping much at Saybrook with Mr. Fenwick, attained to good knowledge of the things of God and salvation by Christ, so as he became a preacher to other Indians, and labored much to convert them, but without any effect, for within a short time he fell sick, not without suspicion of poison from them, and died very comfortably," Winthrop, *Journal of John Winthrop*, 69.

47. Edward Elias Atwater, *History of the Colony of New Haven to Its Absorption into Connecticut* (New Haven: Printed for the Author, 1881), 332–333. It seems that Uncas sold the land sometime in 1639, given the fact that Winthrop records Fenwick and his family settling in the location at that time. See Winthrop, *Journal of John Winthrop*, 299. As Atwater explains, the location gave Uncas easy access to Pequot lands across the Connecticut River. After Uncas treated with Fenwick, he withdrew to the east side of the Connecticut River, "to a region which had formerly belonged to his ancestors, the Pequot sachems, [and] was assigned to him as a portion of the spoils of war," Atwater, *History of the Colony of New Haven*, 333.

48. Williams, *Letters*, 67.

49. Williams, *Letters*, 92.

EIGHT

Reading Tipâcimôwin

and the Receding Archive

Susan Paterson Glover

The rich resources of nineteenth-century Cree syllabic material in the archives of the Methodist and Anglican churches of Canada remain to be explored fully for their contributions to our understandings of Indigenous networks of literacies and communications in northern Canada in the nineteenth century. Much of this material, some of which was produced on handmade printing presses in northern Canada, remains housed in archival and library collections, both physically unavailable to the communities whose ancestors created it, and — increasingly — linguistically difficult to access, as the Cree family of languages continues to evolve. With the inroads of spoken and written English and French, younger members of the communities are increasingly unable to read syllabics, a short-hand based form of writing the language created by Methodist missionary James Evans using variously oriented geometric characters to represent syllables and single segments of words.[1] While digitization of surviving archival texts offers the obvious benefits of preservation and distributed access, the implications are equally obvious; if they are made more readily available, who will be able to read them with comprehension and provide historically informed interpretation?

This chapter explores the introduction of Evans's Cree syllabic system in northern Canada, elements of reader reception that aided the very rapid and widespread adoption and implementation of this system, and the logistical and interpretive challenges in accessing the surviving documents currently held in various archival collections. In so doing, it will illuminate some of the complexities inherent in the implementation of Canada's Truth and Reconciliation Commission's Calls 67 through 70 to museums and archives for reviews of current practices.[2]

The discussion begins with a short contextual account of the missionary activities of the Church of England and the Wesleyan Methodist Church in British North America following the American Revolution. An extensive historical archive has accumulated in Canadian collections providing evidence for both the adoption in print and manuscript form of Cree syllabics, and the reading practices and literacies deployed by the Cree peoples who adopted the system. Finally, it reflects upon some of the logistical and theoretical challenges posed by any consideration of possible digital access to this material. As noticed elsewhere in this collection, difficult questions of competing possessory claims and jurisdictions, intellectual property, the settler-colonial bias of provenance, and the realities of physical storage complicate efforts to extend reconciliation to this component of the colonial archive.

Mission Work and Print in British North America following the American Revolution

The Church of England's missionary work in the North American colonies was undertaken early in the eighteenth century by the Society for the Propagation of the Gospel in Foreign Parts (SPG) established in 1701, and its educational work was supported by the Society for Promoting Christian Knowledge (SPCK), founded two years earlier. Most of the attention during its first century was directed to the thirteen colonies in America, but following the revolution, the focus shifted northwards to Canada. The first Anglican bishop in North America, Charles Inglis, was appointed in 1787, and King's College was established in Nova Scotia in 1789 to prepare clergy. This was, in part, a relocation of the King's College founded by King George II in New York in 1754, reorganized after the revolution as Columbia University.[3] While the primary concern of the SPG was the unchurched settler community, Church of England missionaries were sent to minister to Indigenous communities at the Bay of Quinte, the Grand River (the Six Nations community established on the Grand River north of Lake Erie under Joseph Brant following the revolution), Lake St. Clair, and the north shore of Lake Huron, including Manitoulin Island. Of particular interest to this discussion is the church's focus on education: most of its clergy were university men, and there remains to this day in Canada a strong tradition of Anglican colleges and schools; for example, Canada's largest university, the University of Toronto, began as an Anglican college. In his study of the encounter of Indigenous peoples and Christian missionaries in Canada, John Webster Grant notes the Anglican "insistency on the primacy of the written word, attaching scarcely less importance to schoolmasters than to preachers."[4] At the close of the eighteenth century, the more evangelical Christian Missionary Society was founded in 1799, and in 1820 it sent its first missionary, the Rev. John West, to the Selkirk Settlement in Rupert's Land, the land granted to the Hudson's Bay Company, comprising the entire watershed of Hudson's Bay, to start a school for Indians there. One of his students, Sakacewescan, baptized as Henry Budd, would later become the first Indigenous priest ordained in the Anglican Church in North America.

The mission field was a competitive one, and the efforts of the Anglican Church frequently conflicted with the work of the Methodists, while both engaged in an intense rivalry with their Roman Catholic counterparts. A chance meeting between a young Methodist missionary, James Evans, and the Governor of the Hudson's Bay Company, Sir George Simpson, on the north shore of Lake Huron in the spring of 1839, led to an invitation to the Wesleyan Methodist Missionary Society to send three young men to establish missions in Rupert's Land, with Evans to serve as Superintendent. Although Roman Catholic and Anglican missions were established in the Red River area, the Hudson's Bay Company was motivated less by concern for an equitable settler spiritual offering to the peoples of Rupert's Land than by a strategic interest in halting the drift of hunters to the settlements to the south, as well as the need to at least appear to respond to the condition attached to the Company's charter renewal in 1837 that "it improve the Indians' spiritual condition."[5] As a result, permission was granted to establish missions at Norway House, Rainy Lake, Fort Edmonton, and Moose Factory, the latter first established as a Hudson's Bay Company post in southern James Bay in 1673. The missionaries, and the Mission society and supporters back in England who prayed for and financed them, intended to introduce their approach to Christian faith through personal teaching and preaching, but also through the provision of manuscript and printed texts. These could allow the learning process to continue during the long periods of time when people were away from the forts and missions hunting and travelling, hence the urgency to write out, and later print, translations of hymns, catechisms, the gospels, and portions of the Old and New Testaments. There is anecdotal evidence that people read and prayed together and discussed their texts, serving, as some scholars have pointed out, almost as "lay missionaries" to one another.[6]

Evans arrived at the Rossville Mission near Norway House at the northern end of Lake Winnipeg in the summer of 1840, but had already considerable experience working in Indigenous languages, having taught at several missions in what is now southern Ontario. The Canadian Conference of the Methodist Church had appointed a committee to prepare an orthographic system for the Ojibwa language. By 1836, Evans, one of its members, had devised a syllabary, which the Bible Society in Toronto rejected because of the expense of creating a new font. It is likely that Evans would have also known of the Cherokee writing system to the south that by 1828 had led to a high literacy rate and, among other things, a weekly newspaper. On his arrival at the mission, Evans drew on his experiences and his studies the previous winter to develop a syllabary for the Cree language and began copying out texts for distribution. There are varying claims for the origins of the syllabic system: as a gift to the Cree people from the spirit world, the possible influence of the Lutheran and Moravian missionaries who introduced writing to the Greenland Inuit in the 1700s, and Cree practices of using trail signs and pictographs or other forms of inscribed communication.[7] The discussion here focuses on the decade following the introduction of the system devised by Evans.

The labor involved in manuscript production, and the increasing demand, quickly led Evans to experiment with making a printing press. According to Egerton Young, Evans used the thin sheets of tin from the containers used to ship tea to make metal type, clay for molds, and chimney soot mixed with sturgeon oil for ink. A fur press was modified to press type to paper.[8] After weeks of frustrated efforts, on October 15, 1841, Evans recorded in his journal that the first sheets with images of the syllabic alphabet had been printed.[9] He wrote the following spring to Joseph Stinson, former superintendent of Methodist missions in Upper Canada, of his successful year: in addition to 173 names on the Baptismal Register at Norway House, "I have made a fount of Indian type — press & every thing necessary, & besides making a nearly four months voyage — have printed about 5000 pages in the Mushkego [Swampy Cree] language. Among other things a small volume of Hymns &c., which is bound, 100 copies, of sixteen pages each. For this purpose I prepared a *syllabic* Alphabet such as I presented to the Bible Soc in Toronto in '36. and of which they disapproved."[10] Joyce Banks and Bruce Peel have established that Evans printed at least seven books at Rossville, with the likelihood that a number of other productions have since been lost. His request for a press and font of syllabic characters was finally answered, but not until 1845, and the press arrived shortly before Evans's departure for England. His co-worker and fellow Methodist missionary, William Mason, and his wife Sophia, together with Henry Bird Steinhauer, an Anishinaabe (Ojibwe) teacher at the mission, and another assistant, Metis John Sinclair, continued the work for the subsequent nine years (to be discussed further), but printing in the north then moved to the second press in the region, at the Anglican mission at Moose Factory. As demand increased, printing in syllabics was increasingly done in England at presses with syllabic fonts and sent back on the ships that sailed into Hudson's Bay.

Reader Reception and Networks of Literacy in the North

Even with substantial assistance from Sinclair and Steinhauer, Evans found the process laborious and time-consuming. He wrote to his brother Ephraim of his request to the Hudson's Bay Company in London for permission to import a printing press, fully aware of their policy to allow no such device into their territory: "They doubtless fear that the spread of knowledge will endanger their hold on the hunters."[11] Evans returned from one of his lengthy tours in March of 1841 to learn that the Missionary Society had agreed to send a press, but the Hudson's Bay Company had insisted it could be used only for missionary material, and all work had to be approved by Chief Factor Donald Ross. The Hudson's Bay Company had every reason to fear the printing press; once the communication technology was introduced, it was beyond the control of the Church and the missionaries, and there is ample evidence that the Cree peoples adopted and adapted it to serve their own needs. The Church's possibly naïve intention may have been a unidirectional transmission, but in practice it was a multidirectional exchange of written texts that spread from northern Quebec to the Rocky Mountains.

The surviving documentation does not appear to suggest that the Churches shared the Hudson's Bay Company's concerns about the impact of increased literacies, or worried that the readers and writers might use this new form of communication to share their own forms of spirituality. For example, Jennifer Brown has suggested that the use of syllabics as a form of communication may have contributed to the rise of the prophetic movement begun by Cree leaders Abishabis and Wasitek on the James Bay coast in the early 1840s.[12] Several decades later, John McLean, one of Evans's biographers, wrote tantalizingly of the success of the syllabic system and its widespread use among the Northern and Plains Cree and the Stony Indians, who "read the books printed in this system fluently, and write letters in it; some of which I have in my possession. A short time ago, a band of Indians in the far north sent a letter written in these characters on a piece of birch-bark by one of their number, imparting information concerning their ideas of liberty and government."[13]

In their comparison of syllabic systems in North America and China, R. Alison Lewis and Louis-Jacques Dorais point out that "the Cree soon started using the system towards their own ends, writing letters to relatives and friends, and noting down events such as births and deaths in their family Bibles. Some even wrote up their daily diary. Rather than remaining a mere missionary tool for evangelizing Aboriginals, syllabics thus really became the people's own way of communicating among themselves."[14] Methodist missionary George Barnley recorded that in 1842 an Indian unknown to him came in to trade at Rupert House, now Waskaganish, on James Bay, and requested "'a beaver,' a unit of currency at the trading posts, of writing paper from the manager."[15] The Scottish writer Robert Ballantyne has left a lively and engaging account of his six years with the Hudson's Bay Company. In it he describes canoeing across the lake to the Rossville mission and spending a pleasant afternoon at the parsonage in 1843, "admiring the rapidity and ease with which the Indian children could read and write the Indian language by means of a syllabic alphabet invented by their clergyman."[16] The same year Robert Rundle, to the west at Rocky Mountain House, was receiving letters written in Cree syllabics from the Cree chief Maskepetoon.[17] By May 1844, Evans could write to Simpson with optimistic accounts of the fur produce, the garden yields, and the flourishing school with its fifty-seven students. In reference to his syllabic system he adds, "indeed there are but few, and these principally old people, that are not able to address any of their friends by letter in the Native language, with far greater correctness than half of the lower classes of Great Britain."[18] In their study of the use of Cree syllabics, John W. Berry and Jo Anne Bennett suggest that by the beginning of the twentieth century, literacy rates in syllabic script in Native populations across northern Canada "were probably close to 100%, and certainly higher than among non-Native sectors of the Canadian populations."[19]

To the east, at Moose Factory on James Bay, Barnley also experimented with a handmade press and syllabic printing, but by 1847 the Methodist mission there had been abandoned. The mission was eventually transferred to the (Anglican) Church Missionary Society, and John Horden installed in 1851 as a teacher; he was shortly thereafter ordained, and became the first bishop of Moosonee in 1872. Initially, there was little enthusiasm for the continued production of missionary materials in Indigenous languages, in the belief that the acquisition of English should be promoted. This view changed when Bishop David Anderson visited Moose Factory in the summer of 1852. In his diary entry for July 29 he noted, "to see them with their books is novel to me: these are little paper books, in which Mr. Horden writes out for them in the syllabic character, the Ten Commandments, the Creed, and the Lord's Prayer, with the opening versicles of the Prayer-book, and a few leading texts containing the essence of the Gospel; added to these are a few short hymns; and these they copy out and multiply themselves. . . . I read to them a part of the commencement of the Prayer-book from Mr. Hunter's translation, and they at once turned to it in their books."[20] The next day, he met with Isaac Hardesty, who was assigned as his guide, and asked him to write something, "which he did with ease. I gave him a pencil instead of ink; this he said would do for his children, the eldest of whom he was teaching to write, but that for himself he preferred the ink, as more permanent and durable."[21] He is surprised when a visiting family asks for paper: "I did not at first understand, though knowing well the Indian word," adding that "This, and the petition for ink above, are novel among Indians generally," but in his journal entry for July 31 he notes that Hardesty's wife "writes quite as well as he does himself."[22] He continues: "The great novelty to me is to find Indians looking into a book, and that a book bearing on another world and their souls, and in their own tongue . . . . They have, some of them, a case for their little books, two bark boards, like the oaken boards of old binding; these, tied together with a leather thong, make the treasure. This they will carry sixty miles off, and there they will read it together . . . . Mr. Horden is as yet the chief scribe over them, but many from among themselves are, as it were, scribes of the Lord."[23] These comments, taken from David Anderson's published account of his travels in the James Bay area in the mid-nineteenth century, hint at the enormity of the transition that had begun. Even at the presumably retrospective distance of writing or at least revising in England, the word "novel" proliferates in his narrative — he is clearly unprepared for what he encounters. Observing a young man in the act of reading as he prepares for baptism, Anderson wonders: "Should I then deny him?"[24]

Much of the evidence for these reading practices is anecdotal and, of course, all derives from the colonial archive. Like the Jesuits before them, the missionaries had overseers and benefactors back home for whom they wished to demonstrate at least progress, if not success, in their endeavors. Historians of this field have noted the very difficult — and often unsuccessful — transition evident in journals and letters as young men from England lived through long stretches of time immersed in the northern landscape and Indigenous cultures, struggling with guilt, self-doubt, and faltering faith (see in particular, John Murdoch). Yet there is little evidence of fears or doubts on the part of the Churches about the two-edged sword they had freely given.

Anglican and Methodist Archives

Many of the Church of England missionaries brought with them their Oxbridge backgrounds, their commitment to education, and their libraries. A special issue of the *Journal of the Canadian Church Historical Society* (2008–2012) was devoted to Anglican libraries in Canada, beginning with the libraries established by Thomas Bray, founder of both the SPCK and the SPG; during his lifetime he set up thirty-nine libraries in the North American colonies.[25] In 1985, Karen Evans published a bibliography of native language imprints held in the archives and libraries of the Anglican Church of Canada; there are 746 entries, with eighty-four editions printed between 1780 and 1899.[26] Rare copies of the booklets printed in Cree syllabics at Moose Factory are held in the James Evans Fonds at Victoria University, University of Toronto.

There is also significant manuscript material: the Diocese of Moosonee Fonds, held in the Special Collections of the J. N. Desmarais Library, Laurentian University, includes the undated manuscript for John Sanders's translation of the Psalms into "Ojibway" (Anishinaabemowin) syllabics. Sanders (1845–1902) was born at a Hudson's Bay Company trading post south of James Bay; his father was a canoe maker for the Hudson's Bay Company and Sanders grew up speaking Anishinaabemowin, later learning English and Cree. He eventually became a catechist, teacher, and translator at Moose Factory under Bishop John Horden, who later ordained him as deacon and then priest in 1879.[27] The Moosonee Fonds also holds the manuscript of Thomas Vincent's translation into Cree syllabics of John Bunyan's *Pilgrim's Progress* that he took to England and had published in London in 1886. Vincent's father John was the son of Thomas Vincent, a fur trader who rose to become governor of the Southern Department of the Hudson's Bay Company, and his Indigenous wife Jane Renton. John Vincent's limited prospects as a "half breed Son" may have prompted the family's move to Manitoba, where his son Vincent was able to graduate from St. John's Collegiate School in Winnipeg. Following graduation he worked with the Rev. Horden as a catechist and teacher at Moose Factory, and assisted with the translation and printing of texts at the mission there.[28] In 1863, Vincent was ordained as a priest in the Church of England. He was made Archdeacon of Moosonee in 1883, and was thought by many to have merited appointment as the first Indigenous bishop when Horden returned to England, but his Metis status posed too great an obstacle to a church ostensibly committed to supporting Indigenous ministry.

The Problem of "Access"

The concept of access here connotes a range of possibilities, from simply viewing signs on a (paper or digital) page, to the fraught questions of authorial intention, meaning making, reception, textual interpretation, language and translation, bibliographic evidence, and temporal and cultural barriers, perhaps for both author and reader — all the elements bound up in the noun's connotative signification of "the right to come near or into contact with someone or something."[29] Just what is the reader "accessing" when encountering these texts? As is the case with much archival material arising from Indigenous-settler relations, the most immediate problem remains physical admission to documents; much of this material is held in library, museum, and university special collections, often many hundreds of miles from their points of origin and the communities from which they emerged. To encounter them in person may require extensive (and expensive) travel, a familiarity with library and archival practices, and knowledge of where to look in the first place. Opening hours are limited, archival collections are often closed on weekends, and archival staff resources often stretched.

Once physical access is achieved, one is then faced with both the familiar challenges of "translation" from one language to another, but in this case the more daunting prospect of moving between temporal and epistemological worlds. The digital medium appears to offer at least a partial solution to the problem of physical access, allowing for a much wider readership, but brings its own challenges of deracination, loss of control of access and textual integrity, and a further removal from any land-text nexus that might locate meaning. The matter of translation, an issue particularly relevant to the Indigenous-created texts under discussion here, also raises a number of highly complex research demands: how might we recover that reciprocal exchange of the spiritual imaginary as early nineteenth-century Indigenous catechists, teachers, and clergy worked to carry the scripture and liturgy of the English Churches across into other worlds and languages?

Much has been written about the influence of the King James Bible and the 1662 Book of Common Prayer on English language, writing, and thought; what do we know about the transformation of their metaphors, imagery, and meaning into Indigenous spiritual worlds, imaginaries, languages, and texts? And what might the non-Indigenous reader have to learn from the transformation of familiar texts into other ways of reading? Earle H. Waugh concludes his incisive and thoughtful article, "Religious Issues in the Alberta Elders' Cree Dictionary," with an acknowledgement of the difficulties in "translating" European religious history into Cree understandings of their universe.[30] The intellectual, spiritual, imaginative, and linguistic work of any religious translation is considerable, yet in the study of these historical texts, the work of Indigenous translators — a group that includes the Indigenous wives of missionaries — has been neglected. There has been little attention to Vincent's translation work, for example, apart from that of Arlette Zink and Sylvia Brown, and more recently Stephanie Fitzgerald, Bryan Kuwada, and Phillip Round.[31] By focusing on *Indigenous* readers, the latter article begins to open the kind of analysis that would foster this exploration, but what is needed is more comment and analysis from, in this case, readers of Cree syllabics, a treasured but small and diminishing group.

Passing time lends a certain urgency to this call. In surveying Cree-speaking communities in northern Ontario in the mid-1990s, Berry and Bennett found that while older people in the communities continued to use the syllabic script, increasingly those under the age of forty relied on spoken and written English and Roman orthography.[32] The retired bishop of the Anglican Diocese of Moosonee, the Right Reverend Tom Corston, notes that the Horden translations in the Moose Cree dialect are still in widespread use, but that there are problems with accessibility for those regions that speak other forms of Cree; there are four dialects in the diocese. Many of those who are able to understand and speak Moose Cree are unable to read or write syllabics, and rely on older priests and elders who are still able to read the old translations. He also notes that many of the residents who attended residential schools reported losing their ability to read and write in their language.[33] Several translation projects sponsored by the Cree Initiative, a joint project supported by the Canadian Bible Society and Wycliffe Bible Translators, are currently underway to provide new Indigenous-led translations of scriptural and liturgical material for five of the Cree language groups. The work includes a translation group in Kingfisher Lake, led by Bishop Lydia Mamakwa, area bishop for the Indigenous Spiritual Ministry of Mishamikoweesh, the Anglican Church of Canada's first entirely Indigenous diocese covering territory in northwestern Ontario and northern Alberta. The members are producing translations of portions of the Book of Common Prayer, lectionary readings, and the gospels in their language of Oji-Cree, using the syllabic writing system. There is also a project to reproduce the 1862 Mason Bible; despite the now archaic Plains Cree that few are able to read with comprehension, it is seen as a "legacy Bible as a Cree equivalent of the English King James version."[34] Gayle Weenie, who works on the Plains Cree translation in Saskatchewan, finds it "a way to reverse the impact of the residential schools."[35]

Since the introduction of scriptural texts in syllabics by missionaries in the nineteenth century, speakers of all forms of Cree relied on the Cree Bible translated by Mason, who had succeeded Evans at the mission at Rossville, with the assistance of his Cree-speaking metis wife Sophia, and his Indigenous associates Steinhauer, a teacher, and Sinclair, an interpreter. Steinhauer, an Anishinaabe from Upper Canada, had been educated at the Methodist Cazenovia Seminary at Cazenovia, and the Upper Canada Academy, and Sinclair worked as an interpreter at the mission. This suggests that the Cree translation was very much a collaborative undertaking, even though Mason's name alone appeared on the title page. Elsewhere, he credited his wife's contribution, but did not acknowledge the work of his male assistants. The Masons had left Rossville in 1854 and transferred their allegiance to the Church of England, moving to York Factory that year, and from there travelling to London to oversee first the printing of the translation of the New Testament (1859), and then a printing of the Old and New Testaments that formed the 1862 Bible.[36]

In *Native Tongues: Colonialism and Race from Encounter to the Reservation* (2015), Sean Harvey offers a comprehensive overview of nineteenth-century colonial studies together with analyses of, and interventions into, Indigenous languages, including the introduction of the Cherokee syllabary, and notes the polarizing effect: "Its advocates held it up as the invention of writing that philosophers had conjectured was the harbinger of civilization" while traditionalists argued for its role in an Indigenous education to maintain "cultural and political sovereignty."[37] As reading ability declines, syllabics will increasingly fail on both fronts, and the possibilities of reentering that time of encounter and transfer of knowledge diminishes and fades. Round has called for a reimaging of bibliographic practices that would bring together the most recent, innovative thinking in book history and American Indian Studies in order to highlight "the materiality, ideology, and the social life of texts," and calls particularly for such an initiative to be grounded on the bibliographic work of Donald McKenzie.[38] State, church, and educational institutions have acquired documents in a variety of ways, and the question of provenance and ownership remains largely uncontested. Materials accumulated over more than two centuries through missionary work have fallen by default to church archives, with little thought to matters of copyright or authorial rights, themselves Western concepts that, like property in land, were never "negotiated." The digitization of texts provides a partial circumvention of these constraints, but other factors impede the fuller exploration called for by Round.

In volume six of *The Final Report of the Truth and Reconciliation Commission of Canada* (2015), the Commission lays out a series of ninety-four Calls To Action, designed to address the challenge of "reconciliation" in the wake of the commission's extensive hearings held across Canada into decades of widespread abuse and neglect in Canada's residential schools for First Nations, Inuit, and Métis children.[39] Several of these Calls explicitly address the role of Canada's museums and archives. While the Commission's focus was primarily on documents and records pertinent to the history of residential schools, its recommendations have more far-reaching implications. Call 70 specifically requested funding for the Canadian Association of Archivists "to undertake, in collaboration with Aboriginal peoples, a national review of archival policies and best practices" in order to determine the level of compliance with the *United Nations Declaration on the Rights of Indigenous Peoples* and the *United Nations Joinet-Orentlicher Principles* and to produce a report with recommendations.[40] The Association has responded through its participation in the Steering Committee for Canada's Archives, which has a working group focused on responding specifically to Call 70. Additionally, Library and Archives Canada has announced new initiatives to expand digital access to its documentary holdings and support digitization of Indigenous-language recordings, under the guidance of an Indigenous Advisory Circle.[41] Many smaller institutions, however, lack the resources to undertake this kind of work; when contacted, the collections holding the archival material cited here, for example, indicated that there were no immediate plans to digitize the materials. Some of the manuscript documents in the James Evans Fonds in the Western Archives, Western University are available on compact discs, but there are no facilities for viewing these in the library and researchers are asked to bring their own laptops. Nevertheless, it appears that change is underway, and "the materiality, ideology, and the social life of texts" may indeed become the focus of digital approaches to the Indigenous archive.

In the fall of 2017, Abenaki filmmaker Alanis Obomsawin released a documentary film about the Helen Betty Osborne Ininiw Education Resource Centre, the acclaimed elementary-secondary Cree school at Norway House Cree Nation. Titled *Our People Will Be Healed*, the film reflects Obomsawin's delight in the "new sense of optimism" she experienced at the First Nations school where "children are thriving" in an environment that immerses them in their language and history.[42] Norway House, the site of the Hudson's Bay Company post, is less than three miles from the nearby Rossville mission where Evans developed his form of syllabics. Yet when asked if students at the school were taught to use the syllabic system of writing, a resource teacher there replied, "No . . . no, not at all." Evans introduced his form of inscribing the language there in the early 1840s. Time will tell if this form of language, and the life, thought, and response to encounter it articulated, becomes another of the worlds we have lost.

Notes

1. John D. Nichols, "The Cree Syllabary," in *The World's Writing Systems*, ed. Peter T. Daniels and William Bright (New York: Oxford University Press, 1996), 599.

2. Truth and Reconciliation Commission of Canada, "The Final Report of the Truth and Reconciliation Commission of Canada," Vol. 6. *Canada's Residential Schools: Reconciliation* (Montreal & Kingston: McGill-Queen's Press, 2015).

3. University of King's College, "History," *University of King's College* https://ukings.ca /campus-community/about-kings/history/ accessed August 20, 2017.

4. John Webster Grant, *Moon of Wintertime: Missionaries and the Indians of Canada in Encounter since 1534* (Toronto: University of Toronto Press, 1984), 112.

5. John S. Long, "The Reverend George Barnley and the James Bay Cree," *Canadian Journal of Native Studies* 6:2 (1986): 313–31 http://www3.brandonu.ca/cjns/6.2/long.pdf accessed August 20, 2017.

6. Martha McCarthy, *From the Great River to the Ends of the Earth: Oblate Missions to the Dene, 1847–1921* (Edmonton: University of Alberta Press, 1995), 80, 156, cited in Patricia A. McCormack, *Fort Chipewyan and the Shaping of Canadian History, 1788–1920s* (Vancouver: University of British Columbia Press, 2010), 114. See also Sean Harvey, *Native Tongues: Colonialism and Race from Encounter to the Reservation* (Cambridge, MA: Harvard University Press, 2015), 44.

7. For discussion of syllabics as a gift from the spirit world, see "Another Version of Cree Literacy: The Cree Story of Syllabics," Cree Literacy Network, http://creeliteracy .org/beginning-to-read-plains-cree-in-standard-roman-orthography/another-version -of-cree-literacy-the-cree-story-of-syllabics; David G. Mandelbaum, *The Plains Cree:*

An Ethnographic, Historical, and Comparative Study (New York: Columbia Population Research Center, 1940), 180; Winona Stevenson, "Calling Badger and the Symbols of the Spirit Language," *Oral History Forum d'histoire orale* 19/20 (1999–2000), 19–24.

8. Egerton R. Young, *The Apostle of the North: Rev. James Evans* (Toronto: Fleming H. Revell, 1899), 188–89.

9. Robert Peel, "Rossville Mission Press: Press, Prints and Translators," *Papers of the Bibliographical Society of Canada* 1:1 (1962): 28–43, 29.

10. James Evans to Joseph Stinson, June 11, 1841 in James Evans Fonds, Correspondence of James Evans. Box 1. E. J. Pratt Library, Victoria University, Toronto.

11. James Evans to Ephraim Evans, n.d., quoted in Roger Burford Mason, *Travels in the Shining Island: The Story of James Evans and the Invention of the Cree Syllabary Alphabet* (Toronto: Natural Heritage Books, 1996), 55.

12. Jennifer Brown, "The Wasitay Religion: Prophecy, Oral Literacy, and Belief on Hudson Bay," in *Reassessing Revitalization Movements: Perspectives from North America and the Pacific Islands*, ed. Michael E. Harkin (Lincoln: University of Nebraska Press, 2004), 104–123, 106.

13. John McLean, (Robin Rustler), *The Indians: Their Manners and Customs* (Toronto: Briggs, 1889), 256.

14. Lewis, R. Alison and Louis-Jacques Dorais. "Two Related Indigenous Writing Systems: Canada's Syllabic and China's A-Hmao Scripts," *Canadian Journal of Native Studies* 23:2 (2003): 277–304 .

15. Barnley, National Archives of Canada, George Barnley Journal, MG 20, J40, November 13, 1841, quoted in Hans. M. Carlson, "Home is the Hunter: Subsistence, Reciprocity, and the Negotiation of Cultural Environment Among the James Bay Cree," Ph.D. dissertation, University of Maine, 2005, p. 26.

16. Robert M. Ballantyne, *Hudson's Bay; or Every-Day Life in the Wilds of North America During Six Years' Residence in the Territories of The Honourable Hudson's Bay Company.* A facsimile of the 1848 edition (Edmonton, AB: Hurtig, 1972), 130.

17. John Stewart Murdoch, "Syllabics: A Successful Educational Innovation." (Master's thesis, University of Manitoba, 1981), 5. http://www.bac-lac.gc.ca/eng/services/theses /Pages/theses-canada.aspx accessed September 10, 2017.

18. James Evans to George Simpson May 16, 1844, in Fonds.

19. John W. Berry and Jo Anne Bennett. "Syllabic Literacy and Cognitive Performance among the Cree and Ojibwe People of Northern Canada," in *Scripts and Literacy: Reading and Learning to Read Alphabets, Syllabaries and Characters*, ed. Insup Taylor and David R. Olson, 341–357. (Dordrecht: Springer Science+Business, 1995), 349–50.

20. Anderson, David. *The Bishop of Rupert's Land. The Net in the Bay; or, Journal of a Visit to Moose and Albany*(London: T. Hatchard, 1854), 93–94.

21. Anderson, *The Bishop*, 96–97.

22. Anderson, *The Bishop*, 98.

23. Anderson, *The Bishop*, 99.

24. Anderson, *The Bishop*, 99.

25. Richard Virr, "A Precious Heritage and a Great Challenge: Anglican Libraries in Canada," *Journal of the Canadian Church Historical Society* 50:1 (2008–2012): 5–15, 9. accessed August 31, 2017.

26. Karen Evans, comp., *Masinahikan: Native Language Imprints in the Archives and Libraries of the Anglican Church of Canada* (Toronto: Anglican Book Centre, 1985).

27. Donald B. Smith, "Sanders, John," *Dictionary of Canadian Biography*, s.v. http://www.biographi.ca/en/bio/sanders_john_13E.html accessed August 31, 2016.

28. John S. Long, "Vincent, Thomas," *Dictionary of Canadian Biography*, s.v. http://www.biographi.ca/en/bio/vincent_thomas_1835_1907_13E.html accessed August 15, 2017.

29. "access," *Oxford English Dictionary Online*, s.v. http://www.oed.com.librweb.laurentian.ca/view/Entry/1028?rskey=Vn0cdd&result=1&isAdvanced=false#eid accessed August 15, 2017.

30. Earle H. Waugh, "Religious Issues in the Alberta Elders' Cree Dictionary." *Numen* 48:4 (2001):468–90. doi:10.1163/156852701317092904. http://web.b.ebscohost.com.librweb.laurentian.ca/ehost/pdfviewer/pdfviewer?vid=1&sid=6ec7430a-6306-4281-8b89-b25e2f4bfbee%40sessionmgr103 accessed September 3, 2017.

31. See Arlette Zink and Sylvia Brown, "The *Pilgrim's Progress* Among Aboriginal Canadians," *1650-1850: Ideas, Æsthetics, and Inquiries in the Early Modern Era* 13 (2006): 201-23.; Stephanie Fitzgerald, Bryan Kuwada, and Philip H. Round, "Pilgrims in Print: Indigenous Readers Encounter John Bunyan," *Common-place.org* 15:4 (2015). http://common-place.org/book/pilgrims-in-print-indigenous-readers-encounter-john-bunyan/ accessed August 31, 2017.

32. Berry and Bennett, "Syllabic Literacy," 345.

33. Bishop Thomas Corston, e-mail message to author, August 21, 2017.

34. Dwayne Janke, *Word Alive* 35:1 (2017). https://www.wycliffe.ca/wycliffe/ck_assets/admin/files/wam/wam_2017_jan-apr.pdf accessed August 20, 2017, 14.

35. Janke, *Word Alive*, 14.

36. Joyce M. Banks, "The Printing of the Cree Bible," *Papers of the Bibliographical Society of Canada* 22:1 (1983): 12–24, 17–21. http://jps.library.utoronto.ca/index.php/bsc/article/viewFile/17526/14460 accessed August 21, 2017.

37. Sean Harvey, *Native Tongues: Colonialism and Race from Encounter to the Reservation* (Cambridge: Harvard University Press, 2015), 144.

38. Phillip H. Round, "Bibliography and the Sociology of American Indian Texts," *Textual Cultures: Texts, Contexts, Interpretations* 6:2 (2011): 119–32, 121. http://www.jstor.org.librweb.laurentian.ca/stable/10.2979/textcult.6.2.119 accessed August 14, 2017.

39. Truth and Reconciliation Commission of Canada, "The Final Report," 144.

40. Truth and Reconciliation Commission of Canada, "The Final Report," 144–145.

41. "Indigenous Documentary Heritage Initiatives," Library and Archives Canada, https://www.bac-lac.gc.ca/eng/discover/aboriginal-heritage/Pages/indigenous-documentary-heritage-initiatives.aspx.

42. Nick Patch, "Alanis Obomsawin on Her 50th Film, and Why She Won't Stop," *Toronto Star*, September 9, 2017. https://www.thestar.com/entertainment/tiff/2017/09/09/alanis-obomsawin-on-her-50th-film-and-why-she-wont-stop.html accessed September 10, 2017.

NINE

Re-Incurating Tribal Skins: Re-Imagining the Native Archive, Re-Stor(y)ing the Tribal Imagi(Native)

Gordon Henry

A Post-Colonial Allegory — Vizenor in the Curatorium

Gerald Vizenor's experience in the archive, as way of finding a unique, transformative, historical identity, also opens to one of Bill Ashcroft's thematic components of post-colonial literature and narrative identity formation. Ashcroft argues that "narrativity reproduces metonymically, the teleological progression of the history it records."[1] Thus, we find in Vizenor's narrated history of survivance, absent direct reproduction of teleology of history, a narrative of native presence, a construction of metonymic persona and of social and political systems that suggest that narrative and historical identity are at least partially dependent on an archive, the curatorium, the placeholder and space of event encounter, of artifact, curators and the curated (or curation of the already curated) and, though we aren't there yet, a developed sense of curatorial subjectivity. Further, the curated artifact, in this instance and so many others, engenders a layered curation, or re-curation, within each and every archival artifact.

Vizenor narrates as follows, on his entry into the archive: "during my research on Native writers, tribal leaders, and treaties at the Minnesota Historical Society, a generous reference librarian directed me."[2] Once directed, Vizenor finds the artifacts, the aforementioned "original bound copies of the Progress." In an economy of language, metonymies unfold in this narrative passage. From his role as self-designated researcher to the site of curation to the unnamed librarian to the found artifact, Vizenor tells a story of representation, of organizations, of people and memoranda, standing as abstract representations at the site of his search for native writers, leaders, and treaties.

The Minnesota Historical Society as the site of the archive, as the larger overseer of the curatorium, interpolates three metonymic terms of entry into postcolonial allegory. The Native researcher, in Vizenor's narrative of presence, must enter into a relationship with a tripartite institutional system of oversight, of state affiliation, academic/methodological practice and an affiliated group of curators. The state of Minnesota, the discipline of history, and the history of history and social networks serve as institutional agencies, named here as one in three, but disembodied in narrative, as no one person or representative body Vizenor encounters. Instead, Native presence in becoming a unique subject must interact, temporarily at least, within larger systemic agency, curating, curators, curation, and the curatorium.

Further, the namelessly inscribed librarian, described as "generous," signs a metonymic abstraction of generosity, as if the archive is there to give, through the generosity of an overseeing curatorial representative. Though the librarian's narrative act seems slight, as simply directing the researcher to the artifact, such knowledge of where the artifact lies indicates the presence of a curator, someone who displays, among other things, knowledge of the layout of the curatorium and what is housed where. This one act of directing illustrates one of many roles of the curator/librarian; in this case, the act involves assistance with movement through the archive, to help the researcher locate the body of artifacts he or she is seeking. Thus, we find ourselves steeped in allegory. (We might think here beyond history, or of history as allegory, in this case, perhaps of some Virgilian passage into the land of the dead, Dante trying to cross the river Styx, or of Kafka's countryman, before the law, those literary allegories of helpers, gatekeepers, as the allegorical protagonist enters protected or dangerous sites, perhaps, in what Louis Owens characterized in *Other Destinies*, as an "act of recovery."[3] We might think back still further, to Jacques Derrida's remarks on Archons, guardians of the Archive, guardians of "the house" as sanctioned by the "Greek State."[4])

Vizenor's own metonymic narrative double, "the researcher," seeks within the archive Native writers, Native leaders and treaties, or the representative written documents or artifacts associated with each of those subjects, artifact categories. Thus, the researcher's archival search involves an array of metonymic constructions as well. Native "writers, leaders, and treaties," serve as stand-in representations of larger communities of Native people and deeper more complex processes of engagement between treaty makers and the historical and political Indigenous communities treaties transformed and re-established, in writing and law. All such constructions allegorize broad sets of categories through which one may apply the tools, technics, the knowledge and the critical discernment of a researcher to gather certain tangible proof about the existence, the historical presence, the historical conditions, and the thoughts of Natives past.

Abstract Statement of Theme/Figuration/ the Curatorium

American Indian people and cultures have circled and circulated, and continue to circle and circulate, through, in and around acts of curates, curators, curation, and the lesser and greater installations of American curatoriums by engaging, disengaging, avoiding, resisting, and redressing the people, places, projects, contexts, jurisdictions, and critical interventions involved in the development of the Great American Indian curatorium, whether curated by Natives or non-Natives, or by some combination of both. Curatoriums rely on legal, social, cultural, and political organizational processes of selection, collection, ordering, exclusion, removal, relocation, production, and interpretation, along with structured event development, to recontextualize Native culture, peoples, places, and representations, as filtered through human/technical adaptations. (Let me say that current engagements with and extensions of the digital human archive are but another development of the curatorium.)

In *Digital_Humanities*, Anne Burdick, Johanna Drucker, and Peter Lunenfeld, claim, "Collection-building and curation have always defined humanistic learning: so much so that even the most ancient literary forms adopt listing, cataloging, and inventorying as key features of poetic communication."[5] Thereafter, the authors of *Digital_Humanities* forward a brief list of ancient Greek works of literature, as examples of curation, evidenced by inventories and/or poetic catalogues in those works. But Burdick, Drucker, and Lunenfield push forward, thankfully, to link cultural memory and historical artifacts, to institutional holdings of such, as they further claim, that through such holdings, "a new regime arises within which there exist such proliferations of historical information and cultural material that data from the past can no longer be assumed to possess a priori value. They become supports for the production of knowledge, knowledge's precondition but not its substance."[6]The authors further argue, "Informed critical judgments regarding the relationship between originals and copies, the greater or lesser authority of a given object or set of objects, and the work's meaning all become far more significant than the mere fact of accumulation."[7] From these informed critical judgments, then, new professional figures "emerge, alongside scholars, by the end of the nineteenth century, entrusted with guardianship over the remains of the past and armed with a battery of scientific and analytical techniques: archivists, museum curators, catalogers, and librarians."[8] Thus, a sort of complex develops, in and around which there seems little if any separation between scholars and an array of technical procedures and professionals, including data analysts, librarians, and archivists. From this emergence, the authors contend that (at least) "two parallel institutional worlds emerge that the digital revolution is reconnecting under transformed circumstances"[9] It's as if the near merger of scholars and archival, curatorial professionals, once narrowly separated by parallel lines, meet in some unforeseen beyond, where even the infinite extensions of parallel lines are reconfigured in digital spaces, where floating archival sets wait for engagement with an unknown "outside."

At almost every historical turn, American Indian people have been subjects and producers of such accumulation of artifact and memory, just as the extensions Burdick, Drucker, and Lunenfeld claim for accumulation of archival matter and memoranda have supported "production of knowledge" in general. The accumulation of archived Native cultural material production has also (how shall I say it) spawned a legion of critical interpretive guardians, technicians, and professionals dedicated to what we say about and what we do with the Native curatorium of artifact and memory. Such Native matter and memory, too, has been extended in and through digital environments and online archival spaces as well.

A Post-Colonial Allegory, The Post-Archive Vizenor-Curate

Most readers of American Indian literature are likely familiar with Vizenor's "edited and interpreted" work, *The Summer in the Spring*. This book includes materials from another "old cabinet" of Anishinaabe newspapers and transcripts of recordings of Anishinaabe songs. That is, Vizenor constructed the texts known as *Summer in the Spring* from preexisting archival and published sources. The songs and stories included in the *Summer in the Spring* collections were selected from the work of Francis Densmore and from a turn of the century—not this century, the last one, (some of you remember)—White Earth newspaper, titled the *Progress*.[10] Further, both of the archival sources Vizenor draws from to construct *Summer in the Spring* remain available online, in digital formats.

That given, my attention here will center on decentering Vizenor's editorial/ authorial moves to move song transcriptions into the category of literature. Over the course of nearly thirty years, Gerald Vizenor drew on archival and turn of the century publications on the Anishinaabeg, to produce a number of iterations of *Summer in the Spring*. The first of these, a Nodin Press publication, titled *Summer in the Spring, Lyric Poems of the Ojibway,* appeared in 1965 in a "limited hardbound edition." The second edition, retitled *Anishinaabe Nagamon*, was published in 1970 by Nodin Press as well. A separate publication of Anishinaabe stories, *Anishinaabe Adisokan*, drawn from stories extracted from the *Progress*, came out that same year. A new combined edition of the same previously published songs and stories came out in 1981, with a return to the previous title, *Summer in the Spring: Ojibwe Lyric Poems and Tribal Stories* — with "edited and reexpressed by" under the title, just above Vizenor's name. The final permutation of Vizenor's adaptions of tribal songs and stories appeared in 1993, again with the title *Summer in the Spring*, though in 1993 *Anishinaabe* supplants *Ojibwe* from the 1981 title, as the categories of types of literature, *Lyric Poems and Stories*, remains nearly the same. In addition, "New Edition," is amended as part of the subtitle and the previous subscript "edited and re-expressed" is replaced by "Interpreted." Such titular changes, though seemingly slight, show an attention to language, to particulars and intentionally or not, connote different and extended roles and identity formations for the editor.

As *Summer in the Spring* readers, we are left, then, with texts that have emerged from residual resources and which, in turn, exclude certain material and event elements and factors that went into remaking sources the texts are drawn from. In its many manifestations and manners of use and production and in its over-writing of archival antecedents, *Summer in the Spring* stands as a palimpsest in the material the text contains, in the ways that material is reinterpreted and repositioned as text, and in the ways that certain songs and stories, from sources Vizenor drew from, were never included in any versions of the *Summer in the Spring* palimpsest. For example, as in the previous 1981 edition, the 1993 version includes, an "Introduction" to the text, the songs and poems, Anishinaabe picto-myths, and "Interpretive notes." The 1993 palimpsest also includes a new revised "Introduction," a new section of "Page Notes," and a Anishinaabemowin glossary.

Further, in the 1993 edition of *Summer in the Spring*, Vizenor overwrites previ-ous overwritings of Densmore's text, by adding new passages to the "Introduc-tion." In one such added passage, Vizenor states: "the translation from the heard to the written is a transvaluation of the heard to the seen, the listener once and the reader evermore."[11] In this case, the palimpsest opens to another promise, not of a retention of a voice for a future listener, but instead the songs recorded by Densmore, as edited and interpreted by Vizenor, will have the potential to be seen by readers "for evermore." The new lasting promise issued in the transference of voice to print lies built upon the conceptual promise of transvaluation, which will produce a lasting, readable artifact. The value of the heard voice is overwritten by the value of printed, viewable text. This positions text over voice and reader over listener, and that implies that sound is less permanent than writing or literature, and that listeners will not last as longs as readers. Vizenor has remade song as literature. As we will see in a later passage of this chapter, that remaking of song as literature will be overturned once again, as those same songs are presented online, in a digital archive. There the songs will become songs again, sounding out in audio files, supplemented by text, associated with singers' names. Vizenor's name will be erased at that site, disassociated with songs online, as the songs return to categories of music, from their own print text categorical identities, as "lyric poetry."

The differences between Vizenor's editor's "Introduction," between the last two versions of *Summer in the Spring*, seem slight. But in the 1993 text, our literary curate introduces two new terms, "transvaluation" and "tribal hermeneutics,"[12] perhaps to shed light on how songs and stories might be pulled from the shadows of an archival past and, arguably, how they should be viewed and encountered as literary documents. About those two terms, Vizenor writes: "The translation from the heard to the written is a transvaluation of the heard to the seen. The listener once and the reader evermore."[13] Clearly, Vizenor stakes a claim there for adapting Anishinaabe song and printing it as poetry, with a new extended value, as a kind of literature, that will last beyond the sound of a voice, beyond connected instances of being heard.

Summer in the Spring embodies, then, an overwriting of sources as well as an overwriting of previous publications Vizenor collected and published from those sources.[14] Moreover, Vizenor super-positions his text as publication, as affiliated with him, with his name, and with his title, *Summer in the Spring*. These signify the assignment of the text into rights of possession, a kind of (dare I entrance you with yet another combinatory term, predicated on a passing construction of the use of the prefix trans?[15]) palimpsestic trans-possession of residual resources as part of his body of work, at a certain site of cultural production.

Vizenor's re-inscription of Anishinaabe songs as lyric poetry also connotes a kind of suturing of created form from one cultural context with a creative form of another culture. Songs, "Dream Songs," are sutured, or attached, to lyric poetry. He's building from Densmore's work, no doubt, but remediating, re-curating that work into yet another publication of re-sourced material. This, for better or worse — or something in between — opens the sutured Anishinaabe cultural creation to extended readings and categorical reassignment as literature, or something literary, while suturing the text itself to Vizenor's name and literary identity, under extended copyright from 1965 to 1993.

This suturing and re-designation may also reflect Vizenor's notion of trans-valuation.[16] Whether Vizenor draws his transvaluation from Friedrich Nietzsche, we will never know. Vizenor doesn't elaborate on any connection to Nietzsche's formulation of transvaluation, nor does he provide an explanation of his use of transvaluation. In any case, Anishinaabe song becomes transvalued as poetry. The trans-possessed Anishinaabe value of the song extends now to another context of encounter, with the potential for having an extended value in new and different contexts.

Additionally, in the 1993 Oklahoma Press version of *Summer in the Spring*, Vizenor does not include the individual names of singers along with the songs, as originators or composers of the songs.[17] Further, in the printed texts Vizenor edits, he overwrites not just the names of the singers but the unique vocal identities of the singers. Without sound, part of the dynamic of who the singers were remains silenced, erased, repressed, in another type of topographical impression, as words on a page, represented, re-curated as a type of literature.

Moreover, *Summer in the Spring*, in its various Vizenorian curations stretches the formal category of the dream songs Densmore collected by interpreting those songs as "lyric poems." In *Palimpsest, a History of the Written Word*, Matthew Battles, claims, "Writing needs us more than we need it. Like chess, neoclassical architecture, and religion, it is a thing that feeds on consciousness, requires the human mind in order to survive and propagate."[18] Perhaps such a view moves Vizenor, too. In some ways, his very survivance, his aesthetic interest as an Anishinaabe, as a writer, is informed by his reselection, his collection, his ordering of recast renderings of the songs found in *Summer in the Spring*. The Trickster-fashioning author put together the collection; he created categories for the structure of the book, and his name is on the book, with all the rights associated with writing reserved for such work. His knowledge, his insights, his ingenious conceptual constructions for housing the songs speak to his techne-bilities to curate what he has found in the Densmore collections, with a sharp, ardent sense of the power of dream songs, the power of authorship, the literary and the curatorial subjectivity implicit in the personally transformative and culturally adaptive forms of production he works through to bring Anishinaabe dreams to print, to the call of poetry, to marks of pages.

Matthew Battles also suggests that:

> in the process of evolutionary change, writing has buried its roots deep within our cultures, our very consciousness. Writing is a meme — a whole flock of them, really — a community of beguiling ideas nesting within one another, for whom the mind (extended, distributed) is the essential ecology. And yet unlike with language — unlike even reading of the broad, ineluctably human kind described above — we can get by perfectly well without writing. For tens upon tens of thousands of years, we did get by without it — and millions of people do today. Writing can be absent from the brain without causing trauma in a way that cannot be said of language. And yet once rooted there, it will not be excised.[19]

To his credit, Vizenor does create an Anishinaabe palimpsest, a "tribal hermeneutic," a text or document that (trans) values the cultural continuity of Anishinaabe songs and stories and he credits Densmore and the editors of the *Progress* with publication of the source material he remasters in *Summer in the Spring*. Of the songs he writes, "The lyric poems and dream songs in this book have been interpreted and re-expressed from the original Anishinaabeg song transcriptions integrated with literal translations for the Smithsonian Institution, Bureau of American Ethnology."[20] At the same time, Vizenor applies new critical terminologies to such texts — songs and story reflect reinterpreted, transvalued recollection and reading. On the one hand, he is funneling sources through authorial super-positioning, and on the other, destabilizing his own text, as a shadowed multiplicity of authorial creations and inventions including, perhaps, even the shadows of Native ex-nominum, nominally excluded Anishinaabe singers, as their names and voices, still resonate through other media now, post, post Indian, stored and storied like stories Vizenor found in the archives, through online sites, among so many such webs of palimpsests.[21]

In "Time Perspectivism and the Interpretive Potential of Palimpsests," Alan P. Sullivan III writes: "In common practice, a palimpsest 'refers to a superposition of successive activities, the material traces of which are partially destroyed or reworked because of the process of superposition.'"[22] While Sullivan's work and ideas on the palimpsest derive from the practices and interpretive schema involving archeological work, related to residual cultural material, the ideas and the concerns he outlines offer opportunity for us to rethink, perhaps reimagine, our interpretive relations to American Indian writing, texts, and the cultural and imaginative sources, people, and contexts, those writings and texts written over, repressed, or subjected to "superpositioning."

As Vizenor produces a palimpsest of songs and stories in *Summer in the Spring*, he also moves tribal, cultural resources into a constellation of realized material re-curations. The palimpsest operates as a re-curation of material resources that were previously collected, selected, held in different spatial and formal contexts, and arranged therein for different uses, under different interpretive terms of distribution and possession, legal and otherwise.

In another vein, Harold Scheube reminds us of the palimpsests relationship to stories: "When a storyteller creates, it is always within at least four contexts, (a) the unique story itself, (b) but also involving other stories in the tradition that shadow the unique performance and that provide it with a networking frame, acting as a kind of doppelganger, (c) and including the performer's own history, experiences, and feelings, a palimpsestic arrangement, (d) all within the context of the history, experiences, and feelings of the members of the audience, also a palimpsest."[23]

Whether Vizenor's re-curation might be called storytelling or not remains subject to interpretation, perhaps another curation of a re-curation. To be sure, it enfolds creation of techne-curated Indian palimpsests: a curation of Indian, curated by the curatorial Native; an interpreter/interpretive machine bound to, in Vizenor's case, techne-shinaabe; re-marking, re-writing, through proficiency and interpretive intervention, involving collection and selection analysis; and then, after Vizenor, a re-curated, web-bound palimpsest involving the techne-Indian's digital proficiency in collection, selection, thematic categorization of cultural artifact, suturing Densmore's work to virtual presence and more, while moving further and further away from the subject body that created the materials, from whom the selected, collected, thematic categories are drawn.

Perhaps what we gather and gain in curated published texts *is a story* of losses, along with the promise of accretions. In *Summer in the Spring* we lose the names and voices, the vocal identities of singers, the melodies of the songs; and what was sung in Anishinaabemowin, now appears in print, in English, as text, for supposedly different, or extended audiences, readers more than the listeners. As the transitory material sound of singers' voices once curatorially transformed into recorded audio material, is curated, transformed again to text. And we have hopefully, under Vizenor's curation, gone from ethnomusicology and ethnography to a text reassigned as literature, under the name of an editor and publisher.

In that light, *Summer in the Spring* might be regarded as a precursor to more recent developments of curation associated with digital humanities. I would like to suggest that in his resourcing of archival texts and by re-curating them as literature, Vizenor displays and advances the extension of archived documents and artifacts of Anishinaabe creation through a curatorial subjectivity. That curatorial subjectivity is indicated by his selection, organization, adaptions, and critical interpretations of those artifacts, as he repositions those artifacts against previous presentations of artifact.

In seeing Vizenor's publication of *Summer in the Spring* as curatorial, we might endeavor to assess that curation, his ingenious, deft moves toward curation, selection, categorization, and re-interpretation. But that might be nearly impossible, fraught with irony, dismissed with speculative casts of intentionality. Where does this leave us? Can the material presence of Native publication offer insight into curatorial subjectivity? Probably not. But, for the sake of discussion, in an earlier version of this paper — another palimpsest, perhaps, I pose a series of ironic theorems as an appendix to this essay, to test curatorial subjectivity or, perhaps, the presence of some kind of Native/curate/persona. To be sure, to characterize or attempt to assess curatorial acts with the complex of the curatoria, subjective interior and material exterior, may be an irreal, impossible proposition, but we can always leave the archive, depart from any discussion of the archive, with nothing, with no conclusive sense of the past, with no better understanding of the archival subject persona. But for now, we must move forward with these beguiling nests of ideas.

Websites such as *Drumhop* house the same sets of Anishinaabe songs Vizenor arranges, and more. But the *Drumhop* website recounts the history of the Anishinaabe songs as Densmore's work with no mention of Vizenor or his publications of the songs. Further, curation at that site seems driven by archival promise and superpositioning as well. At *Drumhop* though, curation finds a different purpose, setting forth a different set of intentions for preservation: "This music is provided here as a reference for other singers, researchers, and the general public to enjoy. It is not offered as music to be downloaded or shared, but only accessed for these reasons. The music in this library comes from a variety of sources including private and published recordings. If you like what you hear, you can find some of this and similar music for sale at some of these organizations . . . (Drumhop Music)."[24] Ironically, Vizenor's name does not appear at the Drumhop site. His poetic rendering of audio and previously published songs goes unnamed, unacknowledged. Yet the songs remain, with the voices and the names of singers and electronic print copy, dispersed, like Nobel Laureate Bob Dylan's "holy kiss" to "fall on strangers, travel free," in a virtual afterlife, living, well after life as song, literature, or poetry.[25] To be sure, the songs are never referred to as poetry at Drumhop and there is no reference to the songs re-incurated in texts, edited by our Imagi(native) literary curate, Gerald Vizenor.

In many respects, the continued regeneration of the songs, across generations, through a variety of media may tell a bigger imagi(native) story; perhaps, songs and stories cannot be contained, cannot be retained as personal, they remain trans-possessive, transpossessions. That being, those song-beings continuously replicate, whether aurally, or visually, in sound, in vibration, in text font, or in some ineluctable modulation, on the cusp of re-transmission through some new human medium, stretching forward and backward, in a living moment of striving for emotive authenticity.

This sort of immaterial presence, whether an immanence, a potential, or some un-nameable undisclosed agency, may be indicated by certain, ghostly, structural features in the Anishinaabe language. Richard Rhodes writes: "Algonquian languages are radically head marking, so much so that their lexicons and productive syntax are organized so as to largely avoid oblique nominal." Or, to read it another way, "Algonquian languages have a surfeit of agent suppressing (or object highlighting) operations, a middle, two clearly distinct passive constructions, and, in some languages, a productive indefinite actor construction, alongside the type of inverse agreement system that reverses subjects and primary objects syntactically."[26] With that view, songs as communicative, emotive enunciations, in all their palimpsestic overwrites and derivations, may be reminding us that songs and stories travel as para-agents, as beings, surpassing possession through human agency, as songs can live more than locally, outside of human jurisdiction, as they cannot be restrained in their creation, their re-generation, their becomings and their goings on.[27]

No doubt, we must celebrate Vizenor's insights on Anishinaabe stories and songs, as we must admire his masterful selection, ordering, presentation, and conceptualization of the songs in *Summer in the Spring*. By reprinting the songs as poetry, as perhaps an interpretive gesture suggesting the transcultural literary value of Anishinaabe song, art, and poetry, Vizenor opened our eyes to possibilities for rereading the Anishinaabe imagi(native), as if the literature were already living in the songs, waiting to be released, from a previous existence, whether in archives or as subjects of study, of ethnomusicological song types, signifying the preservation of a cultural past. In Vizenor's renderings of songs as poetry, readers must re-encounter the Anishinaabe imagi(native). Yes, in the end he leaves out singers' names, the resident subject, an archived subjectivity, as one imagi(native) gives way to the emergent subject, a subjectivity of overwritten skins, as palimpsest, both the residual and emergent reminder of a remainder of an event, a remainder of an experience, emerging in an integrative thinking event, transformative in its happening, perhaps as an attempt to express, perhaps an authenticity, oblique, un-nameable, in remainders of material, words, artifacts, in the hands, through the eyes of an imagi(native) other.

Post Script — Curation as Survivance, the Afterlife

In the conclusion of "Aesthetics of Survivance," Vizenor, recalls Derrida's words from *Archive Fever*. The passage reads: "Derrida observes that the afterlife [survivance] no longer means death and the return of the specter, but the surviving of an excess of life which resists annihilation."[28] By this view, the losses we experience in the collection, selection, organization, even in the interpretation of archival material, as representative of Native culture, of the tribal imaginary, by some excess, by some creative encounter, perhaps by who we are as we re-imagine the archive, remains alive, though in different form, in alternate places and extensions of space. The songs, the names of singers are not lost, then, they float among an unnamed potential, extending possibility beyond even our current notions of curation, curator, curatorium, to other story contexts, to sites reminding us of the lasting excess of the tribal imaginary, a curatorium without jurisdiction.

As evidenced in a layered reading of Vizenor's cultured palimpsests, such reading may involve creation of a delayered reading of text beneath, the curated and the uncured, as in the kind of reading we must now conduct to find names of Anishinaabe singers in the media complex of transmission of their songs, the songs of almost forgotten men and women, overshadowed by others, though their voices have remained, where we find once again their names, adjacent to a webhosted digital sound file, still sounding out their words, sounding out like a formation of cranes passing overhead, moving over palimpsests of landscapes, of tribal and digital landscapes, singing as if one with the world of sky and nature, not yet driven to death by the technical adaptions for curating their moving presence, but living, still moving, just seeking a still greater promise of another place to land.

Notes

1. Ashcroft, Bill, *Postcolonial Transformation,* (New York and London: Routledge, 2001), 105.

2. Vizenor, Gerald, *Survivance: Narratives of Native Presence,* (Lincoln, Nebraska, USA, University of Nebraska Press), 2008, 6

3. Louis Owens, *Other Destinies: Understanding the American Indian Novel* (Norman: University of Oklahoma Press, 1992), 129.

4. Derrida, Jacque, *Archive Fever: A Freudian Impression.* (University of Chicago Press. 1996), 2.

5. Anne Burdick, Johanna Drucker, and Peter Lunenfeld, *Digital_Humanities* (Cambridge, MA: The MIT Press, 2012), 32–33.

6. Burdick et al., *Digital_Humanities,* 32–33.

7. Burdick et al., *Digital_Humanities,* 33.

8. Burdick et al., *Digital_Humanities,* 33.

9. Burdick et al., *Digital_Humanities,* 33.

10. Vizenor also uses pictographs in *Summer in the Spring,*

11. Gerald Vizenor, *Summer in the Spring: Anishinaabe Lyric Poems and Stories, New Edition* (Norman and London: University of Oklahoma Press, 1993), 4.

12. Vizenor extends tribal hermeneutics to trickster hermeneutics in some passages.

13. Vizenor, *Summer in the Spring,* 4.

14. I use the term "embodies" advisedly here, but a text is a material artifact, a figurative body, or body part, of a body without organs, connected to social and cultural functions of larger institutional, political and cultural bodies, ordering and processing flows of knowledge and interpretations of historical, cultural and natural relationships and events. I also prefer the term "overwriting" to "rewriting," since Vizenor's collections and interpretations involve the assignment of different categories, classifications, and presentations of the source material he publishes in *Summer in the Spring.*

15. We have all used trans-portation, the movement from, to, across, through, and inside of portals, doors, points of departure, arrival; we all remain transcendently human, capable of abstract constructions of experiences which empirically, spiritually, mechanically, or naturally, as in dreams, remind us we might go beyond — our bodies, this life, this experience; and of late Vizenor has delivered us to transmotion, movement to movement, across movement, through movement, as movement, moving even the notion of motion, to another possibility of positioning, as if our very presence were an infinite rehearsal for a motion transcending motion, a migration away from ourselves, to another moving without ourselves, trans-selved, in other greater bodies of motion, motioning us away, in transit, transitory, transmigratory, untranslatable, trans human, trans-emotional, trans-pathic, trans-graphic, trans-ogenic, trans-bio-scopic, trans-aural, trans-neural, trans-whatever was as trans-never is, just is — a song, with the personality of a singer, singing while no one remembers the melody of the song, the voice of the singer, hanging there somewhere, moving, motion within motion, the very stirring of motion as vibration, carried by wind

perhaps, by particles of water, carrying particles of dust, the singer in that somewhere, singing, moving toward another motion still.

16. I am not sure if Vizenor is building from Nietzsche here, or not, if so, he does not directly, or indirectly, refer back to philosophical or critical sources or influences of terms and he doesn't unpack terms he employs as he re-imagines songs as lyric poetry.

17. Vizenor does mention the name of Gagandac, one of singers in "Page Notes" in the text. Vizenor, however, does not link individual songs to singers/composers in the "lyric poems" section of the text. In the "Introduction" and "Page Notes," Vizenor provides the name of Anishinaabe orator, Keeshkemun. As for the stories drawn from the *Progress*, Vizenor informs readers that "Theodore Hudon Beaulieu wrote in the original introduction to the series published in the *Progress* that two members of the midewiwin, Day Dodge and Saycosegay, told stories of the religious life of Tribe in Anishinaabemowin, the oral language of the Anishinaabe. These stories were then translated by the editor and published under his name. These are oral versions of the trickster stories; the author does not indicate when he first heard these stories. The editor and publisher of the *Progress* were both crossblood members of the tribe and lived on the White Earth Reservation" (16–17). One might suggest, in his publishing of songs and stories included in *Summer in the Spring*, Vizenor is following publishing practices associated with forbearers, previous Anishinaabe editors and publishers.

18. Matthew Battles, *Palimpsest: A History of the Written Word* (New York and London: W.W. Norton, 2015), 3.

19. Battles, *Palimpsest*, 2–3.

20. Vizenor, *Summer in the Spring*, 140.

21. See Drumhop website, http://drumhop.com/music.php; and electronic versions of the *Progress*, http://chroniclingamerica.loc.gov/lccn/sn83016853, as well as Bureau of Ethnology online facsimiles of text, for example, https://archive.org/details /bulletin451910smit, October 21, 2017.

22. Harold Scheube, *Story* (Madison: University of Wisconsin Press, 1998), 33.

23. Scheube, *Story*, 16.

24. Again see http://drumhop.com/music.php: the site lists additional websites where other organizations and institutions hold collections of tribal music. Those sites include Canyon Records, Indian House, Indian Records, New World Records, and Smithsonian Folkways.

25. From "Love is Just a Four Letter Word," composition and lyrics by Bob Dylan.

26. Richard Rhodes, "Missing Obliques: Some Anomalies in Ojibwe Syntax," *Current Studies in Linguistics: Hypothesis A / Hypothesis B: Linguistic Explorations in Honor of David M. Perlmutter*, eds. Donna B. Gerdts, John C. Moore, and Maria Polinsky (Cambridge, MA: The MIT Press, 2010), 428, 427.

27. I am not sure I have the linguistics absolutely right in my interpretation of Rhodes' work. I wasn't going for an absolute, I was, am still heading toward a kind of "non-relational," view of language and the influence of imagi(native) beings on the relational enunciation of songs, stories, and language/texts. Suffice it to say, I am doing a kind of open reading of the hard linguistics. I consulted Rhodes via email and another linguist who shall go unnamed at this point and didn't receive a conclusive answer about how to read Rhodes' remarks. I took some liberties with my interpretation. Call it a move toward a non-linguistic reading, a literary extrapolation, from a linguistic argument, looking for the "outside" of linguistic structures and sets.

28. Derrida, Jacque, *Archive Fever: A Freudian Impression.* (University of Chicago Press. 1996), 60.

PART III   *Interventions*

TEN

The Occom Circle at Dartmouth College Library

Laura R. Braunstein, Peter Carini,

and Hazel-Dawn Dumpert

Samson Occom (1723–1792) was a Mohegan Indian and one of the earliest Native American students of Eleazar Wheelock, a Congregational minister who established Moor's Indian Charity School in Lebanon, Connecticut in 1754 and founded Dartmouth College in 1769. Trained as a missionary and eventually ordained as a Presbyterian minister, Occom became an itinerant preacher, serving Native and white communities throughout the Northeast. After breaking with Wheelock in the early 1770s because Wheelock turned his efforts away from educating Natives, Occom helped to found and lead an independent Indian community in upstate New York called Brothertown. The Dartmouth College Library's *Occom Circle* project, led by English professor Ivy Schweitzer and funded by a grant from the National Endowment for the Humanities, has produced a scholarly digital edition of Occom's papers, including journals, letters, sermons, herbals, and accounts.[1] In addition to Occom's papers, the project also includes documents that discuss Occom by others in his "circle," including Eleazar Wheelock; Nathaniel Whitaker, a fellow minister with whom Occom traveled on a fundraising tour to England and Scotland; Joseph Johnson, his son-in-law and student of Wheelock; David Fowler, his brother-in-law and another Wheelock student; and George Whitefield, the famous English revivalist whom Occom stayed with in London. The digital edition is fully searchable, with annotated indexes of people, organizations, places, and events. The documents in the edition, all of which are held in the archives of the Dartmouth College Library, are a foundational collection of primary sources in Native American Studies, colonial history, and American religious history.

Digitizing Occom's papers has been an organization-wide endeavor for the Dartmouth College Library, involving staff from many departments, including Special Collections, Preservation, Cataloging and Metadata Services, and Reference. Professor Schweitzer framed the project in terms of current research on Indigenous sovereignty and designed it in consultation with scholars, librarians and archivists, digital humanists, and members of the Mohegan Tribe.[2] A half-time project manager directed the transcription and markup process, which involved library staff, faculty, undergraduate students, and the English subject librarian. This chapter will describe the development of the project management process, which has been accomplished almost entirely within the existing organizational culture of the library. The library does not have a separate digital humanities department, program, or center, but it has a long tradition of producing digital projects; it is in the early stages of developing staff dedicated to leading and supporting large-scale, ongoing digital humanities projects. *The Occom Circle* provides a case study in organizational change and an example of how subject specialists and department liaisons can work within their libraries' existing cultures to develop new skills and connections to support and foster the digital humanities and Indigenous archives.

Samson Occom, 1723–1792

"I was Born a Heathen and Brought up in Heathenism" — so opens Samson Occom's 1768 autobiography.[3] Occom was born a Mohegan Indian in eastern Connecticut in 1723. In his teenage years, he had two experiences that shaped the rest of his life. The first was a religious awakening that first made him fear for his soul and then brought him to Christianity and literacy. The second was watching deliberations related to the infamous Mason case, a controversy over Indigenous land rights that turned on the Connecticut colony's exploitation of Indian illiteracy.[4] These two experiences — one spiritual and one political — led him to seek a Christian education with the New Light minister Eleazar Wheelock in 1743. Occom and Wheelock had a complicated relationship. On the one hand, Wheelock provided Occom with a classical education (including Latin, Greek, and Hebrew) not offered even to most white students at the time. On the other, Wheelock kept Occom beholden to him for support, both financial and moral.

Occom was ordained in 1759 after serving as a lay minister and teacher for many years at Montauk on Long Island. He always struggled financially and was well aware that he was supported much less extravagantly than English ministers doing similar work. In 1764, he and his growing family moved back to Mohegan. He soon ran afoul of local clergy because he was drawing Native parishioners away from their services. He also became embroiled in the Mason land case in an attempt to protect the Mohegans from financial ruin. It wasn't long before accusations of misconduct were leveled against Occom. Disgusted by these accusations, Wheelock convened a synod that acquitted Occom of all charges, save those related to the Mason controversy. Fearing Occom's further involvement in local issues, Wheelock sent him to England in 1766 in the company of local minister Nathaniel Whitaker to raise money for Wheelock's Moor's Indian Charity School. In England, Occom and Whitaker, who was something of a hustler, traveled the country; Occom preached while Whitaker took up collections. Their tour raised an astounding £12,000 — equivalent to approximately $2.4 million today.

On his return to the colonies in 1768, Occom found himself without means of support. Wheelock had neglected Occom's family and, feeling his attempts to educate Natives had failed, turned his attention from his former pupil and his missionary work in order to pursue the founding of a college on the New Hampshire frontier to educate white missionaries. Occom and Wheelock fell out over the use of the funds raised in England, which Wheelock channeled into establishing the institution that became Dartmouth College. Occom never visited the College, nor saw his former mentor in person again. This was a turning point in Occom's life, and his first step toward spiritual and intellectual independence.

In 1772, a Mohegan Indian named Moses Paul was convicted of murdering a white man while under the influence of alcohol. He was sentenced to death and asked Occom to preach his execution sermon. Occom spoke to a large, mixed-race audience on the subject of temperance, an issue of deep concern to the English establishment in its relationship to Indian communities. At the urging of others, Occom had the sermon printed, and it went through more than twenty editions (including a Welsh translation), making Occom the sixth-most published American author of the 1770s. The sermon launched him on a new path of celebrity.[5]

Over the next fifteen years, Occom became increasingly disenchanted with white settler culture, while at the same time he deepened his connection to his Christian faith. In 1787, he wrote a sermon titled "Thou Shalt Love Thy Neighbor as Thyself" in which he declared that those who held slaves — which included almost all white men of station at the time — were not Christian. Even in an environment where several states had moved to outlaw slavery, this was a radical statement. Frustrated by his own circumstances and by those of his Christian brethren across a number of tribes, he and several other graduates of Moor's School set up a Christian Indian settlement called Brothertown in Oneida territory in upstate New York. Occom moved back and forth between Oneida and Mohegan for many years and finally died in Brothertown in 1792.

While much about Occom made him unique among his peers — his education, his experiences in England, his international acclaim and recognition, his straddling of two cultures — he stands out most prominently today as the foremost colonial Native American to have left behind a published body of written work. Many consider him the first Native public intellectual. It is this body of work, along with the opinions and perceptions of his Anglo-American contemporaries, that makes Occom of particular and compelling interest to modern scholars of eighteenth-century history, literature, and culture. The largest body of Occom's papers are housed in Rauner Special Collections Library at Dartmouth College.

The Occom Circle

Rauner Library is committed to integrating its collections into the intellectual life of Dartmouth College. In most academic years, over 100 classes hold multiple sessions in Rauner, using materials from the rare book, manuscript, and archival collections. Ivy Schweitzer, Professor of English and Women's, Gender, and Sexuality Studies, has regularly brought her Early American Literature class in to use Rauner's collections. Her teaching collaboration with College Archivist Peter Carini led to an invitation to present and discuss Samson Occom's papers as part of Dartmouth's annual Pow-Wow, an event celebrating Native American culture held annually since the College refocused attention on supporting Native American education in the early 1970s.[6] Their presentation during the May 2007 Pow-Wow was attended by members of the Mohegan tribe. During the session with Schweitzer and Carini, a member of the Mohegan Tribal Council asked why, if Occom was such an integral and important part of the College's early history, was he not more visible at Dartmouth — at the time, the only space in Hanover named for Occom was a large pond on the periphery of campus. This question sparked a lively discussion and inspired the idea for The Occom Circle.

Over the next few months, Schweitzer and Carini had several discussions about the possibility of digitizing Occom's writings. At the crux of the discussion was the recent publication of Joanna Brooks's book *The Collected Writings of Samson Occom, Mohegan: Leadership and Literature in Eighteenth-Century Native America*, a critical edition of Occom's written work that included a number of documents that were not part of Dartmouth's holdings.[7] Rather than simply repeat Brooks's work in digital form, Schweitzer decided that a digital scholarly edition of Occom's writings at Dartmouth, combined with documents from his contemporaries (particularly regarding their perception of Occom), would provide a new and important angle, while at the same time facilitating her pedagogical use of the documents in the classroom.

In consultation with Carini and David Seaman, Associate Librarian for Information Management, Schweitzer applied for a grant from the National Endowment for the Humanities and was awarded $250,000 to create a scholarly digital edition of approximately 530 eighteenth-century documents, comprising letters, accounts, journals, sermons, and other documents by, about, and related to Samson Occom.[8] The grant proposed to digitize the documents, transcribe them, and mark up the transcriptions using the Text Encoding Initiative (TEI) XML schema. The markup would allow scholars to search and sort the documents in ways that a simple plain-text transcription would not allow. It would also make it possible to present the documents in both a scholarly diplomatic version (as literal a transcription as allowed in text) and a modernized version that would regularize variations in spelling and handwriting common to eighteenth-century documents, making the material more accessible to undergraduates, as well as to K–12 students and general readers.

The Occom Circle, funded in part by the National Endowment for the Humanities and supplemented by the Dartmouth College Library, has resulted in 586 scanned documents either by or about Occom, as well as a number of other documents pertaining to other Native American students taught by Eleazar Wheelock at Moor's Indian Charity School in Connecticut. These scanned documents amount to 3,098 images (or pages), each of which has been catalogued, transcribed, and marked up using TEI. The final product presents the transcriptions side-by-side with the scanned documents to allow scholars and students to judge and interpret the documents and transcriptions for themselves.

The Project and the Process

The Occom Circle is one of the Dartmouth College Library's most complex projects to date. The leaders of the initial project team were primary investigators

Schweitzer and Carini, with five additional members from library departments including Library Leadership, Cataloging and Metadata Services, the Digital Library Technologies Group, and Preservation Services. Hazel-Dawn Dumpert, an experienced editor, was hired from outside the library as project manager, and members of Dartmouth College's Web Design and Development team served as consultants. The project involved at least forty individuals from the library, Computing Services, and the grant team. It has also employed a number of Dartmouth undergraduates and graduate students, and postdoctoral fellows from Dartmouth and other institutions.

Not initially included among the team members were department liaisons from the disciplines most relevant to the project: English, History, and Native American Studies. This was neither a deliberate exclusion nor an oversight, but rather a function of the way new digital projects had been initiated within the current organizational structure of the library. Project leaders within the library — in this case, Carini, the subject specialist for college history — made proposals to a cross-departmental, cross-functional committee, which then decided how to move forward in accommodating new projects. Department liaisons often initiated new projects in the library's digital program, on their own or in collaboration with faculty, but their roles once projects were underway had not been defined. The process of developing and carrying out *The Occom Circle* served to reveal both the strengths and the challenges of the current organizational structure and to suggest additional ways of involving department liaisons in digital projects in order to improve both library services and the projects themselves.

While the project was defined to a certain extent by the grant, a number of specifics needed clarification. To ensure that all parties were clear about the expectations and outcomes from the project, the project team drew up a success statement. The success statement included a narrative that laid out in broad strokes the technical expectations for the final product, as well as the expected functionality of *The Occom Circle* website, such as: "The encoding will allow linking to contextualizing information about people, events, places, and organizations mentioned in the letters as well as facilitating research related to textual elements within the documents." This was followed by an itemized list of actions that spelled out in more detail the expectations for each step in the process. This document was important both for keeping the project on track and for managing expectations, as well as being a reminder of commitments made by various library departments. The project team began by setting out a timeline and identifying milestones. For the first two years, the team met on a monthly basis to report progress, sort out details of work, and discuss technical problems.

The first step in launching *The Occom Circle* relied on the College Archivist's expertise in identifying all of the relevant documents. Carini, assisted by an undergraduate student, identified all of the documents written by Samson Occom in Dartmouth's manuscript holdings and then made a first review to determine other documents in the collection that discussed Occom. Ivy Schweitzer then identified additional materials, including documents by other Native American students of Eleazar Wheelock. Each of the relevant documents was examined and verified to make sure its content was consistent with catalog records. During the 1950s and 1960s, photocopies of documents not owned by Dartmouth had been added to the collection, so potential documents had to be checked to ascertain that they were in fact eighteenth-century manuscripts and not modern copies. A very basic condition check was also conducted at this time. Once the documents were inventoried and verified, they were sent to Preservation Services for assessment and treatment. Treatments included minor repair and stabilization and, occasionally, more extensive treatment. Several documents had pressure tape on them and had to be sent to the Northeast Document Conservation Center in Andover, Massachusetts, to have the tape and residue removed. Once the documents were treated, they went to the library's Digital Production Unit for scanning. The documents were scanned at 600 dpi. The decision was made to scan all of the pages, including blank pages, so that scholars using the digital collection could be sure they were seeing the entire document.

As the documents were scanned, the transcription team began the laborious process of transcribing the contents. This was by far the slowest and most painstaking part of the process. Not only did the transcription involve deciphering eighteenth-century handwriting, it meant puzzling out the hands of multiple writers, each with their own idiosyncrasies. These included an original version of shorthand and a wide variety of abbreviations. The final step in the process was marking up the documents using the standards of the TEI. Transcribers provided a simplified initial markup at the beginning of the process, but the final markup and the development of TEI headers that in turn facilitated the creation of Encoded Archival Description and Machine-Readable Cataloging (MARC) records for each document was performed by members of the text encoding team from Cataloging and Metadata Services. The final results are documents for which specific elements have been consistently noted by the team to facilitate searching and to improve access to and comprehension of the documents. For example, TEI allows us to regularize variant spellings in the collection so that if someone searches for Occom, he or she will find all the documents where Occom is mentioned, even if the spelling is "Occum." The markup also provides clarification of unique abbreviations or strike-throughs, such as "Chh," which the team determined stood for church.

Managing *The Occom Circle*

The grant for *The Occom Circle* provided for a half-time project manager, Hazel-Dawn Dumpert, who was hired from outside the Dartmouth College Library. The ultimate aim of the project manager (PM) should be the establishment of a smooth and steady workflow and the facilitation of an easy interchange of labor between departments and team members. In the case of *The Occom Circle*, which was a ground-up effort, the PM began with the very basic task of meeting individually with each team member to get a feel for his or her duties, goals, and ideas, and thus to envision a preliminary network of how each member's distinct tasks fit into the project as a whole.

From there, the PM's next task was to assist the project director in hiring student assistants. As anyone who has employed student workers knows, this can be a hit-or-miss endeavor. To help refine the search for reliable assistants, *The Occom Circle* PM gave promising candidates a short presentation to relate what their duties would entail, encouraging them to give the work serious thought before joining up. The development early on of an easily repeatable training program ensured consistency and a steady learning curve. Likewise, the PM learned to quickly identify, and dismiss, those students whose performance or work habits did not show promise or improvement.

One of the PM's more challenging endeavors was deciding which tasks to delegate, and to whom. While having an overview of a project's processes is not only helpful but necessary, a PM can risk becoming the sole keeper of that overview. For example, a particularly resourceful student worker was promoted from the transcription of letters to the researching of names, places, and organizations contained in the documents. This student soon became invaluable to both the project and the PM, building a narrative of the players and events involved in the Occom documents. Although other research assistants were also recruited, they did not prove to be as effective. In hindsight, it would have proved beneficial to the project and the PM to be more proactive about delegating some long-term duties to other permanent team members, thereby distributing project information more evenly and increasing the exposure of project documents to those who could help to ensure accuracy and consistency.

Connecting with Department Liaisons

The library's existing organizational structure assigned one lead contact for digital projects — in the case of *The Occom Circle*, the College Archivist, who is the subject specialist for college history — to coordinate the project both inside and outside of the library. Laura Braunstein, department liaison to English (the home department of principal investigator Ivy Schweitzer), had heard about the project from library and faculty colleagues and from the PM, and was looking to learn more about the digital humanities — both as a field in general and in terms of learning skills and competencies that she would need to support faculty, students, and researchers doing new work in this area.

Braunstein approached the PM in the summer of 2013 and asked to contribute in any way useful — not necessarily using her disciplinary expertise as a department liaison, but by learning the project from the ground up. She negotiated with her manager to contribute five hours per week to the project and began with the same training program used for the student assistants. She learned eighteenth-century paleography and transcribed letters, journals, and accounts using the simple markup developed for the project. She worked with student assistants, the PM, and principal investigator Schweitzer to proofread document transcriptions. Later, she learned the TEI markup language in order to complete the headers and markup for individual documents. This part of the process had heretofore been accomplished solely by the PM and by staff on the text markup team in the library's Cataloging and Metadata Services department. While Braunstein could have asked to join the text markup team, joining the project as if she were a student assistant offered additional opportunities to view the project as a whole from the perspective of the PM. Learning TEI through participating in *The Occom Circle* was a challenging process, but was enormously helpful in demonstrating the sheer scale of work and army of collaborators involved in producing a digital edition of this size. Understanding a project from the inside helps department liaisons advise other faculty and researchers who are interested in initiating new digital projects, and provides valuable experience for librarians working within their libraries' existing cultures to build digital humanities programs.

Lessons Learned

The Dartmouth College Library has a long history of involvement in producing digital editions, but none have approached the scale of *The Occom Circle*.[9] The road has not always been smooth, but we are lucky to have been able to draw upon the expertise and experience of our staff, who met technical and organizational challenges as they arose. When producing a large digital edition, defining the scope of the project and having a detailed understanding of the actions and expected outcomes are extremely important. Having the success statement as a reference point and guide kept the project on track as individual documents moved through the process. Having a set of milestones and a carefully thought-through workflow helped assure that the "large number of people" involved knew where their tasks fit into the whole.

Even with these planning and reference tools in place, the project — like most endeavors of its kind — ran into several technical problems. Some of these problems were minor, while others had a significant impact on the project. An example of a relatively minor problem was the discovery that several separate letters were often written on a single document. Special Collections had cataloged each letter at the item level without regard to whether it was originally written on a separate piece of paper. Since the eighteenth-century authors did not give any thought to future digital projects when they were writing — and paper was expensive! — these letters often ended or began on the same page as an earlier letter by another author. This situation complicated the process of relating individual transcriptions to specific images within the database.

A similar issue that had a much larger impact on the project was also related to scanning. When the collection was originally scanned, some larger documents — generally folio sheets — were scanned a single page at a time, while smaller documents — such as multi-page quarto-sized journals — were scanned open so that two pages appeared in one image. This presented some problems in making a one-to-one match between page images and transcriptions, with the end result that several large sets of double images had to be split apart digitally.

From the project management perspective, digital projects such as *The Occom Circle* can often be an education in lessons learned the hard way. Scrupulous record keeping can help minimize back-to-the-drawing-board delays. Something that appeared to be inconsequential at the beginning of the project — for instance, building a list of each and every manuscript number related to each individual mentioned in the documents — would be of great importance further down the road. A detailed daily work journal, as well as a spreadsheet to keep track of all of the project's various lists, proved to be of enormous benefit in corralling all the various aspects of the project.

Another aspect of the project that came to light only after a great deal of time had passed was the fact that the markup of certain documents would differ significantly from others. Although the transcription of letters — which comprised the majority of the project documents, and so were tackled first — was often difficult in terms of deciphering handwriting, their TEI encoding was a fairly straightforward and even pleasant task. When it came time for journals and accounts, however, team members were somewhat dismayed to find themselves faced with a whole new set of unforeseen problems, including but not limited to the difficulties of transcribing ledgers in ways that would ultimately display correctly on the published site and the sheer volume of person and place names contained in the journals (some of which ran longer than forty pages, contained nearly 100 names, and entailed exacting specifications in their TEI markup). Only in hindsight did the PM realize that a healthy sampling of each type of document at the outset would have helped to sketch out timelines and prevent "coding fatigue" later in the project.

Our advice for department liaisons who want to support and foster new digital humanities projects at their libraries would be to pay close attention to what processes the organization already has in place for initiating, organizing, and operating existing projects, from the smallest to the largest. It would be unnecessarily complex, not to mention nearly impossible, to include every relevant library staff member on every project and doing so should certainly not be a goal for even the most ambitious team. Yet given that much of department liaison work is outreach to and information sharing with faculty, students, and community members, there is always room to improve project communication. This can be an avenue for the departmental liaison to take positive action. Ask questions of anyone who will answer; spend time "informational interviewing" colleagues; don't assume that digital humanities projects will function in the same way as other cross-departmental initiatives; and get comfortable with the possibility that channels of communication may occasionally have some static. If the project does not appear to have a place for the traditional contributions of a department liaison, consider it an opportunity to learn something new. Is there a process to which you can contribute? Is there a technical skill that you can learn? At the very least, commit to understanding what it would take for the library to support and foster new projects that your faculty might want to propose. Faculty members, students, and other scholars often hear about opportunities for collaboration from their colleagues; they might not comprehend the scale, technical resources, and staff time involved in producing many digital humanities projects.

Samson Occom worked tirelessly until his death to speak to and for his people. His journal entries over many years describe his itinerant preaching to Native and white communities throughout the Northeast. A detail that he noted at nearly every stop on his travels was that "a large Number of People" had gathered to listen to him. A large number of people at Dartmouth College have worked to produce a scholarly digital edition of Occom's writings to bring his voice to new readers and to honor Native American intellectual traditions. Part of the project's funding comes from the National Endowment for the Humanities' We the People initiative, which specifically supports public humanities scholarship to enhance civic life.[10] Through our edition of his works, Occom speaks to an even larger number of people in audiences he could have never anticipated. *The Occom Circle* testifies to the transformative potential of the digital humanities as a field of community-based knowledge and scholarship.

The authors wish to thank Ivy Schweitzer and Jay Satterfield for their feedback in revising this chapter. Reprinted, with permission, from Digital Humanities in the Library: Challenges and Opportunities for Subject Specialists, edited by Arianne Hartsell-Gundy, Laura Braunstein, and Liorah Golomb (Chicago: ACRL, 2015).

Notes

1. Ivy Schweitzer, ed., *The Occom Circle*, Dartmouth College Library, https://www.dartmouth.edu/~occom accessed August 1, 2014.

2. For a description of this process, see Ivy Schweitzer, "Native Sovereignty and the Archives: Samson Occom and Digital Humanities." *Resources for American Literary Study* 38 (2015): 21–52.

3. Samson Occom, "Autobiographical Narrative, Second Draft (September 17, 1768)," in *The Collected Writings of Samson Occom, Mohegan: Leadership and Literature in Eighteenth-Century Native America*, ed. Joanna Brooks (Oxford: Oxford University Press, 2006), 52.

4. For background on the Mason case, see Michael Oberg, *Uncas: First of the Mohicans* (Ithaca, NY: Cornell University Press, 2003), 207–13.

5. Samson Occom, *A Sermon, Preached at the Execution of Moses Paul, an Indian* (New London, CT: T. Green, 1772).

6. See Dartmouth Native American Program, "History of the Dartmouth Pow-Wow," Dartmouth College, www.dartmouth.edu/~nap/powwow/history.html accessed August 1, 2014.

7. Occom, *The Collected Writings of Samson Occom.*

8. Bonnie Barber, "Schweitzer Awarded National Endowment for the Humanities Grant to Digitize Occom Papers." *Dartmouth Now* (blog), Dartmouth College, July 24, 2010, http://now.dartmouth.edu/2010/07/schweitzer-awarded-national-endowment-for-the-humanities-grant-to-digitize-occom-papers

9. The search interface for the Dartmouth Dante Project was co-designed in the early 1980s by the library's Digital Library Technologies Group. See Robert Hollander, Steven Campbell, and Simone Marchesi, eds., *Dartmouth Dante Project* website, Dartmouth College, http://dante.dartmouth.edu, accessed August 1, 2014, and the Dante Project's successor, Dante Lab, http://dantelab.dartmouth.edu accessed August 1, 2014. For more recent examples, see the Dartmouth Digital Library Program, http://www.dartmouth.edu/~library/digital accessed August 1, 2015.

10. See NEH, We the People website, http://wethepeople.gov/index.html accessed August 1, 2014.

ELEVEN

The Audio of Text: Art of Tradition

Alan Ojiig Corbiere

Anishinaabemowin Situation

I currently work at Lakeview Elementary School on the M'Chigeeng First Nation on Manitoulin Island, Ontario. My job is to create a more culturally enhanced curriculum through the medium of language instruction. Currently, the Anishinaabemowin Revival Program (ARP) works with elders fluent in Anishinaabemowin[1] to translate various documents, as well as create lessons. The ARP staff also records these elders speaking, thus creating an archive as the project progresses.

Manitoulin Island has six reserves on it with two more in very close proximity. Manitoulin still has a significant Anishinaabemowin speaking population, but the speakers are aging and as they pass there have been no younger speakers filling the void they have left. The population in M'Chigeeng is approximately 900 people, with the majority of speakers above the age of sixty-five. To provide a specific example, in 1974 Lakeview had twenty-four students who graduated grade eight, only six of those graduates were fluent speakers of Anishinaabemowin.[2] The age of speakers precipitously drops with those born in 1970 and onward having virtually no significant Anishinaabemowin.[3] Since 1975, Lakeview School has taught Ojibwe as a subject. Currently, the students of Lakeview School are not fluent nor are there any passive bilinguals. Anishinaabemowin has left the home, and now the school is viewed as the principal place to revive the language.

As this language situation has become more dire, there has been a call for increased instructional time and the implementation of a different pedagogy. An array of programming for different age groups has been offered with evening classes for adults and online resources for parents.[4] This call for additional resources has been issued with a stipulation to use resources that are from our area, by our elders, and in our dialect. Furthermore, the call has added the stipulation that lessons be more tactile, interactive, and engaging. Although we still have a good corps of language speakers, many grew up in a time of Christianity, farming, and logging, and the active condemnation of Anishinaabe culture and teachings by church and state. In such a situation, many of the elders may have heard the aansookaanan (sacred stories), but they cannot necessarily retell them. Thus, Lakeview's ARP has sought to augment its corpus of Anishinaabemowin resources by searching archival collections.

This pursuit for more material, especially those materials written in Anishinaabemowin by Anishinaabeg, led to a search of various archives for documents and manuscripts. Fortunately, in 2009, Michael McNally published the manuscript titled "The Art of Tradition" prepared by Gertrude Kurath, Jane Ettawageshik, and Fred Ettawageshik. This collection of stories seemingly fit the bill, the Anishinaabemowin stories were in a dialect very close to the Manitoulin dialect and written by an Anishinaabe from an Anishinaabe point of view. McNally decided to publish the Anishinaabemowin Stories as transcribed by Jane and Fred Ettawageshik — that is to say, they are published in an obsolete orthography that teachers and students will have a great deal of trouble understanding.

This chapter will detail issues encountered when trying to utilize materials written in an obsolete orthography to develop Anishinaabemowin curriculum that is comprised of aansookaanan (sacred stories), Anishinaabe language, and traditional knowledge and skills. The stories selected for analysis from this published collection are, "Why Some Trees Have Knobs on Them & Birch Trees Grow in Clumps," and the second, "Why the Birchbark Has Streaks." These stories were selected because many people on Manitoulin Island, including some speakers, still harvest birch bark to make crafts for sale and barter.

Manitoulin — Harbor Springs Relationship

The stories were collected "between 1946 and 1954 from Odawa informants living in Emmet County, Michigan, the site of the old Indian settlement of L'Arbre Croche."[5] There are historic, and continuing, ties of kinship between the

Anishinaabe people of Upper State Michigan and Manitoulin Island. After the War of 1812, many of the Anishinaabeg who had fought alongside the British faced increased aggression from American authorities. The Andrew Jackson administration took power and on March 28, 1836, the Odawa and Chippewa (Ojibwe) of modern day Upper Michigan entered into treaty with the Americans.[6] After signing the treaty, the Anishinaabeg, particularly the chiefs of L'Arbre Croche (modern day Little Traverse Bay Band of Ottawa, and Grand Traverse Bay Band of Ottawa), understood that they had guaranteed their homelands with the treaty by specifying reserves for themselves and their progeny. However, the clause in the treaty that established the reserves was unilaterally modified by the Senate. Instead of guaranteeing the reserves forever, on May 20, 1836, the Senate imposed a five-year limitation on the reserves.[7] Thus, the Anishinaabeg could have been removed from their ancestral territory to lands west of the Mississippi.

Since 1815, the British had continued to honor past treaty obligations with the Anishinaabeg by delivering presents to them annually at posts on the British side of the border. Those Anishinaabeg living on the American side annually traversed the great lakes of Superior and Michigan to Lake Huron to attend the renewal of this alliance and to receive presents. After hearing the news of the Senate's actions, the Anishinaabeg of upper Michigan welcomed the offer to have Manitoulin Island set aside as one big reserve for many Anishinaabeg. Many Odaawaa from L'Arbre Croche and surrounding area moved to Wikwemikong in the 1830s and continued to pass back and forth in subsequent years. In fact, many of the surnames at Cross Village are the same as those at Wikwemikong. So the people are related and the dialect is virtually the same. In fact, Fred Ettawageshik, the storyteller/author of the two stories covered in this chapter, is related to the people named Assiginack, Apakozigan, and Sampson here on Manitoulin Island.[8]

Dialect Issues

The dialect spoken on Manitoulin Island has been called Ottawa/ Odawa or Central Ojibwe.[9] The dialect on Manitoulin is the same as the dialect at Harbor Springs. However, there are some differences, because every dialect is composed of idiolects as well. Specific instances in the story, "Why the Birchbark Has Streaks,"[10] include the two words that were not recognized by three Manitoulin Island speakers. Ettawageshik used the word wi-gwas-ke-mij [wiigwaaskemizh] for birch (paper birch, or betula papyrifera).[11] The incorporation of the medial morpheme — ke- is notably absent in various dictionaries that list birch/paper birch as Wiigwaas, wiigwaasaatig, wiigwaaso-mtig, or Wiigwaasmizh.[12] Even the Ojibwe dialect in Minnesota had Wiigwaas, wiigwaasi-mitig, or wiigwaasaatig.[13] Consulting both Bishop Frederic Baraga and Reverend Edward Wilson's earlier dictionaries yielded no results for wiigwaaskemizh.[14]

The second word Ettawageshik used that was unrecognizable to the Manitoulin speakers was written as gi-go-dagwisid and translated in the English gloss as climb. The closest word to that is kodaanzii vai, climb, climb up.[15] The rest of the vocabulary used by Fred Ettawageshik in the two stories was readily recognized by the Manitoulin speakers.

Orthographic Issues

The stories written in Odawa in "Art of Tradition" were written in Anishinaabemowin by Jane and Fred Ettawageshik. Jane admittedly could not speak Anishinaabemowin at the time. She relied on her husband Fred to transcribe and translate stories, but she did phonetic transcriptions. She reported that for one of the popular historical tales, "this is the story told by Fred, which I transcribed phonetically and he translated."[16] Fred Ettawageshik reportedly recorded some stories at the American Philosophical Society (APS) in 1947. Jane noted that "Fred Ettawageshik, my husband, read a prepared Odawa script when he recorded myths and legends . . . These stories have been translated by Fred and are included in this collection along with one that Fred recorded and then translated in 1948. I made phonetic transcriptions with interlinear translations of three other stories told by Fred."[17]

Brian Carpenter of the APS graciously consulted the collection and furnished a copy of the hand written notes of this collection. Included was a handwritten transcription of the story entitled, "Why Some Trees Have Knobs on Them and the Birches Grow in Clumps."[18] Also included in the forwarded files was a word list for the story. "Why Birchbark Has Streaks."[19] Comparing these two documents, it is evident that the handwriting and the alphabetic symbols are different. The handwritten document of "Why Some Trees Have Knobs on Them" has a stylized signature at the end of the story but no written name. This has to be the Ettawageshik doodem Piipiigwenh (Pe-pe-gwe) noted by Fred and Andrew J. Blackbird. In the other document, the phonetically rendered words incorporate diacritics that do not appear in the published version. Jane reported that, "The Odawa script that Fred Ettawageshik uses is based on our English alphabet and his own interpretation of the way it should be used to write Odawa. He does not know just when he began to write Odawa. I am of the opinion that he was influenced by his father, Joe, who also wrote Odawa. The Odawa written by Joe Ettawaweghik [sic] is very similar, if not identical, to Fred's rendition. A number of Odawas write their language and there is considerable variation among them."

It is likely that Fred Ettawageshik learned to read and write Odawa from his father. The orthography, however, did have its origins in the orthography devised and utilized by Catholic priests. Jane noted that this was the likely source and stated that, "It is probable that modern writers of Odawa owe a debt to Fr. Baraga, who translated hymnals and prayer books into Odawa in the mid-nineteenth century, yet I have not seen any recently written Odawa that is exactly similar to his." In the end, Jane Ettawageshik somewhat frustratedly reported that, "I have tried to pin Fred down a number of times about the origin of his Odawa script, but he usually ends by saying, 'I write the words the way they sound to me.'"[20]

The French inspiration is evident in Fred's orthography, specifically the consistent use of the letter "e" for the long e sound, as in the terminal sound in Anishinaabe. The manner in which Fred used other vowels also adhered to the orthography inspired by French orthographic conventions, namely the letter "a" for long and short "a"; the letter "i" represents both the short and long "i" and the letter "o" represents both short and long "o." Another telltale sign is the use of the consonant cluster "dj" to represent the hard "j" sound in Jesus or jeopardy. Fred also used the consonant cluster "tch" for the "ch" sound; Baraga used both of these consonant clusters in the same manner. However, one of the most revealing signs of French orthographic inspiration is the use of the letter "j" for the "zh" sound as in wiigwaasmizhiig, which Fred rendered as wigwaske-mijig.

The fact that Ettawageshik and his father employed the French inspired orthography should not come as a surprise because as early as 1828 the Odaawaa of L'Arbre Croche had adopted Roman Catholicism.[21]

Recording Versus Text

Unfortunately, the stories as published in "Art of Tradition" are practically unusable in an elementary school program. The process to render them usable to students and teachers started in 2013. Bear in mind, that we did not have access to the recordings or the handwritten notes, just the publication. I completed an initial transliteration, converting the Anishinaabemowin words into the modern double vowel (Fiero) orthography.[22] Any words that I did not know, I highlighted and then we gathered as a group (Alvin Ted Corbiere, Lewis Debassige, and

Evelyn Roy) and read the stories. The interlinear English provided essential clues to many of the words that had either been idiosyncratically written or were mistakenly typed from handwriting to publication.[23] One of the team's goals was to maintain as much of the original wording as possible. In 2013, the elders and I transliterated and where necessary, edited, nineteen of the stories that were published in "Art of Tradition." Included in that set of stories was "Why the Birchbark Has Streaks" and "Why Some Trees Have Knobs on Them & Birch Trees Grow in Clumps."

Once the recordings became available online we could double check our work against Fred's writing and against Jane's writing. Corbiere and I sat down to listen to the recordings and followed along with the transcript. Understandably, not every word or sentence made it into the transcript. Notably one whole coda line was missing at the end of "Why Some Trees Have Knobs on Them." Also the Anishinaabemowin titles of these two stories were not published in the book, just the English titles. We also took the opportunity to check words that I had earlier highlighted as problematic. Some of the recordings are poor, especially in areas where questions have arisen about the spelling or choice of word. There remain two words that we could not make out positively. Fred Ettawageshik may have written the stories out in Odawa and read them, but he also adlibbed during the recording.

The main point is to urge any institutions that have recordings in their collections to get them out to the language programs that need them.[24] The elders and I put in many hours transcribing these stories, yet I am not sure having access to the recordings would have necessarily saved much time.[25] It was worth the effort because of the dialogue amongst the elders in choosing alternative words or phrasing a clause differently than Fred Ettawageshik did. It is hard to listen to the original recordings, and this makes it unsuitable for inclusion in an elementary school second language program. In the end we did need a transliteration of the story and, hopefully, someday, we will have illustrations to accompany the story.

Developing a Curricular Unit and Lesson Plans

The stories, "Why the Birchbark Has Streaks" and "Why Some Trees Have Knobs on Them & Birch Trees Grow in Clumps," were integral to forming the curricular unit focused on birch bark to be taught to the elementary school students (the materials will be repurposed later for adult students). We had translated Daphne Odjig's "Nanabush Loses His Eyeballs." In this story Nanabush blinds himself through his antics, but while blinded the birch tree did not assist him; in fact, the birch tree antagonized him and scolded him. In contrast, the spruce tree assisted Nanabush, gave him some spruce gum, which Nanabush used to remake his eyes. Once he could see again, he grabbed a willow switch and whipped the birch tree for his callous behavior. That is the reason the birch tree has streaks. In the version written down by Emerson and David Coatsworth from the Anishinaabeg of Mnjikaning (Rama), the culture hero named Nenbozhoo asked the birch tree to watch his deer meat as it dried. Birch tree fell asleep and some birds came and ate up all the meat. Enraged, Nenbozhoo took a branch from the balsam tree and whipped the birch tree for not doing his job.[26] Some of the details differ but the story is the same. In Ettawageshik's version, Nenbozhoo killed a bear and cooked the meat. Then the birch tree started to squeak because the wind came up and two branches were interlocked. Nenbozhoo went to untangle them but got himself stuck. Once he extricated himself he was angry; he then whipped the birch but the kind of switch is not identified in Ettawageshik's version. The second story has Nenbozhoo punching the birch tree and then the birch trees fleeing together to escape his wrath. This is the explanation for why birch trees grow in clusters.

I had assumed that this story and the other would be categorized as a morality tale or a "creation/origin" tale. However, after going on a trip with an elder to harvest birchbark, I am convinced there is more transmitted in the story than mores and the consequences of breaking them. In the summer of 2013, I asked Ted Toulouse if I could tag along and record him speaking in Anishinaabemowin while he harvested birchbark for his wife Myna, an award winning quillbox maker. As we walked along, I asked various questions. We passed some birch trees and I said, "Those are too small?" and he said, "Yes, but look here." Then he pointed out some birch in among some spruce trees. He said "Gaa go gegoo nizhshiziiwag giwi ayaawag, wiigwaasag, gaawaandagoonsag bdakshinwaad, dgogziwaad (The birch are not nice when they grow in among where spruce grow)." Then he proceeded to peel the bark from a birch that was surrounded by spruce. The inner bark had all kinds of scarring and was not of much use for a craftsperson. I postulate that the story encodes the knowledge that the bark of the birch is compromised when it is in contact with spruce. This is what people call "traditional ecological knowledge."

None of the versions of the story consulted or published have all of these elements in it. The various versions of the episode are mixed and matched with other episodes of the Nenbozhoo story. Sometimes, the episode of the squeaking tree is the origin for why the cedar has a twisted grain,[27] other times the squeaky tree is the punishment of the birch and the origin of the streaks on the bark. As a people, the Anishinaabeg have used the birch tree for multiple purposes. It is natural that a story would be told about its appearance as well as about its preferred habitat. The Anishinaabeg, however, did not formulate this knowledge in an almanac, they encoded it in the aansookaanan (sacred stories of Nenbozhoo).

The resources used to complete this curricular unit[28] were drawn from multiple sources from multiple locales, published accounts, archival documentation, digitized wire recordings and, of course, the continuous lived artistic practice of Anishinaabe people. It is a curricular unit that embraces the regional knowledge and speech of the Anishinaabeg of the central great lakes.

Notes

1. Anishinaabemowin is more commonly known as Ojibwe. The Ojibwe, Odawa, and Potowatomi people refer to themselves as Anishinaabe (Anishinaabeg plural) and the word for the language is Anishinaabemowin.

2. Personal communication with Eria Beboning, August 29, 2016. We looked at her grade eight class photograph and she identified her classmates that could speak Anishinaabemowin. Eria and most of her classmates were born in 1961.

3. I was born in 1969. During my time at Lakeview there were a few passive bilinguals (those who can understand all that is said to them in Anishinaabemowin) two grades below me, and only one fellow student in my class that could speak. He was raised by his grandmother.

4. In the fall of 2013 Kenjgewin Teg Educational Institute established the immersion school called Mnidoo Mnising Anishinaabe Kinoomaagegamig, starting at kindergarten and following a cohort for following five years. This is also located in M'Chigeeng First Nation. The M'Chigeeng First Nation has passed a resolution to gradually implement immersion at Lakeview School, year by year.

5. Kurath, Gertrude, Jane Ettawageshik, and Fred Ettawageshik. *The Art of Tradition: Sacred Music, Dance and Myth of Michigan's Anishinaabe, 1946 - 1955* (East Lansing: Michigan State University Press, 2009), 273.

6. James M. McClurken, *We Wish to be Civilized: Ottawa-American Political Contests on the Michigan Frontier.* (Thesis, East Lansing, Michigan State University, Department of Anthropology, 1988), 240.

7. McClurken, "We Wish to be Civilized," 244.

8. Andrew J. Blackbird wrote that anybody of the "Pe-pe-gwenh" tribe were relations. Blackbird also recorded that Makadebinessi (Blackbird's father), Assiginack, Apaukozigan, and Wing were brothers.

9. Richard A. Rhodes, *Eastern Ojibwa-Chippewa-Ottawa Dictionary* (New York,: mouton de gruyter, 1985); Randolph J. Valentine, *Nishnaabemwin Reference Grammar* (Toronto, ON: University of Toronto Press, 2001).

10. Ettawageshik, Ettawageshik, Kurath, *The Art of Tradition*, 323–324.

11. Usually "-ke" is a verbalizer. It is added to Ojibwe nouns to convey the idea of making, picking, harvesting, or fixing. Wiigwaasike in John D. Nichols and Earl Nyholm, *A Concise Dictionary of Minnesota Ojibwe* (St. Paul: University of Minnesota Press, 1995);, and wiigwaaske in Rhodes (1985), is translated as harvest birch bark, pick birch bark.

12. Nishnaabemwin Online Dictionary, http://nishnaabemwin.atlas-ling.ca/#/results accessed August 22, 2016. Rhodes 1985, 361.

13. Ojibwe People's Dictionary, http://ojibwe.lib.umn.edu/en/search?utf8 =%E2%9C%93&q=birch&commit=Search&type=english accessed August 22, 2016.

14. Baraga lists birch as wigwass (p. 28 and 414) and Wilson lists birch as wigwaus (p. 171). Neither listed wiigwaasaatig nor wiigwaasmizh nor wiigwaaso-mitig. Frederic Baraga, *A Dictionary of the Ojibway Language* (St. Paul: Minnesota Historical Society Press, 1992). Edward F. Wilson, *The Ojebway Language: A Manual for Missionaries and Others Employed Among the Ojebway Indians* (Toronto, ON: Rowsell and Hutchison for the Venerable Society for Promoting Christian Knowledge, 187[4]).

15. Both Baraga and Wilson listed akwaandawe (spelled in their respective orthographies) but neither listed kodaanzii. Kodaanzii is listed in the Nishnaabemwin Dictionary, http://nishnaabemwin.atlas-ling.ca/#/results accessed August 22, 2016

16. Kurath, Ettawageshik and Ettawageshik, *The Art of Tradition*, 279.

17. Kurath, Ettawageshik and Ettawageshik, *The Art of Tradition*, 273.

18. Published in Kurath, Ettawageshik and Ettawageshik, *The Art of Tradition*, 328.

19. Published in Kurath, Ettawageshik and Ettawageshik, *The Art of Tradition*, 323–324.

20. Kurath, Ettawageshik and Ettawageshik, *The Art of Tradition*, 436 n2.

21. Alan Corbiere, "Exploring Historical Literacy in Manitoulin Island Ojibwe," in H.C. Wolfart, editor, *Papers of the 34th Algonquian Conference,* (Winnipeg: Algonquin Conference, 2003), 57–80.

22. The adopted orthography that many Anishinaabemowin teachers use today was developed by Charles 'Chuck' Fiero. It is distinguished by the use of two vowels to indicate the length of said vowel. The orthography has since come to be known as the 'double vowel orthography' and/ or the Fiero writing system.

23. One such error in typing occurred in "Why Some Trees Have Knobs on Them" — Fred had written ab-mondang but he did not complete the top of the O so it was mistaken for the letter U; however, the orthography that Fred wrote does not use the letter U. Also in this same story Fred wrote "gindj-kadesi (he became anry [sic])." So Fred erred as well, not just the typist. The word for "he got angry" would be written as gi-nishkadisi

(gii-nshkaadzi in Fiero). We know that this is a spelling error because of the recording. Fred clearly said "gii-nshkaadizi."

24. The American Philosophical Society has posted these recordings onto a secure website requiring the user to procure a password. This is a good policy because some of the stories may not be appropriate to disseminate indiscriminately.

25. We have also employed this processing method with stories from William Jones's collection of Ojibwe stories, as well as some from Alexander F. Chamberlain and Paul Radin, none of which had any recordings.

26. Emerson Coatsworth and David Coatsworth, *The Adventures of Nanabush: Ojibway Indian Stories* (Toronto, ON: Doubleday, 1979), 9–11.

27. Reverend Frost's version of one of "Nenbozhoo's adventure's related to him by Indian Minisino (Min-is-i-no)= Warrior, at Garden River 18 years ago." *Indian Legends.* Reverend F. Frost, 1892, Bell Papers, LAC, MG 29, B15, Vol. 54, File 8. Also refer to "Why the White Cedar is Twisted." *Indian Legends* by Rev. Fr. DuRanquet, Bell Papers, MG 29, B15, Vol. 54, File 4.

28. The unit is yet to be implemented and tested.

TWELVE

Writing the Digital Codex: Non/Alphabetic, De/Colonial, Network/Ed

Damián Baca

Since the 2008 publication of my study, *Mestiz@ Scripts, Digital Migrations, and the Territories of Writing*, I have been working on non-Hellenocentric, non-Eurocentric, de-colonial modes of knowing and representation, with a focus on non-alphabetic writing systems. My current project investigates the expressive potential of Mexican codex writing in the realm of new media and web-based digital information. Specifically, I want to study how digital codices modeled after pre-Columbian manuscript sign systems might catalyze in contemporary Mexican-origin student writers a deeper understanding, not only of ancient Mesoamerica, but also of their own lives and traditions in the present.

The fundamental premise of this research is that the field of digital humanities has overlooked the obvious connection between ancient non-alphabetic story systems and the twenty-first-century graphical user interface (GUI). Indeed, modern literacy scholarship and pedagogy has so naturalized the representation of logo-syllabic speech in digital environments that there are surprisingly few tools — commercial or otherwise — that are specifically designed to help storytellers write with pictures, the pervasive interface idiom dominating popular computing for the past two decades. The codices — or amoxtli — of ancient Mesoamericans offer an intriguing model for addressing this missed opportunity. These manuscripts rely entirely on multimodal pictographic and logographic inscription systems that consist of figural representations and symbols.[1]

I employ the historically recent Western anthropological word "Mesoamerica" here as an umbrella term, not to suggest a sweeping generalization, nor an erasure, but a recognition of long processes of interrelated yet diverse cultures in a constant state of transformation. The expression is not necessarily fixed along a chronological scale and has been used as an enduring cultural identifier in a perpetual state of change. Mesoamerica did not disappear, in a matter of speaking, but continues to adapt today.

Ancient codex writing is a configuration of permanently recorded marks that signify thoughts, ideas, objects, events, identities, temporalities, and relations rather than visible speech (i.e., specific words and sentences). As a result, this writing system is both syntactically flexible and conceptually robust, so that all graphic and tactile practices — pictograms, ideograms, logograms, and iconography — can be combined in a single interface and interpreted across linguistic borders. Notably, this writing practice fuses into a single symbolic account of what, for Western minds, are separate and hierarchical concepts of writing and art. For example, tlacuiloliztli, the Nahuatl verb for "writing," translates as "the spreading of color on hard surfaces" and disrupts the hierarchical Western distinction between "writing" and "painting."[2]

Despite writing's vibrant history that continues to thrive as a twenty-first century tradition, scholarship in the digital humanities still asserts the Western alphabet as its foundational and primary marker of literacy. Such scholarship neglects Mexican rhetorical and literary contributions,[3] and Chicanx-designed research methods.[4] The Digital Codex Project intends to address these oversights directly through the creation of a suite of software tools that will allow writers to review and revise historical and contemporary codices alike. Using an innovative GUI, writers might develop life stories through a process of continuous symbolic engagement with Mesoamerican stylistic devices and Mexican, Mexican American, and Chicanx rhetorical strategies. By fusing and embellishing Mesoamerican pictography with European inscription practices in digital environments, codex technologies promote a new dialectic, a new strategy of inventing and writing among worlds.

Of significant influence is the work of Chicana feminist artist Delilah Montoya, notably her *Codex Delilah: Journey from Mexicatl to Chicana*, completed in 1992 during the quincentenary of European invasion of the Americas. Montoya's contemporary re-visioning of the Amoxtli tradition notably affirms the roles of Mexican women in Indigenous codex production. Here, Montoya weaves pictographs with alphabetic literacy to tell of initiation into Ticitl or Curanderisma, the practice of Indigenous Mexican folk medicine. By depicting her journey *toward* Aztlán, the mythic homeland of the Mexica, Montoya transposes the great migration narrative referenced in the 1541 *Codex Boturini*, which depicts the great eleventh century migration of the Mexica from Aztlán southward to Tenochtitlán. Montoya's representation of self-discovery and initiation does not seek an idealized or nostalgic pre-Columbian identity but, instead, sets in motion a distinct present-day Mexican and Chicana subjectivity. Furthermore, *Codex Delilah* takes its name from its composer, thereby symbolically opposing the earlier European appropriation and ongoing control of Mesoamerican codices.

In addition to its composing tools, the Digital Codex Project will include an editing studio with an interactive collection of post-Columbian Codex materials dating from the late fifteenth century to the twenty-first. These items will:

1. Allow writers to actively navigate across and through hyperlinked Codex materials, beginning with *Codex Delilah*.
2. Educate writers about power dynamics, cultural history, and identity formation practices of both ancient Mesoamericans and modern day Mexicans north and south of the militarized us/Mexico border.
3. Educate writers about Chicana feminist methodologies and ways of reading codices.
4. Prepare writers to engage in the invention of codex composition strategies.

An alpha development stage will include a web-based digital environment designed to inspire thinking beyond the dominate Greco-Latin and alphabetic horizon, and to engage writers in thinking and composing processes that originated in the Americas/Abya Yala/the so-called Western Hemisphere, at the dawn of globalization beginning in 1492.

The editing studio function in the Digital Codex Project will offer codex students a suite of image, animation, and sound manipulation tools to facilitate hands-on exploration, invention, and critical engagement with a multitude of writing systems of the Americas, including glyphs, ideograms, logograms, iconography, oral and performed texts, and Nahuatl, Spanish, English, and Spanglish alphabetic scripts. Specifically, the tool will provide access to an inventory of digital assets — codex pictography, us/Mexico border imagery, NAFTA-era political discourse, stencil and graffiti art, and so on — from which writers may select and invent. This will allow writers to design and construct hyperlinked, multi-hued, vertically and horizontally oriented, and non- or multi-lineal codices.

The digital codex editing studio will also assist novice codex composers by introducing them to a set of "themes." Projected themes include Border Crossing; Literacy Migrations; Genealogy; Labor; and Borderland Identities, to name a few. Each theme will include embedded "guidance materials" to help such novice users develop their first digital codex. In addition, the editing studio aspect of the digital codex will facilitate the sharing of codices with other creators who have used the studio and developed work on the project network. Further, the editing studio section of the digital codex and the codex writ large will provide online assistance to codex users. Online assistance will include a glossary of key terms from the interaction collection. That glossary will hold definitions for key Nahuatl, Spanglish, and Spanish expressions and phrases, along with how-to pages with short instructional help videos and a web forum where writers may share tips and request help from more experienced codex composers.

Upon completion of the alpha development stage of this project, we will do a preliminary goals assessment to examine key outcomes on navigation and usage of the digital codex site. Such assessment will determine whether codex writers were sufficiently prompted to examine the movement of writing systems across continents, oceans, and shifting borders under varying colonial situations and contexts. Assessment will also address whether the codex provided adequate conditions for allowing writers to rethink the history of writing technologies, both forward and in reverse, as a potential means for reading technology in the humanities "against the grain" of instantiated forms, modes, patterns, and application of hegemonic Western practices of inscription as used in technologies of reading and writing. With that, post alpha development of the project will also examine if writers discerned that power, colonial or otherwise, is enacted in all scenes of writing and with all technologies of writing. Another important aspect of assessment will determine if the project invited writers to consider the results and consequences of decolonial historiography and whether the process of composing personal codices led writers to interrogate and redefine such terms as "literacy," "writing," and "technology" in the humanities. Finally, assessment of the alpha stage implementation of the codex project will examine if writers felt challenged to think with, against, and beyond their own alphabets.

Simultaneously, the alpha stage of this project also addresses the problem that few researchers have examined: how Mexican-origin writers and other writers compose codex cultural materials in the digital realm in order to critique dominant historical narratives as well as advance "new" histories of identification in the global Americas. This involves the development and production of a content-based digital codex — that is, a digital interface design that reactivates the non-linear, multi sign-system codex through which users may navigate. This new media codex will provide an interactive web-delivered means of making, reproducing, and reimagining codex materials. Users will apply historical and cultural knowledge gained in the interactive archive to produce their own narratives, their own literacy journeys, and their own real and metaphorical migration stories through new technologies. Specifically, historically grounded cultural acts of making and remaking digital codices requires complex yet accessible knowledge of codex histories and their contemporary variations.

Hopefully, the University of Arizona Library will make available a digital adaptation of Delilah Montoya's *Codex Delilah*, allowing users to "drag" the manuscript from left to right and right to left. Pictographs and icons will hyperlink to primary and supplemental historical data that guides users through the mythic journey of Six Deer, the character embodying the contact between Mesoamerican and Spanish culture in her trip "pal norte" towards Aztlán.[5] Further, I hope to receive a seed grant from my university's new Center for Digital Humanities, though funding is of course still uncertain. The digital codices will be public and integrated into undergraduate seminars in the coming semesters; this may also coincide with a certificate in Professional & Technical Writing that is under development in my program and department. The certificate is a small step toward what my colleagues and I hope will become new undergraduate major in Writing Studies.

As students in such courses complete "new" born-digital projects based on their use of the digital codex, we will exhibit these as samples of what can be achieved using this interface. This effort to reimagine a forgotten and ignored history integrates several visual and narrative elements to affirm the importance of both historical and contemporary intermixing for Mexican and Chicanx cultural survival. Montoya's powerful journey will serve as a source of inspiration, as users will construct their own narratives and visions of Chicanx, Mexican, and Indigenous futures.

Codex technologies support the idea of writing as an inclusive term of the complexity inherent to Mexican symbolization. It is precisely through the direct graphic weaving of Mesoamerican pictography with the Western alphabet that readers and writers are confronted with the hierarchical discord between them. To look at pictographs as disembodied, de-contextualized systems is to misunderstand and underestimate the communicative power they continue to hold. The Digital Codex Project encourages new definitions of both writing and technology that depend less on the notion of preserving visible speech and more on the permanency and visibility of particular signs as they appear in electronic spaces. In addition to illustrating wider notions of literacy that surpass the boundaries of alphabetic speech, this project will expand conventional acts of archiving by blurring distinctions between storage and production. Mesoamerica is not a fixed historical moment within the colonial division of time, but an interactive living tradition that can reveal much about the future.

Notes

1. Elizabeth Hill Boone and Walter Mignolo, eds., *Writing Without Words: Alternative Literacies in Mesoamerica and the Andes* (Durham, NC: Duke University Press, 2004).

2. Damián Baca, *Mestiz@ Scripts, Digital Migrations, and the Territories of Writing* (New York: Palgrave Macmillan, 2008), 96.

3. David Carrasco and Eduardo Matos Moctezuma, *Moctezuma's Mexico: Visions of the Aztec World* (Boulder: University Press of Colorado, 2003); Guillermo Gómez-Peña, Enrique Chagoya, and Felicia Rice, *Codex Espangliensis: From Columbus to the Border Patrol* (San Francisco: City Lights Books, 2000).

4. Gloria Anzaldúa, "Border Arte: Nepantla, El Lugar de la Frontera," in *La Frontera/ The Border: Art about the Mexico/United States Border Experience*, ed. Natasha Bonilla Martínez (San Diego: Centro Cultural de la Raza, Museum of Contemporary Art, 1993), 113; Mary Pat Brady, *Extinct Lands, Temporal Geographies: Chicana Literature and the Urgency of Space* (Durham, NC: Duke University Press, 2002); Ana Castillo, *Massacre of Dreamers: Essays on Xicanisma* (Albuquerque: University of New Mexico Press, 1994); Aida Hurtado, *Voicing Chicana Feminisms: Young Women Speak Out on Sexuality and Identity* (New York: New York University Press, 2003); Cherríe Moraga, *The Last Generation: Prose and Poetry* (Boston: South End Press, 1993); Laura Pérez, *Chicana Art: The Politics of Spiritual and Aesthetic Altarities* (Durham, NC: Duke University Press, 2007); Sonia Saldívar-Hull, *Feminism on the Border: Chicana Gender Politics and Literature* (Berkeley: University of California Press, 2002).

5. Montoya has agreed to allow her manuscript to be digitally scanned for this project specifically, though the copyright on the material will remain hers.

THIRTEEN

An Orderly Assemblage of Biases:
Troubling the Monocultural Stack

Jason Edward Lewis

> The digital earth is where I'm Indigenous.
> *Blake Hausman*[1]

Riding the Trail of Tears is a novel by Cherokee writer Blake Hausman. It is a surrealistic sci-fi take on virtual reality, featuring an immersive tourist trap through which visitors relive the Cherokee Removal in the winter of 1838–1839. The novel's first section is narrated by Nunnehi, a Little Person or creature from the old Cherokee stories. Nunnehi describes the genesis of the Tsalagi Removal Exodus Point Park (TREPP) and recounts how he and others like him came to be alive and resident within the ride. By the end of the book, Nunnehi and his siblings complete a long-gestating insurrection, lay claim to the digital territory delineated by TREPP, and start rewriting the narrative to re-center the story of the Trail of Tears around the Cherokee experience rather than the settlers' gaze. Early on, Nunnehi says: "the virtual Trail of Tears . . . [is] my homeland. I'm probably more Indigenous than you, and the digital earth is where I'm Indigenous."

This chapter is about the digital earth, its composition, and how we might be Indigenous in it. It is about new ways of understanding our role in the computational ecosystems we are building, and how we might make kin with the other entities that we create in it and emerge from it. It is about nurturing the digital earth from which it will all grow — silicon soil in which our descendants will stick their virtual toes, wiggle them around, and think, "This is a good place to be Cherokee. This is a good place to be Mohawk. This is a good place for our people."

The Stack and Its Corruptions

Let us start with where we are at.

As I have written elsewhere,[2] modern computing systems work via a very narrow logic, admit only certain kinds of information as data, and can perform operations representative of only a small, impoverished subset of the operations we enact as humans every day. These systems exist as components of the stack, the vertically interrelated and interdependent series of hardware configurations and software protocols that make high-level media computation and networking possible. The software stack sits on top of the hardware stack. Moving up the hardware stack is to move from circuits to micro-chips to computers to networks; moving up the software stack is to move from machine code to programming languages to protocols to systems. As you go upward, you are moving from custom solutions to generalized solutions, from specifics to abstractions. As you make this traversal from the deep structure to the surface interface, ever more of the details of the underlying configurations are hidden from you. With the increasing opacity, your ability to assert fine control over the execution of the underlying algorithms decreases. Eventually you get to the software application or web service layer of the stack. It is at this highly abstract level that most people interact with computational systems, as they use Microsoft Word, Google Search, play a video game, or enter into an immersive environment.[3]

The sheer complexity of these layers, both horizontally, as different components interact with one another, and vertically, as different layers distribute data to the human interface and back, making it difficult to impossible for any single human actor to understand or effectively manipulate the whole system. Yet we are subject to the regimes the stack places upon us. In the same way the law embodies and polices the dominant culture's expectations about people's behavior, computational systems materialize and constrain the dominant culture's expectations of what counts as data, what algorithms are appropriate for processing that data, and what are valid results of that processing.

Cultural bias coupled with the pervasiveness of computational technology means that we are creating computer systems that are dangerous in their blindness. The last few years have seen this realization penetrating Silicon Valley culture, as technology developers at Google, Facebook, and others begin to comprehend that "unbiased algorithm" is as much an oxymoron as "pure meritocracy." Scholars such as Kate Crawford,[4] D. Fox Harrel,[5] and Safiya Umoja Noble,[6] among others, have brought the discussion of these biases into greater focus. This has brought the critique out of the academy, where the argument about how computational systems reflect the culture within which they are developed has a long history, and into the public sphere.[7]

Algorithmic bias exists in the non-digital world, of course. One of the most notable examples is the color reference cards first used in the 1940s to calibrate image printing processes. These "Shirley" cards "generally showed a single white woman dressed in bright clothes" to facilitate calibration as "color film chemistry at the time was designed with a bias towards light skin."[8] Communications scholar Lorna Roth has conducted extensive research into the use of Shirley cards. In 2009 she wrote: "Until recently, due to a light-skin bias embedded in color film stock emulsions and digital camera design, the rendering of non-Caucasian skin tones was highly deficient and required the development of compensatory practices and technology improvements to redress its shortcomings."[9] Roth points out how this practice continued for decades after the first complaints were made, with the first substantive change only made in the 1970s. At that time, image calibration cards were redesigned not out of a desire to rectify their skin tone bias but rather to satisfy furniture and chocolate makers who had been complaining that the cards did a poor job of representing the darker tones of their commercial products.

Much of the current interest in looking at bias in computational systems stems from artificial intelligence yet again becoming a locus of substantial research, development, and deployment. Numerous studies over the last decade show how bias is embedded into every aspect of such systems. Examples include machine systems for learning human languages incorporating the human prejudices embedded and expressed in the corpora of natural languages on which the systems are trained,[10] and machine systems for learning to recognize people learning that beauty is a trait possessed primarily by white people.[11] One of the most egregious classes of these biases discovered to date is that embedded in the criminal justice system. The investigative journal *ProPublica* conducted an investigation into the risk assessment software that is increasingly used in the United States to provide advice to judges, lawyers, and parole officials throughout the judicial process — determining bail, setting sentences, guiding parole conditions, etc.[12] The authors quote US attorney general Eric Holder addressing the use of such software in 2014: "I am concerned that [risk assessment software] inadvertently undermine[s] our efforts to ensure individualized and equal justice . . . they may exacerbate unwarranted and unjust disparities that are already far too common in our criminal justice system and in our society." In 2016, *ProPublica* raised concerns that suggest that Holder's concern was justified. Its investigation into the use of COMPAS software turned up "significant racial disparities . . . falsely flagging black defendants as future criminals . . . at twice the rate as white defendants" and misidentifying white defendants as "low risk more often than black defendants."[13]

Social scientists such as Crawford have pointed out how difficult it is to rid ourselves of the deep bias in the datasets feeding the algorithms driving these systems. Many times "new" datasets are actually based on or include information from older datasets that were collected using outmoded or discredited methods. "Classifications," notes Crawford, "can be sticky, and sometimes they stick around a lot longer than we intend them to even when they are harmful."[14] This stickiness means that, even if system designers made the effort to counter the bias in their algorithms, the data they feed those algorithms may taint the entire endeavor.

White Supremacy: Not Just for People Anymore

Media scholar Lisa Nakamura notes that, "[t]hough computer memory modules double in speed every couple of years, users are still running operating systems which reflect phantasmatic visions of race and gender. Moore's Law does not obtain in the 'cultural layer.'"[15] In other words, the exponential evolution in computational processing power since the early 1980s has not been accompanied by a comparably rapid evolution in equality in North America. Statistics comparing Indigenous people and African Americans to the majority population in Canada and the US, respectively, show just how far both societies are from eliminating racial bias.[16] It should be no surprise that our computational systems reflect a worldview in which this is not only accepted but — given the stickiness of the phenomenon — perhaps preferred by the majority population. Expecting our tools to be more enlightened than we ourselves is a foolish self-delusion.

Computational artist Trevor Paglen has observed that, "one of the philosophical dangers of using widespread automation . . . is that it fixes meaning."[17] That inertia, combined with the data bias identified by Crawford and the extension of racial bias into cyberspace identified by Nakamura, drastically increases what is at stake when these systems are designed and deployed. The underlying algorithms must make assumptions about the world in order to operate; even if these assumptions themselves are not biased, they may make use of biased classification methods. And even if the classification is not biased, the data feeding the process may be biased. All these aspects of computational systems are often obscured, either purposively in order to protect intellectual property or as a byproduct of a technical complexity that prohibits non-specialists from understanding and evaluating them. The system becomes a fact of the world, stubborn and difficult to unfix. The result is that, in a society where it is increasingly difficult to do anything without touching on a computational interface of some sort, the decisions that developers are making all the time have profound and long-lasting consequences for how we live our lives.

Indigenous people are intimately familiar with how the old ways of thinking and looking at the world become sedimented into our contemporary worldviews. Marcia Cosby and others have written about how the "Imaginary Indian" was constructed to justify the theft of Indigenous lands,[18] and that imaginary person remains the dominant image that most settlers have of Indigenous people. This is the image settlers draw upon when they parse news about life in Indigenous communities, when jurors and judges consider court cases involving Indigenous people, and when the mall security guard is deciding who looks suspicious and who does not. As Harrel's work on phantasmal media shows, these are exactly the sorts of images that get embedded into our computational systems. "Computational media," he writes, "play roles in constructing ideas that we unconsciously accept as true and constructive of reality yet are in fact imaginatively grounded constructions based in particular worldviews."[19] Or, in Crawford's more blunt assessment, "[These systems are] not free of bias; this is just bias encoded."[20]

As we struggle to "write the thoughts of systems," in the words of computational philosopher and poet David Jhave Johnston,[21] and as those systems become ever-more pervasive, we are beginning to see that it is a political act to define the protocols that guide these systems' thoughts. It is about how power is exercised, and by whom.

The Fast and the Slow

Nakamura, in her extensive research on race in cyberspace, notes that "in order to think rigorously, humanely, and imaginatively about virtuality and the post-human, it is absolutely necessary to ground critique in the lived realities of the human, in all their particularity and specificity. The nuanced realities of virtuality — racial, gendered, Othered — live in the body."[22] When we pay attention to the bodies producing these protocols, we can see they are not just a random collection of homo sapiens. They are clustered in certain geolocations, particularly Silicon Valley, but with outposts in places like Seattle, Boston, Waterloo, and Oxford. They are working within an intellectual lineage that stretches back to the Greeks, even if they themselves might not be descendants of Europeans. Their education and professional practice rarely incorporate ideas or even data that comes from Africa, or South America, or large swathes of Asia. They are overwhelmingly white and male, and underwhelmingly brown and female[23] — and, even when brown bodies appear, "they participate in the 'cultural hegemony that privileges a white race.'"[24]

Going back to Winograd and Flores (1987) theorizing about the contextually coupled nature of cognition,[25] Haraway's (1991) critique of the interpenetrating relationship between human, non-human, and machine bodies,[26] and Reeves & Nass's (1996) experiments showing that "[i]ndividuals' interactions with computers, television, and new media are fundamentally social and natural, just like interactions in real life,"[27] critical approaches to computational culture have argued for acknowledging the deep entanglements among the cultural and computational layers of the stack. Now, after three decades in which computational systems have grown ever more ubiquitous and complex, we are starting to see clearly the consequence of the radical disjuncture between the high velocity evolution of our digital tools and the much slower evolution of our societal configurations.

Making Space

We founded the Aboriginal Territories in Cyberspace (AbTeC) research network in 2006 to ensure that Indigenous people were present in cyberspace and possessed the knowledge necessary to bend it to our needs. We were also interested in speeding up the rate at which Indigenous people increased their understanding of computational media. One hope was that this would help address and counter the white supremacy being baked into the computational layer, and resist its replication into cyberspace. AbTeC did this by exploring the question of what it means to be Indigenous in cyberspace — how do we make, maintain, and vivify Indigenous places within that archipelago of websites, immersive environments, social media, and video games that increasingly interpenetrates "real" space?[28]

How Indigenous people related to cyberspace had been a topic of conversation within Indigenous media arts circles at least a decade before AbTeC launched. Cree filmmaker Loretta Todd's groundbreaking 1996 essay, "Aboriginal Narratives in Cyberspace," asked the question: "Can [Indigenous] narratives, histories, languages and knowledge find meaning in cyberspace?" She considers how cyberspace might be (re)conceptualized as an Indigenous space, starting with the kinds of questions that should be asked by those building and inhabiting it: "Will cyberspace enable people to communicate in ways that rupture the power relations of the colonizer and the colonized? Or is cyberspace a clever guise for neo-colonialism, where tyranny will find further domain? What if with each technological advancement the question of its effect on the seventh generation was considered?"[29] Mohawk artist and AbTeC co-founder Skawennati wrote, for the 1998 edition of the pioneering CyberPowWow online gallery, "[t]he www is an awesome tool for information-sharing and for meeting people with similar interests whom you may never have met otherwise . . . If we are going to help shape this medium, let's do it right . . . We can use the www to present our stories, to inform people about our issues, and to explore solutions to some of our problems."[30]

Over the last decade, AbTeC has mounted numerous projects designed to address Todd and Skawennati concern with consciously shaping cyberspace to serve Indigenous ends. We have worked with numerous North American Indigenous youth and artists to develop their technical and conceptual capacities for manipulating computational media in order to tell their stories their way (Skins Workshops on Aboriginal Storytelling and Digital Media Design[31]); supported the creation of original artwork that uses cyberspace as a medium (*TimeTraveller™*,[32] *2167*,[33] *She Falls for Ages*[34]); and built tools for manipulating digital media (Mr. Softie,[35] NextText[36]). Each project claims new territory in cyberspace.

Making Cyberspace

In 2014, AbTeC started the Initiative for Indigenous Futures (IIF) to understand how Indigenous people are envisioning the future.[37] One way we do this is to ask people what it means to make cyberspace Indigenous. We have delineated territory and turned its resources toward our own ends in video games, websites, machinimas, and virtual reality environments created by Indigenous minds, rooted in Indigenous worldviews, telling Indigenous stories, for Indigenous audiences. But all that activity takes place within a wider technological environment made by and structured through white cultural hegemony. We are Indians *in* cyberspace; how do we become Indians who *make* cyberspace?

Making cyberspace means, in part, articulating protocols through which the various entities inhabiting it — human and machine — communicate with one another. Indigenous communities are good at thinking in terms of cultural protocol; I would like to suggest that it is time we start drawing on that deep knowledge of how to properly order human-human interaction and consider how it can be used to order human-computer interaction.

In her essay "Codetalkers Recounting Signals of Survival," from the *Coded Territories: Tracing Indigenous Pathways in New Media Art* collection, Métis/Cree artist Cheryl L'Hirondelle (Cree-non status treaty/French) makes an argument that Indigenous protocol can be found in the deep history of cyberspace:

> [The] paths [laid down by our ancestors] became trade routes between bands and territories as we established networks and trade languages and built a knowledge base around what we knew about each other. So when the first Europeans came to "explore" the land, our ancestors naturally led them along these well-established paths, which, over time, as the newcomers settled, became roadways and thoroughfares. With the advent of the telegraph and the telephone, wire was hung along these thoroughfares that literally became the beginnings of the physical network that . . . allows . . . packets of information to move as freely as our ancestors.[38]

Where L'Hirondelle discerns Indigenous protocol embedded at the bottom layer of the stack, Cree artist Archer Pechawis, in his *Coded Territories* essay, imagines it spreading everywhere: "I am looking to a future in which Indigenism is the protocol, an all-encompassing embrace of creation: the realms of earth, sky, water, plant, animal, human, spirit, and, most importantly, a profound humility with regards to our position as humans within that constellation."[39]

I am interested in what happens if we embrace L'Hirondelle's Indigenous reading of the foundations of the network and extend Pechawis' circle of relationships to include our machine creations in an attempt to articulate, in the words of Tuscarora art historian Jolene Rickard, "a more complex view of how [digital networked technology] is situated in people's cultures."[40]

Very little of the current work being done on algorithmic and dataset bias or the ethics of artificial intelligence grapples with the fundamental corruption of the stack — the willful flattening of people's cultures that is a consequence of its monocultural origins. That corruption flows from numerous original sins: Platonic ideals; Aristotelian classification methods; Old Testament dominion over the natural world; Cartesian duality; Boolean binarism; Darwinian fitness. Even if the general state of accepted knowledge complicates, troubles, and sometimes rejects aspects of these knowledge frameworks, they still haunt our data and the design of our computational systems.

The question, then, becomes this: how do we breathe humanity into our computational creations in a way that avoids Western anthropocentric conceits?

Re-imagining Relations

Remember Nunnehi, the Cherokee Little Person from *Riding the Trail of Tears*? Hausman does not clarify whether he and his siblings emerged out of the complexity of the code running the Trail of Tears virtual reality ride or if already-existing Little People used the environment to manifest themselves. Either way, the computational infrastructure running TREPP evolves into an ecosystem operating far beyond the parameters envisioned by the original designers.

By the end of the novel, all hell has broken lose. Nunnehi and his kin have compromised the system, reordering it to better support themselves and to resist the chopped up, remixed, settler self-serving story TREPP has become and more accurately reflect the terror and loss inflicted on their Cherokee ancestors. Other virtual entities have phased into being, engendering ongoing battles over who gets to control the simulation. Towards the end, the main character, Tallula — whose Cherokee grandfather designed the virtual experience — exhausted and confused by the epistemological and ontological battleground that TREPP has become, struggles to make sense of it all. She says to one of the "native-born" non-human entities, "I never imagined this group of people even existed." He replies: "Could be something wrong with your imagination."[41]

We are experiencing a similar failure of imagination in the present moment. We are confronting challenges in understanding the computational systems in which we have now enmeshed ourselves, as they become more complex and as we write more autonomy into them. The algorithmic bias discussed above exemplifies how such systems often end up subverting their intended purposes, largely because we refuse to see ourselves clearly. Motes in our eye become glitches in the code, which then go on to become "global protocol."

What if we took a fundamentally different approach to understanding the digital beings we are creating, particularly those collections of code that act with some degree of autonomy — from network daemons[42] to the most complex artificial intelligence? What if, instead of treating them as tools and servants, we made a place for them in our circle of relationships?

After a century of subordinating the hard work of making common culture to the imperatives of the market, and failed after failed experiment in using technology to compensate, the Western consciousness has been left ill-prepared to lead such a conversation. The hegemonic social imaginary reduces all such talk to superstition and stymies any attempts to widen the kinship circle beyond the human by insisting empiricism is the final word in understanding who we are.[43]

Yet many Indigenous communities remember. We retain the protocols for understanding a kinship network that extends to all aspects of the world around us — animals and plants,[44] wind and rocks,[45] mountain and ocean.[46] Our languages contain the conceptual formations that enable us to engage in dialogue with our non-human kin, and help create mutually intelligible discourses across vast differences in material, vibrancy, and genealogy. As Blackfoot philosopher Leroy Little Bear observes, "the human brain is a station on the radio dial; parked in one spot, it is deaf to all the other stations . . . the animals, rocks, trees, simultaneously broadcasting across the whole spectrum of sentience."[47]

Because we created them, we think we should know how to tune into the stations on which our machine creations communicate. Yet we are only now waking up to the corruptions permeating all levels of the stack. Our difficulties in articulating the ontology of increasingly complex computational processes, and our inability to foresee the results of these complex processes interacting with one another and with the human and natural world, all point to the conclusion that we do not actually understand them. And if we do not understand them, they most likely do not understand us. Such profound mutual incomprehensibility is a recipe for disaster. Ask any Indian.

Notes

1. Blake Hausman, *Riding the Trail of Tears* (Lincoln: Bison Books, 2011), 13.

2. Jason Edward Lewis, "Preparations for a Haunting: Notes Towards an Indigenous Future Imaginary," in *The Participatory Condition in the Digital Age*, ed. Darin Barney, Gabriella Coleman, Christine Ross, Jonathan Sterne, and Tamar Tembeck (Minneapolis: University of Minnesota Press, 2016), 229–49.

3. One can get even more abstract, as Benjamin Bratton does in *The Stack: On Software and Sovereignty* (Cambridge: The MIT Press, 2016), and articulate the stack in terms of

globally spanning megastructures. At that level, however, all the lived politics involving real bodies — and thus the utility outside of academic argument — have been drained out.

4. Kate Crawford, "The Hidden Biases in Big Data," *Harvard Business Review*, April 1, 2013, https://hbr.org/2013/04/the-hidden-biases-in-big-data.

5. D. Fox Harrell, *Phantasmal Media: An Approach to Imagination, Computation, and Expression* (Cambridge: The MIT Press, 2013).

6. Safiya Umoja Noble, *Algorithms of Oppression: How Search Engines Reinforce Racism* (New York: New York University Press, 2018).

7. Will Knight, "Google's AI Chief Says Forget Elon Musk's Killer Robots, and Worry about Bias in AI Systems Instead," *MIT Technology Review*, October 3, 2017, https://www.technologyreview.com/s/608986/forget-killer-robotsbias-is-the-real-ai-danger/.

8. Michael Zhang, "Here's a Look at How Color Film Was Originally Biased Toward White People," *Petapixel*, September 19, 2015, https://petapixel.com/2015/09/19/heres-a-look-at-how-color-film-was-originally-biased-toward-white-people/.

9. Lorna Roth, "Looking at Shirley, the Ultimate Norm: Colour Balance, Image Technologies, and Cognitive Equity," *Canadian Journal of Communication* 34:1 (2009): 1, https://doi.org/10.22230/cjc.2009v34n1a2196.

10. Aylin Caliskan-Islam, Joanna Bryson, and Arvind Narayanan, "Semantics Derived Automatically from Language Corpora Necessarily Contain Human Biases," *Science* 356:6334 (May 2017): 183–86, https://doi.org/10.1126/science.aal4230.

11. Jordan Pearson, "Why An AI-Judged Beauty Contest Picked Nearly All White Winners," *Motherboard*, September 5, 2016, https://motherboard.vice.com/en_us/article/78k7de/why-an-ai-judged-beauty-contest-picked-nearly-all-white-winners.

12. Julia Angwin, Jeff Larson Surya Mattu, and Lauren Kirchner, "Machine Bias," *ProPublica*, May 23, 2016, https://www.propublica.org/article/machine-bias-risk-assessments-in-criminal-sentencing accessed.

13. ProPublica's findings have since been complicated by researchers disputing their analysis. However, even these critics acknowledge the need to question how such algorithms come to incorporate questionable classification and measurement methodologies that disproportionately and negatively affect certain populations. See Sam Corbett-Davies, Emma Pierson, Avi Feller, and Sharad Goel, "A Computer Program Used for Bail and Sentencing Decisions Was Labeled Biased against Blacks. It's Actually Not That Clear," *Washington Post*, October 17, 2016.

14. Kate Crawford, "The Trouble with Bias," (keynote presentation, Conference on Neural Information Processing Systems, Long Beach, CA, December 5, 2017). https://www.youtube.com/watch?v=fMym_BKWQzk. 33mm46ss.

15. Lisa Nakamura, "Cybertyping and the Work of Race in the Age of Digital Reproduction," in *New Media, Old Media: A History and Theory Reader*, ed. Wendy Hui Kyong Chun and Thomas Keenan (New York and London: Routledge, 2006), 319. Moore's

Law is a proposition made by Gordon Moore, then chairman of the computer chip maker Intel, in 1965, that the number of transistors on a chip would double every two years. This doubling of capacity as well as increases in transistor speed are the material foundations on which the rapid pace of computational advances have been built over the last five decades.

16. Scott Gilmore, "Canada's Racism Problem? It's Even Worse than America's," *Macleans*, January 22, 2015. http://www.macleans.ca/news/canada/out-of-sight-out-of-mind-2.

17. "This Artist Shows Us How Computers See The World," interview with Trevor Paglen, *VICE News*, July 25, 2017, video, 5:27, https://www.youtube.com/watch?v=HEI8cuGKiNk.

18. Marcia Crosby, "Construction of the Imaginary Indian," in *Vancouver Anthology: The Institutional Politics of Art*, ed. Stan Douglas (Vancouver: Talonbooks, 1991), 267–91.

19. Harrell, *Phantasmal Media*, 28.

20. Crawford, "The Trouble with Bias."

21. David Jhave Johnston, *Aesthetic Animism: Digital Poetry's Ontological Implications* (Cambridge: The MIT Press, 2016), 14.

22. Nakamura, "The Work of Race," 320.

23. Julianne Pepitone, "How Diverse Is Silicon Valley?" *CNNMoney,* http://money.cnn .com/interactive/technology/tech-diversity-data/ accessed January 5, 2018.

24. Radhika Gajjala, "Transnational Digital Subjects: Constructs of Identity and Ignorance in a Digital Economy," keynote presentation, Conference on Cultural Diversity in/and Cyberspace, College Park, MD, May 2000, quoted in Nakamura "The Work of Race," 331.

25. Terry Winograd and Fernando Flores, *Understanding Computers and Cognition: A New Foundation for Design*, 1st ed. (Boston: Addison-Wesley Professional, 1987).

26. Donna Haraway, *Simians, Cyborgs and Women: The Reinvention of Nature*, 2nd ed. (London: Free Association Books, 1996).

27. Byron Reeves and Clifford Nass, *The Media Equation: How People Treat Computers, Television, and New Media like Real People and Places* (Stanford: CSLI Publications, 1996).

28. Jason Edward Lewis and Skawennati Tricia Fragnito, "Aboriginal Territories in Cyberspace," *Cultural Survival Quarterly* 29:2 (July 2005): 29–31.

29. Todd, "Aboriginal Narratives in Cyberspace," 3.

30. Skawennati Tricia Fragnito, "The CyberPowWow FAQ, or Why I Love WWWriting," *CyberPowWow*, 1997, http://www.cyberpowwow.net/nation2nation/triciawork.html.

31. Beth Aileen Lameman, Jason E. Lewis, and Skawennati Fragnito, "Skins 1.0: A Curriculum for Design Games with First Nations Youth," in *Proceedings of the International Academic Conference on the Future of Game Design and Technology* (Vancouver, BC: Association of Computing Machinery, 2010), 282.

32. Skawennati, *TimeTraveller*™, 2008–2014, machinima (video), 78mm. www .timetravellertm.com.

33. *2167*, various artists, 2017, virtual reality. http://www.imaginenative.org/2167.

34. Skawennati Tricia Fragnito, *She Falls for Ages*. 2017. Machinima, 19mm. http://skawennati.com/SheFallsForAges/index.html.

35. Bruno Nadeau and Jason Lewis, *Mr. Softie: A Typographic Text Editor*, Mac OS; Windows; Linux, 2010–2014. www.mrsoftie.net.

36. Jason Lewis, Elie Zananiri, and Bruno Nadeau, *NextText: Library for Interactive and Dynamic Texts*, 2008–2014, http://www.nexttext.net.

37. "The Initiative for Indigenous Futures," Initiative for Indigenous Futures, http://abtec.org/iif/.

38. Cheryl L'Hirondelle, "Codetalkers Recounting Signals of Survival," in *Coded Territories: Tracing Indigenous Pathways in New Media Art*, ed. Steve Loft and Kerry Swanson (Calgary: University of Calgary Press, 2014), 152.

39. Archer Pechawis, "Indigenism: Aboriginal World View as Global Protocol," in *Coded Territories*, 38.

40. Jolene Rickard, "Considering Traditional Practices of 'Seeing' as Future," lecture, 1st Annual Symposium on the Future Imaginary, TIFF Bell Lightbox, Toronto, October 16, 2015, http://abtec.org/iif/symposia/a-new-beginning/#rickard.

41. Hausman, *Riding the Trail of Tears,* 313.

42. Fenwick McKelvey, *Internet Daemons: Digital Communications Possessed* (Minneapolis: University of Minnesota Press, 2018).

43. Attempts to widen the animacy lens and flatten the species hierarchy from within the Western tradition do exist, of course: Spinoza's monadism, Haraway's cyborg, Timothy Morton's hyperobjects, Jane Bennet's vibrant matter, Graham Harmann's object oriented philosophy, etc. My aim here, though, is to introduce sources for thinking about the question of machine relationships from outside the Western canon. In addition, I side with Zoe Todd's ethical critique of the myopia of these intellectual genealogies: "here we were celebrating and worshipping a European thinker for 'discovering', or newly articulating by drawing on a European intellectual heritage, what many an Indigenous thinker around the world could have told you for millennia." See Zoe Todd, "An Indigenous Feminist's Take on the Ontological Turn: 'Ontology' Is Just Another Word For Colonialism," *Journal of Historical Sociology* 29:1 (April 1, 2016).

44. Kim TallBear, "Beyond the Life/Not Life Binary: A Feminist-Indigenous Reading of Cryopreservation, Interspecies Thinking and the New Materialisms," in *Cryopolitics: Frozen Life in a Melting World*, ed. Joanna Radin and Emma Kowal (Cambridge: The MIT Press, 2017).

45. Don Hill, "Listening to Stones: Learning in Leroy Little Bear's Laboratory: Dialogue in the World Outside," *Alberta Views*, September 1, 2008, https://albertaviews.ca/listening-to-stones/.

46. Martha Warren Beckwith, trans., ed., *The Kumulipo: A Hawaiian Creation Chant* (Honolulu: The University Press of Hawaii, 1972). http://www.ulukau.org/elib/cgi-bin/library?e=d-obeckwit2-000Sec-11haw-50-20-frameset-book-1-010escapewin&a=d&d=D0&toc=0.

47. Hill, "Listening."

CONTRIBUTORS

DAMIÁN BACA is an associate professor of English and Mexican American Studies at the University of Arizona and faculty at the Bread Loaf Graduate School of English. He is author of *Mestiz@ Scripts, Digital Migrations, and the Territories of Writing* (New York: Palgrave Macmillan, 2008) and lead editor of *Rhetorics of the Americas: 3114 BCE to 2012 CE* (New York: Palgrave Macmillan, 2010).

LAURA R. BRAUNSTEIN is the digital humanities librarian at Dartmouth College. She is the coeditor, with Arianne Hartsell-Gundy and Liorah Golumb, of *Digital Humanities in the Library: Challenges and Opportunities for Subject Specialists* (ACRL, 2015).

PETER CARINI is the college archivist at Dartmouth College. He frequently presents and publishes on teaching with archives and special collections. He was the co-principal investigator for the three-year Occom Circle NEH grant and led the project team.

ALAN OJIIG CORBIERE, Bne doodemid (Ruffed Grouse clan), is an Anishinaabe from M'Chigeeng First Nation on Manitoulin Island. Currently he is the Anishinaabemowin Revitalization Program Coordinator at Lakeview School, M'Chigeeng First Nation, where he and his team are working on a culturally based second language program that focuses on using Anishinaabe stories to teach language. He is currently conducting research and editing a manuscript written in 1927 by George Gabaoosa of Garden River.

ELLEN CUSHMAN is a Cherokee Nation citizen and dean's professor of Civic Sustainability at Northeastern University. Her book, *The Cherokee Syllabary: Writing the People's Perseverance* (Oklahoma University Press, 2012), was based on six years of ethnohistorical research with her tribe. She is currently developing a digital archive for Ojibwe and Cherokee Manuscript Translation.

CHRISTINE DELUCIA, associate professor of History at Mount Holyoke College, will be joining the History faculty at Williams College in 2019 after a long-term fellowship at the Newberry Library. She is author of *Memory Lands: King Philip's War and the Place of Violence in the Northeast* (Henry Roe Cloud Series on American Indians and Modernity, Yale University Press, 2018), and writes on Indigenous and colonial memorializing, material culture, and placemaking.

HAZEL-DAWN DUMPERT is a writer and freelance editor. She has reviewed films for *LA Weekly*, and writes for the *Village Voice* and *New England Today*. She served as the project manager for the NEH-funded Occom Circle.

SUSAN PATERSON GLOVER is an associate professor of English at Laurentian University, where she teaches British, colonial, and Indigenous texts of the eighteenth and early nineteenth centuries. She is the author of *Engendering Legitimacy: Law, Property, and Early Eighteenth-Century Fiction* (Lewisburg, PA: Bucknell University Press, 2006) and a critical edition of Sarah Chapone's *The Hardships of the English Laws in Relation to Wives* (New York: Routledge/Taylor and Francis, 2018).

GORDON HENRY is an enrolled member of the White Earth Anishinaabe (Chippewa) Tribe in Minnesota, professor of English at Michigan State University, and senior editor of the American Indian Studies series at Michigan State University Press. He is also a published poet and fiction writer. In 1995, he received an American Book Award for his novel *The Light People* (East Lansing: Michigan State University Press, 2003). Henry also co-edited a graphic literature anthology, with Elizabeth LaPensee, titled Not (Just) (An)other with Michigan State University Press, 2018). His multi-genre poetic work, The Failure of Certain Charms, was translated into Catalan and published by the University of Valencia Press in 2018.

JASON EDWARD LEWIS is the university research chair in Computational Media and the Indigenous future imaginary and professor of Design and Computation Arts at Concordia University in Montreal. His research interests include investigating computation as a creative and cultural material, as well creating interactive media art. He is Cherokee, Kānaka Maoli, and Samoan, born and raised in northern California.

JENNIFER R. O'NEAL is a member of the Confederated Tribes of Grand Ronde (Chinook, Cow Creek, Cree), the university historian and archivist at the University of Oregon, and is affiliated faculty with Native Studies, Robert D. Clark Honors College, and the History department. She has led the development and implementation of best practices, frameworks, and protocols for Native American archives in non-tribal repositories in the United States. Her research and teaching are dedicated to centering Indigenous traditional knowledge, decolonizing methodologies, applying Indigenous research methods, and implementing place-based education.

THOMAS PEACE is an assistant professor of Canadian History at Huron University College focusing on the histories of education and settler colonialism in northeastern North America at the turn of the nineteenth century. Along with Kathryn Labelle, he is the editor of *From Huronia to Wendakes: Adversity, Migration, and Resilience, 1650–1900* (University of Oklahoma Press, 2016) and an editor and regular contributor to ActiveHistory.ca, a website focused on making the work of historians more accessible to the public.

TIMOTHY B. POWELL was a faculty member of the Religious Studies department at the University of Pennsylvania and a consulting scholar at the Penn Museum. He was a past director of the Center for Native American and Indigenous Research at the American Philosophical Society and directed Educational Partnerships with Indigenous Communities (EPIC) through the Penn Language Center. He was dedicated to supporting the digital repatriation of archival documents to the Indigenous communities where these materials originated. He died on November 1, 2018 and will be sorely missed by all who knew him and worked with him.

IVY SCHWEITZER is a professor of English and past chair of Women's, Gender, and Sexuality Studies at Dartmouth College. She is the editor of *The Occom Circle*, a digital edition of works by and about Samson Occom (https://www.dartmouth.edu/~occom/), and co-producer of a full-length documentary film entitled *It's Criminal: A Tale of Prison and Privilege* (director: Signe Taylor, 2017 https://www.facebook.com/ItIsCriminal), based on the courses she coteaches in and about jails. She is currently blogging weekly about the year 1862 in the creative life of Emily Dickinson (https://journeys.dartmouth.edu/whiteheat/).

MARIE BALSLEY TAYLOR is a research associate at the University of Minnesota. Her current book project examines the influence that Indigenous diplomatic practices had on the language of the seventeenth-century New England mission. She has published and forthcoming articles in *Quakers and Native Americans* (Brill, 2018) and *Early American Literature.*

MELANIE BENSON TAYLOR is an associate professor of Native American Studies at Dartmouth College and also executive editor of the journal *Native South.* She is the author of *Disturbing Calculations: The Economics of Identity in Postcolonial Southern Literature, 1912–2002* (University of Georgia Press, 2008), *Reconstructing the Native South: American Indian Literature and the Lost Cause* (University of Georgia Press, 2012), and most recently edited *The Cambridge History of Native American Literature* (Cambridge University Press, forthcoming)..

KELLY WISECUP is an associate professor of English at Northwestern University. She is the author of *Medical Encounters: Knowledge and Identity in Early American Literatures* (Amherst: University of Massachusetts Press, 2013) and co-editor of a joint forum on the relations between Native American and Indigenous Studies and Early American Studies, published in *Early American Literature* and the *William and Mary Quarterly.*

INDEX

Page numbers in italics refer to illustrations.

for Ojibwe and Cherokee manuscripts, 12; objection to alphabetic orthography, 130; public school curriculum, 61; Ridge word lists, 14, 120–23, 129–31, *131*, 134–35; writing system and publications, 12, 73, 120, 159, 166. *See also* Indigenous Language Manuscript Translation Project

Chippewa Tribe. *See* Ojibwe Tribe

Christen, Kimberly, 4–5, 25, 29

Christianity: Anglican and Methodist archives, 163–64; Anglican missionary work, 157–59; Brothertown settlement, 8; conversion as conquest, 77, 140, 143–48, 151–52; erasure of kinship in missionary literature, 143–44, 148–52; French imperialist missionaries, 108; historiographical and archival bias and, 110; Indigenous literacy and, 160–63; Indigenous missionary writings, 102; Natick Praying-Town era, 82–83; Native Christian educators, 98–99; Native Christianity as resistance, 6–7; Occom ministry, 191; reciprocal spiritual imaginary, 15; rise of Methodism, 108–9, 158; Sawatanen affiliations, 107; schooling and dispossession relationship, 104; translation of religious doctrine, 165–66

Clement, Tanya, 148

Coatsworth, David, 208

Coatsworth, Emerson, 208

codetalkers, 225

Codex Delilah (Baca), 16

Coeur d'Alene Tribe, 25

collaboration: archivist approach to, 56–57; as centering-of-traditional-knowledge aim, 50; collaborative translation, 12, 63, 75–76; Indigenous Language Manuscript Translation Project, 61; Mason Cree Bible translation, 166; *Occom Circle* collaboration, 6; Powell-Ojibwe collaboration, 16; U'mista Cultural Center collaboration, 37. *See also* Indigenous Archives

Collected Writings of Samson Occom, Mohegan, The (2007), 7–8

collection: afterlife as interrogation of, 11; as archival context, 52; Densmore collection method, 39; extractive/entitled mentality for, 83; Lewis and Clark expedition and, 28–29; Natick as collecting site, 80, 82–83; non-colonial collection, 9; tenets of imperialist thought and, 61–62

colonialism. *See* decolonization

Columbus, Christopher, xiii–xiv

"common pot" experiential model, 5, 8, 15, 107, 142

community-based digital archives, 24–25, 35–36, 37

Confederated Tribes of Grand Ronde, 12

Confederated Tribes of the Colville Reservation, 25

Confederated Tribes of the Umatilla Reservation, 25

Confederated Tribes of Warm Springs, 25

conversion narratives, 77, 140, 143–48, 151–52

Corbiere, Alan, x–xi, 16, 206–7, 233

Corston, Tom, 165

Cosby, Marcia, 222

Crawford, Kate, 220–21

Creek Nation, 129, 132

Cree Nation, 14–15, 156–57, 159–66

curation, 4, 15, 54–55, 174–75, 177–83

Cushman, Ellen, 8, 12, 15, 233–34

Dakota Access pipeline protest, 9–10

Dartmouth College, 6–9, 13, 96–101

Debassige, Lewis, 206–7

decolonization: colonial-era universities and, 7; colonialist/decolonialist technology approaches, 4; Decolonizing Indigenous Research model, 51–52; institutional resources for, 87; language translation protocols for, 69–73, 75–76; *longhouse* interpretive framework and, 110; non-colonial preservation sites, 9; self-archiving as decolonization, 11; Western time concepts and, 62. *See also* recontextualization; settlerism

Natchez Tribe, 131–33

Natick Historical Society, 83–84

National Anthropological Archives (Smithsonian Institution), 24, 25, 29, 35, 64

nationalism, 1

National Museum of the American Indian (Smithsonian Institution), 25

Native American Graves Protection and Repatriation Act (1990), 83

Neilson, John, 107

New-York Historical Society (NYHS), 120–21

Nietzsche, Friedrich, 178

Niranjana, Tejaswini, 75–76

Noble, Safiya Umoja, 220

Norby, Patricia, 10

Northwest Museum of Art and Culture, 25

Norton, John, 108

Norwich (Vermont), 9

Notes on the State of Virginia (Jefferson), 14, 121

Oberg, Michael, 98–99

Obomsawin, Alanis, 168

O'Brien, Jean, 14, 83–85, 142, 150

Occom, Samson: biographical sketch, 189–92; as Brothertown founder, 100, 189, 192; Dartmouth Indigenous students and, 97–99, 101; importance of, 27; as Indigenous writer, 102–4, 191–92, 200; Mohegan Land Case and, 100; "Native space" of, 140; Wheelock relationship with, 7. See also *Occom Circle, The*

Occom Circle, The (digital collection): development of, 15; "Indigenous Archives in the Digital Age" conference, 6, 8–11; kinship networks in, 140; *longhouse* interpretive framework and, 113; Mohegan contemporary experiences and, 27; Occom historiography and, 102; overview, 189–90, 192–200; as re-envisioning initiative, 96–97; second phase development, 17–18; transcultural network associations in, 7. See also Occom, Samson

O'Connell, Barry, 108

Odawa Nation, 204

Odjig, Daphne, 207–8

Ojibwemowining Resource Center, 38

Ojibwe Tribe: Digital Archive for Ojibwe and Cherokee manuscripts, 12; Frances Densmore recordings, 38–39; *Gibagadinamaagoom* coalition, 4–5, 11; Jackson treaty with, 204; *Midewiwin* ritual protocols, 38–39; Ojibwe migration map and story, 30–35; orthographic system, 159; Powell collaboration with, 16

O'Malley, Johnson, 61

O'Neal, Jennifer, 12, 15, 23, 29, 234–35

Oneida Tribe, 8, 100

Opp, James, 148

Osgood, Thaddeus, 97, 106

otherness, 61, 76, 80

overwriting, 15, 80, 177, 184n14

Owens, Louis, 173

ownership: acquisition history and, 167; archives as anti-communal, 9; "common pot" experiential model and, 5, 8, 15, 107, 142; digital media and, 86–87; erasure of kinship and, 142; identification of narrators, 178, 185n17; narrative ownership protocols, 30–34; repatriation, 28, 37, 38–39, 48, 123; "respectful repatriation" and, 123; transpossession, 177, 182, 184n15. See also sovereignty

Paglen, Trevor, 221–22

palimpsests, xii, 15, 176–83

Paul, Moses, 191

Peace, Thomas, 13, 235

Pechawis, Archer, 225

Peel, Bruce, 159–60

Penobscot Tribe, 25, 30–35, 107

Pequot Tribe, 14, 18, 108–9, 140, 143–48

Peter, Hugh, 144–45

Phoebe A. Hearst Museum of Anthropology, 26

physiognomy, 126

Pickering, John, 76, 130

Pimachiowin Aki Corporation, 34

Pine Tree Tribe / Community, 104, 108

place. *See* removal/relocation; spatiality

Plateau Peoples' Web Portal, 25

Popul Vuh, 10

potlatch ceremonies, 36–38

Powell, Timothy, 4, 5, 11, 16, 67, 235

power: archival governance structures, 95; archival silence and, 111–13; control of the archive and, 1; Derrida "House of the Archive" structure, 96, 101; Indigenous practices and, 3. *See also* resistance

preservation: access restrictions and, 85–86; digital preservation of language, 4–5, 16; digital preservation of movement and speech, 35–36; as imperialist tenet of thought, 61; non-colonial preservation sites, 9

Progress (White Earth newspaper), 172, 175, 179, 185n17

"Protocols for Native American Archival Materials" (PNAAM, 2006), 1, 46–57. *See also* archives (settler archives); community-based digital archives; digital archives; Indigenous Archives

Putnam, Lara, 112–13

race: anthropological racial bias, 76; archive access and, 85–86; Christian racial bias, 97–98; colonialist paradigm and, 4; color calibration algorithmic bias, 219–20; criminal justice racial bias, 220–21; cyberspace raciality, 222–26; digital humanities racial bias, 23, 219–21, 226–27; ethnic archives as counter-hegemonic, 1–2; First Fire prophecy and, 31; vanishing race myth, 2. *See also* slavery

recontextualization: celebrity Indigenous writers and, 103; centering of traditional knowledge, 47–51, *50*, 56; Cherokee manuscript digital collections, 73; Cherokee wampum belts and, 61–62; compromised documents and resources, 86; curatorial loss/gain and, 180–83; decolonization of

time and, 62; of digital technology, 5; early Indigenous literature and, 139; history/ memory as contested territory and, 84–85, 95–96; Indigenous kinship and, 141–44, 148–52, 227; narrativity and native presence, 172; restoration of communal circumstances, 14; as settler strategy, 134. *See also* decolonization

Recovering Voices (Smithsonian Institution), 28, 35

removal/relocation: Charles River removal/ trauma, 79–80; Dartmouth-area relocation negotiations, 100; Fourth Fire prophecy and, 31; "Imaginary Indian" image and, 222; Jefferson interest in, 14; linguistic translation and, 123–24, 129–30; return practices and, 131–33; schooling and dispossession relationship, 104; settler-tribal alliances and, 108; "trail of tears" Cherokee Removal, xiii, 218, 226; Treaty of Indian Springs, 120, 122, 129; Treaty of New Echota, 122. *See also* land; trauma

repatriation, 28, 37, 38–39, 48, 123. *See also* ownership; sovereignty

resistance: afterlife and, 9; archival silence and, 111–13; to archiving/collecting, 9; Haudenosaunee Confederacy, 105; Indigenous writing and, 2–3; multi-tribal alliances, 81; Native Christianity as, 6–7; Northeastern Indigenous intellectual network and, 108–9; schooling as resistance, 105, 107–8. *See also* advocacy and activism; power

revitalization (of Indigenous communities): overview, 24–25; revitalization ceremonies, 36–38; revitalization of languages, 24–25, 27–28; Seventh Fire prophecy and, 31–32

Rhodes, Richard, 182

Richter, Daniel, 105

Rickard, Jolene, 225

Ridge, John Rollin, 14, 120–24, 129–35

Rivett, Sarah, 146

Ross, Donald, 160